WALKING THE LAKE DISTRICT FELLS
CONISTON
THE OLD MAN OF CONISTON, SWIRL HOW, WETHERLAM, DUDDON VALLEY AND ESKDALE

MARK RICHARDS

CICERONE

© Mark Richards 2021
Second edition 2021
ISBN: 978 1 78631 039 2

Originally published as Lakeland Fellranger, 2009
ISBN: 978 1 85284 542 1

 Printed in China on responsibly sourced paper on behalf of Latitude Press Ltd

A catalogue record for this book is available from the British Library.
All photographs are by the author unless otherwise stated.
All artwork is by the author.

 Maps are reproduced with permission from HARVEY Maps, www.harveymaps.co.uk

Updates to this Guide

While every effort is made by our authors to ensure the accuracy of guidebooks as they go to print, changes can occur during the lifetime of an edition. Any updates that we know of for this guide will be on the Cicerone website (www.cicerone.co.uk/1039/updates), so please check before planning your trip. We also advise that you check information about such things as transport, accommodation and shops locally. Even rights of way can be altered over time. We are always grateful for information about any discrepancies between a guidebook and the facts on the ground, sent by email to updates@cicerone.co.uk or by post to Cicerone, Juniper House, Murley Moss, Oxenholme Road, Kendal, LA9 7RL.

Register your book: To sign up to receive free updates, special offers and GPX files where available, register your book at www.cicerone.co.uk.

Front cover: Looking to Brown Pike, Dow Crag, from Torver Beck
Title page: Fox Haw and Caw from Stickle Pike

CONTENTS

Map key 5
Volumes in the series 6
Author preface 7
Starting points 8

INTRODUCTION 13
Valley bases 13
Fix the Fells 14
Using this guide 15
Safety and access 18
Additional online resources 18

FELLS 19
1 Black Combe 19
2 Black Fell 35
3 Brim Fell 42
4 Buckbarrow 49
5 Caw 54
6 Coniston Old Man 61
7 Dow Crag 72
8 Great Carrs 81
9 Great Worm Crag 87
10 Green Crag 91
11 Grey Friar 102
12 Hard Knott 110
13 Harter Fell 116
14 Hesk Fell 128
15 Holme Fell 132
16 Muncaster Fell 138
17 Stainton Pike 147
18 Stickle Pike 152
19 Swirl How 158
20 Wallowbarrow Crag 168
21 Walna Scar 172

22	Wetherlam	180
23	Whitfell	194
24	Yoadcastle	202

RIDGE ROUTES 209
1	Two Hard Knotts	209
2	The Swirl Round	212
3	Coniston Triple Treat	216
4	Fox Haw, Caw and Pikes	220

More to explore 223

Useful contacts 224

A fellranger's glossary 225

Alphabetical list of fells in the Fellranger series 229

Old dam south of Hodge Close Quarry (photo: Maggie Allan)

MAP KEY

Key to route maps and topos

 Route on a defined path

 Route on an intermittent or undefined path

▲ **Fell summit featured in this guide** (on maps)

 Fell summit featured in this guide (on maps)

 Route number (on maps)

12 **Starting point**

4 **Route number** (on topos)

N

0 — 500 m
1:40,000

Harvey map legend

 Lake, small tarn, pond

 River, footbridge

— Wide stream

— Narrow stream

Peat hags

Marshy ground

Contours change from brown to grey where the ground is predominantly rocky outcrops, small crags and other bare rock.

Improved pasture
Rough pasture
Fell or moorland
Open forest or woodland
Dense forest or woodland
Felled or new plantation
Forest ride or firebreak
Settlement

 Boundary, maintained
Boundary, remains

On moorland, walls, ruined walls and fences are shown. For farmland, only the outer boundary wall or fence is shown.

Contour (15m interval)
Index contour (75m interval)
Auxiliary contour
Scree, spoil heap
Boulder field
Scattered rock and boulders
Predominantly rocky ground
Major crag, large boulder
O.S. trig pillar, large cairn
Spot height (from air survey)

══════ Dual carriageway
────── Main road (fenced)
▬▬▬▬▬▬ Minor road (unfenced)
— — — — Track or forest road
- - - - - - Footpath or old track
-- -- -- -- Intermittent path
• • Long distance path
+—+—+— Powerline, pipeline
▪▪ ▫▫ ⌐ Building, ruin or sheepfold, shaft

The representation of a road, track or footpath is no evidence of the existence of a right of way.

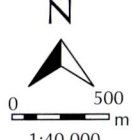

WALKING THE LAKE DISTRICT FELLS – CONISTON

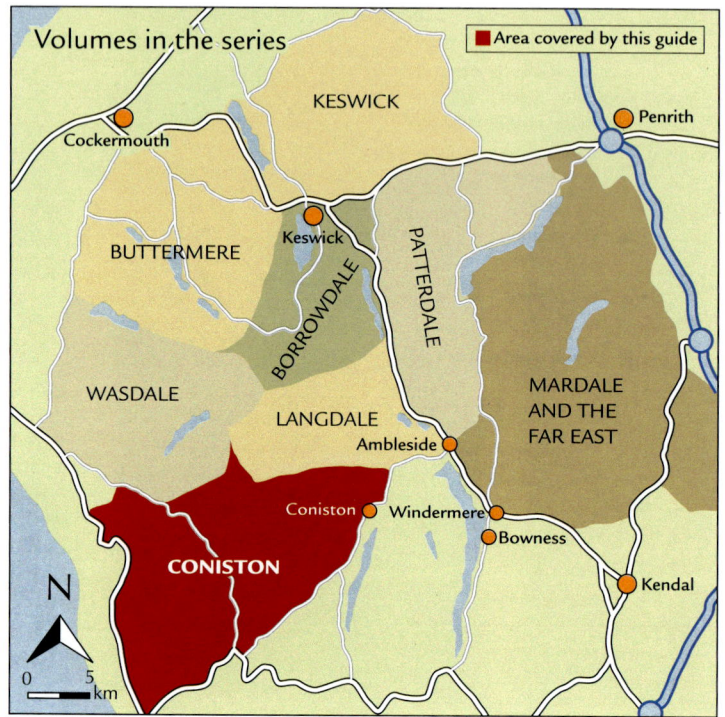

AUTHOR PREFACE

This land of living dreams we call the Lake District is a cherished blessing to know, love and share. As we go about our daily routines, we may take a fleeting moment to reflect that someone, somewhere, will be tramping up a lonely gill or along an airy ridge, peering from a lofty summit or gazing across a wind-blown tarn and taking lingering solace from its timeless beauty. The trappings of modern life thrust carpet and concrete under our feet, and it is always wonderful to walk the region's sheep trods and rough trails, and to imprint our soles upon the fells. This series sets out to give you the impetus and inspiration to make space in your schedule to explore them time and again, in myriad different ways.

However, the regular paths of long tradition deserve our care. Progressively many of the main paths are being re-set with cobbles and pitching by organisations such as Fix the Fells, to whose work you have contributed by buying this guide. But in many instances, the best consideration we can give these pathways is rest. The modern fellwanderer should show a new 'green' awareness by choosing to tread lightly on the land and to find new ways around the hills. One of the underlying impulses of this guide is to protect these beloved fells by presenting a diversity of route options for each and every fell – and also, in this new edition, recommending 'fell-friendly' routes to each summit which are less susceptible to erosion.

Another feature of this latest incarnation of Fellranger, apart from the smaller size to slip in your pocket or pack, is the addition of a selection of inspiring ridge routes at the end of each volume for those of you who like to spend a little longer with your head and feet in the heavenly realms, relishing the summit views and the connections between the fell-tops, as well as some accompanying online resources for readers with a digital bent.

Mark Richards
www.markrichardswalking.co.uk

STARTING POINTS

	Location	Description	GR	Access	Ascents described from here
1	Mosedale	Verge parking on N side of road	NY 242 017	FP	Hard Knott
2	Hardknott Pass	Small layby E of pass summit	NY 232 015	FP	Hard Knott, Harter Fell
3	Hardknott Castle (Roman fort)	Layby parking E of Roman fort	NY 221 014	FP	Hard Knott
4	Jubilee Bridge	Layby E of cattle grid at foot of pass	NY 213 011	FP	Harter Fell
5	Brotherilkeld	Generous verge parking	NY 210 011	FP	Hard Knott
6	Woolpack Inn	Car park beside pub and café	NY 190 010	FP	Green Crag, Harter Fell
7	Stanley Ghyll	Car park in woods	NY 171 003	FP	Green Crag
8	Birkerfell Road (Devoke Water track-end)	Verge parking beside track to High Ground farm	SD 171 977	FP	Great Worm Crag, Green Crag, Yoadcastle
9	Birkerfell Road (Woodend Bridge)	Verge parking	SD 179 963	FP	Great Worm Crag, Hesk Fell
10	Eskdale Green	Large layby W of Forge Bridge (no parking at La'al Ratty stations)	SD 148 994	FP	Muncaster Fell
11	Brantrake	Modest tree-sheltered layby	SD 145 985	FP	Yoadcastle
12	Ravenglass	Large town-centre car park and station car park	SD 085 964	PP, T	Muncaster Fell
13	Dyke	Layby beside farm access lane	SD 113 951	FP	Stainton Pike, Yoadcastle
14	Corneyfell Road (Fell Lane)	A595 verge S of junction	SD 113 942	FP	Stainton Pike, Whitfell, Yoadcastle
15	Corneyfell Road (Buckbarrow Bridge)	Small layby beside bridge	SD 134 903	FP	Buckbarrow, Whitfell
16	Corneyfell Road (road summit)	Layby parking	SD 150 896	FP	Black Combe, Buckbarrow
17	Bootle	Small car park beside church	SD 107 883	FP, T	Black Combe, Buckbarrow
18	Whitbeck	Parking on old road in front of church	SD 119 839	FP	Black Combe

	Location	Description	GR	Access	Ascents described from here
19	Whicham church	Church car park	SD 135 827	FP	Black Combe
20	Beckside	Layby	SD 153 847	FP	Black Combe
21	Hallthwaites	Layby/verge opposite church	SD 178 856	FP	Black Combe
22	Cragg Hall	Verge S of access lane to Swinside Farm	SD 181 872	FP	(Sunkenkirk stone circle – see Black Combe chapter)
23	Brackenthwaite	Verge where track diverges by a gill	SD 179 920	FP	Whitfell
24	Bobbinmill Bridge	Tiny layby opposite cottages on W side of bridge	SD 190 926	FP	Hesk Fell
25	Ulpha	Plentiful verge and layby parking on common	SD 199 919	FP	Stickle Pike
26	Kiln Bank Cross	Layby on common	SD 215 932	FP	Caw, Stickle Pike
27	Broughton Mills	Roadside parking beside bridge	SD 222 907	FP	Stickle Pike
28	Water Yeat (forest gate)	Verge parking beside forestry gate (don't block access)	SD 238 928	FP	Caw, Walna Scar
29	Hummer Lane	Limited verge parking	SD 268 934	FP	Walna Scar
30	Torver (church hall)	Church hall car park (donation)	SD 285 943	FP, B	Coniston Old Man, Dow Crag, Walna Scar
31	Walna Scar Road (fell-gate)	Large parking area beyond fell-gate	SD 288 970	FP	Brim Fell, Coniston Old Man, Dow Crag, Walna Scar
32	Coniston (Lake Road)	Large formal car park; further car park in town by tourist office	SD 308 970	PP, B	Brim Fell, Coniston Old Man, Swirl How, Walna Scar, Wetherlam
33	Tilberthwaite	Generous layby beside beck	NY 306 010	FP	Holme Fell, Wetherlam
34	Hodge Close	Parking area above quarry	NY 315 017	FP	Holme Fell
35	Oxen Fell (High Cross)	Small layby just N of junction with bridleway	NY 328 018	FP	Black Fell, Holme Fell
36	Tom Gill	NT car park off road bend	SD 322 999	NT	Black Fell, Holme Fell

STARTING POINTS *continued*

	Location	Description	GR	Access	Ascents described from here
37	Tarn Hows	Large NT car park with toilets	SD 326 995	NT	Black Fell
38	High Cross	Forestry Commission car park	SD 332 986	PP, B	Black Fell
39	Silverthwaite	Car park	NY 341 037	PP	Black Fell
40	Little Langdale	Roadside parking	NY 319 033	FP	Great Carrs, Holme Fell, Swirl How, Wetherlam
41	Cathedral Quarry	Small layby near ford	NY 315 028	FP	Holme Fell
42	Castle Howe	Verge parking	NY 294 032	FP	Great Carrs
43	Wrynose Pass	Laybys E and W of Three Shire Stone	NY 277 027	FP	Great Carrs, Swirl How
44	Wrynose Bottom	Verge parking	NY 265 022	FP	Great Carrs, Grey Friar
45	Cockley Beck Bridge	Layby and verge parking near bridge	NY 246 016	FP	Grey Friar
46	Birks Bridge	Forestry Commission car park	SD 235 995	FP	Harter Fell
47	Troutal	Small layby for 1–2 cars N of house	SD 235 988	FP	Grey Friar
48	Fickle Steps	Layby just N of road bend	SD 231 974	FP	Green Crag, Grey Friar, Harter Fell, Wallowbarrow Crag
49	Seathwaite	Layby just N of church	SD 229 962	FP	Caw, Dow Crag, Green Crag, Grey Friar, Harter Fell, Wallowbarrow Crag, Walna Scar

FP – free parking

PP – pay parking

NT – National Trust (free to members)

B – on a bus route (in season)

T – on a railway line

Dow Crag from the eastern shore of Goat's Water

Great How Crags from Raven Tor, Brim Fell

INTRODUCTION

Valley bases

The Southern Fells rise from three primary valleys: Coniston Water to the east, Eskdale to the north and the Duddon in their midst, although there are also numerous quieter approaches from the western seaboard. The greatest drama is to be found in the north, where the rugged fells crescendo towards the Scafells. The Duddon harbours a succession of delightful, wooded craggy aspects – no wonder Wordsworth held such poetic passion for this valley. Eskdale too is a treasure, defended by the passes from the throngs that clog the narrow twisting roads of the Langdales.

In general terms, the promised adventure springs from small dale-floor settlements. Two high motor passes form a bridge allowing access to the Western Fells from Little Langdale via the upper Duddon.

Facilities

Coniston is a service-centre village, rare in Lakeland, where the visitor and the local can find most things to meet their needs – from launches to lunches, micro-brewing to cultural exhibitions – the principal attraction, the Ruskin Museum, quite the most absorbing of its kind. Here you can not only learn

↑ *Coniston Old Man from Wetherlam*

the robust detail of an agrarian and industrial heritage, but also witness the influence of great people on the locality, from Donald Campbell to John Ruskin himself. Visit and be inspired!

The whole area has a long tradition of provision to welcome and refresh the walker. Accommodation is available at Torver and, to the south, the Broughton-in-Furness area is reasonably well geared. You can also find some accommodation within the Duddon valley, and certainly camping, notably at Turner Hall. Eskdale rivals Coniston for places of refreshment and lodgings. Little Langdale has just one pub and some holiday lets, but is a stone's throw from popular Elterwater, Skelwith Bridge, Hawkshead and the major tourist hub of Ambleside.

Getting around

On the public transport front, the Coniston Rambler 505 bus runs from Ambleside to Coniston via Hawkshead, while the X12 plies between Coniston and Ulverston. Buses are otherwise absent in this southwestern fell quarter. The Cumbria Coastal Line can be joined from the West Coast Mainline at Lancaster and Carlisle, but is convenient only for walks from Silecroft and Ravenglass.

Parking is not to be taken for granted anywhere in this popular park. Always allow time to find an alternative parking place, if not to switch to a different plan for your day or just set out directly from your door – perfectly possible if you find accommodation within any of the main valleys. Always take care to park safely and only in laybys and car parks, not on the side of the narrow country roads. Consult the 'Starting points' table to find out where the best parking places (and bus stops) are to be found. Note that although, in general, one preferred starting point is specified for each route, there may be alternative starting points nearby should you arrive and find your chosen spot taken.

Fix the Fells

The Fellranger series has always highlighted the hugely important work of the Fix the Fells project in repairing the most seriously damaged fell paths. The mighty challenge has been a great learning curve and the more recent work, including complex guttering, is quite superb. It ensures a flat footfall where possible, is easy

Using this guide

White Pike on Walna Scar from Caw Moss

to use in ascent and descent, and excess water escapes efficiently, minimising future damage.

The original National Trust and National Park Authority partnership came into being in 2001 and expanded with the arrival of Natural England, with additional financial support from the Friends of the Lake District and now the Lake District Foundation (www.lakedistrictfoundation.org). But, and it's a big but, the whole endeavour needs to raise £500,000 a year to function. This enormous figure is needed to keep pace with the challenges caused by the joint tyranny of boots and brutal weather. The dedicated and highly skilled team, including volunteers, deserve our sincerest gratitude for making our hill paths secure and sympathetic to their setting. It is a task without end, including pre-emptive repair to stop paths from washing out in the first place.

Bearing in mind that a metre of path costs upwards of £200 there is every good reason to cultivate the involvement of fellwalkers in a cause that must be dear to our hearts… indeed our soles! Please make a beeline for www.fixthefells.co.uk to make a donation, however modest. Your commitment will, to quote John Muir, 'make the mountains glad'.

Using this guide

Unlike other guidebooks which show a single or limited number of routes up the Lakeland fells, the purpose of the Fellranger series has always been to offer the independent fellwalker the full range of approaches and paths

WALKING THE LAKE DISTRICT FELLS – CONISTON

The Coniston Fells from near Low Parkamoor on Bethecar Moor (photo: Natalie Simpson)

available and invite them to combine them to create their own unique experiences. A valuable by-product of this approach has been to spread effects of walkers' footfall more evenly over the path network.

This guide is divided into two parts. 'Fells' describes ascents of each of the 24 fells covered by this volume, arranged in alphabetical order. 'Ridge routes' describes a small selection of popular routes linking these summits.

Fells

In the first part, each fell chapter begins with an information panel outlining the character of the fell and potential starting points (numbered in blue on the guide overview map and the accompanying 1:40,000 HARVEY fell map, and listed – with grid refs – in 'Starting points' in the introduction). The panel also suggests neighbouring fells to tackle at the same time, including any classic ridge routes. The 'fell-friendly route' – one which has been reinforced by the

Using this guide

National Park Authority or is less vulnerable to erosion – is also identified for those particularly keen to minimise their environmental impact.

After a fuller introduction to the fell, summarising the main approaches and expanding on its unique character and features, come the route descriptions. Paths on the fell are divided into numbered sections. Ascent routes are grouped according to starting point and described as combinations of (the red-numbered) path sections. The opportunities for exploration are endless. For each ascent route, the ascent and distance involved are given, along with a walking time that should be achievable in most conditions by a reasonably fit group of walkers keen to soak up the views rather than just tick off the summit. (Over time, you will be able to gauge your own likely timings against these figures.)

In many instances a topo diagram is provided alongside the main fell map to help with visualisation and route planning. When features shown on the maps or diagrams appear in the route descriptions for the first time (or the most significant time for navigational purposes), they are highlighted in **bold**, to help you trace the routes as easily as possible.

As a good guide should also be a revelation, panoramas are provided for a small number of key summits, and panoramas for every fell in this guide can be downloaded free from www.cicerone.co.uk (see 'Additional online resources'). These name the principal fells and key features in the direction of view.

Advice is also given at the end of each fell chapter on routes to neighbouring fells and safe lines of descent should the weather close in. In fellwalking, as in any mountain activity, retreat is often the greater part of valour.

Ridge routes

The second part of this guide describes some classic ridge routes in the Coniston area. Beginning with an information panel giving the start and finish points, the summits included and a very brief overview, each ridge route is described step by step, from start to finish, with the summits highlighted in **bold** in the text to help you orientate yourself with the HARVEY route map provided. Some final suggestions are included for expeditions which you can piece together yourself from the comprehensive route descriptions in 'Fells'.

Appendices

For more information about facilities and services in the Lake District, some useful phone numbers and websites are listed in 'Useful contacts'. 'A fellranger's glossary' offers a glossary to help newcomers decode the language of the fells, as well as explanations of some of the most intriguing place names you might come across in this area. The 'Alphabetical list of fells in the Fellranger series' is a comprehensive list of all the fells included in this 8-volume series, to help you decide which volume you need to buy next!

Safety and access

Always take a map and compass with you – make a habit of regularly looking at your map and take pride in learning how to take bearings from it. In mist this will be a time-saver, and potentially a life-saver. The map can enhance your day by showing additional landscape features and setting your walk in its wider context. That said, beware of the green dashed lines on Ordnance Survey maps. They are public rights of way but no guarantee of an actual route on the ground. Take care to study the maps and diagrams provided carefully and plan your route according to your own capabilities and the prevailing conditions.

Please do not rely solely on your mobile phone or other electronic device for navigation. Local mountain rescue teams report that this is increasingly the main factor in many of the incidents they attend.

The author has taken care to follow time-honoured routes and keep within bounds of access, yet access and rights of way can change and are not guaranteed. Any updates that we know of to the routes in this guide will be made available on the Cicerone website, www.cicerone.co.uk/1039, and we are always grateful for information about discrepancies between a guidebook and the facts on the ground, sent by email to updates@cicerone.co.uk or by post to Cicerone Press, Juniper House, Murley Moss, Oxenholme Road, Kendal, Cumbria, LA9 7RL.

Additional online resources

Summit panoramas for all of the fells in this volume can be downloaded for free from the guide page on the Cicerone website (www.cicerone.co.uk/1039). You will also find a ticklist of the summits in the Walking the Lake District Fells series at www.cicerone.co.uk/fellranger, should you wish to keep a log of your ascents, along with further information about the series.

1 BLACK COMBE 600M/1969FT

Climb it from	Whitbeck **18**, Whicham church **19**, Beckside **20**, Hallthwaites **21**, Corneyfell Road summit **16** or Bootle **17**
Character	A great whale-backed maritime fell in the extreme southwest of the district
Fell-friendly route	7
Summit grid ref	SD 135 855
Link it with	Buckbarrow

Embracing the West Cumbrian seaboard from Ravenglass down to the Whicham valley, the Lake District National Park takes in both a fascinating shore and a fine fell massif. Black Combe will forever draw admiration from those who live and work in its near shadow. It has a presence that might even delude the innocent into thinking it greater than the mighty Scafells. Although local lore that it is an extinct volcano has proven unfounded, what it lacks in volcanicity it more than makes up for in solidity, resting squat, resolute and reassuring, a cornerstone bulwark marking the fells' southwestern limit.

In shape, Black Combe is reminiscent of the Howgills – rounded ridges falling to the west and south with the northern slopes more Pennine in character. Whitecombe Beck etches deep into the southern slope, giving the fell its greatest

↑ *The southern aspect of Black Combe from Kirksanton, with the railway and Brocklebanks old brewery*

dramatic statement – the splintered screes falling into eastern hollows, those nearest the summit most often in shade, giving rise to the fell's titular blackness.

Remote from common fellwalking affairs, Black Combe is deserving of more than a perfunctory inspection. Indeed, many walkers do make regular forays to the top, as the view of land and sea is quite stunning and infinitely variable through time and tide.

Most visitors climb the fell by the Whicham path (4); however, the fell's Christmas-pudding shape means that anyone seeking to make a circular outing invariably chooses to advance up the Whitecombe Beck valley (6), wending to its head then leaving the summit by one or other of the ridges flanking Blackcombe Screes (7–8). Few walkers climb from Bootle, although there is a steady grassy way (11–13). There is only one northern and one eastern approach (12 and 9 respectively), of value in grand traverses but awkward when it comes to making a tidy circuit. Walkers interested in ancient sites should make a point of visiting Sunkenkirk stone circle (10), potentially at the start of a full linear traverse of the fell.

Ascent from Whitbeck **18**

Via the north ridge →*7km/4¼ miles* ↑*570m/1870ft* ⏰*2hr 20min*

A really pleasant, seldom-trod grassy plod to the top

1 Follow the lane by **Townend Hall**, passing the fascinating, sensitively renovated old mill at the foot of **Millergill Beck**. The bridleway continues, northbound initially, with the intake wall close on the left. It then crosses an undulating section, a clear way firmly striking through the dense bracken, with the hint of a shepherds' path veering right at the first rise to climb onto a natural shelf of the near ridge. (This may be a good direct line of ascent or descent but has not been tested.) The route instead keeps faith with the lower path, passing the derelict **Fell Cottage** and a curious ridge feature with an even more intriguing name: **Tarn Dimples**. Just before the path fords **Holegill Beck** a footpath (Route **2**) enters from the field-gate left.

Cross the ford. The ruined **Hall Foss** can be seen over the wall to the left as the path next fords **Hallfoss Beck** and begins to rise beside the wall, then a fence, onto the fell. Go right, up the ridge, as the ground levels opposite a gate in the intake wall. Route **13** from Bootle joins at this point. The

WALKING THE LAKE DISTRICT FELLS – CONISTON

main ascending path winds up the shallow ridge eastward, mounting above a ruined fold and all too briefly through heather, onto **Hentoe Hill** and thence to the summit of Black Combe. (Just before the summit of Hentoe Hill, a lovely old shepherds' path breaks left across the northern slopes by the ruined square of Charley Fold, enabling you to take in the full sweep of Whitecombe and Blackcombe Screes in an extended ascent if you so wish.)

2 This route begins at a gate off the busy A595 opposite the Barfield Tarn lane. The path traverses the cattle pasture and goes through successive gates to reach the open fell at the ford, where you join Route **1**.

Link to Whicham path via Seaness → *2.3km/1½ miles* ↑*200m/655ft* ⏲*40min*
3 An alternative option from Whitbeck starts out with Route **1** but turns immediately before the mill. Rise up the garden edge almost to the pond to veer right on a clear path above the enclosure wall. Ford **Townend Gill**, then continue beside the fence on a firm farm track which duly angles up the slope, petering out on the fell shoulder; a quad-bike track dwindles to a sheep trod as you reach **Seaness**. Visit the first cairn; however, the southernmost cairn has the loveliest view down the coastal margin to the cluster of wind turbines adjacent to Haverigg prison. Bear left, regaining a clear path to join the popular path (Route **4**) rising north from Kirkbank.

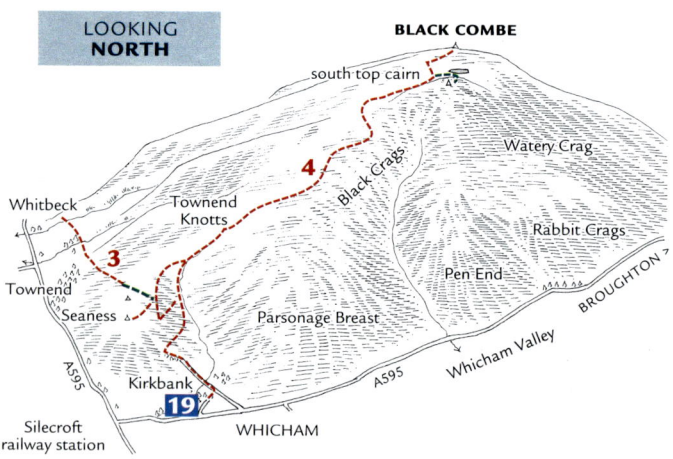

White Combe and the pastoral Whicham valley from above Po House

Ascent from Whicham church 19

Direct →*3.2km/2 miles* ↑*565m/1855ft* ⏲*1hr 20min*

The way of the many

4 Begin from the church car park. (Should a service be in progress, there is a layby just before the turn into the church.) Slip through between the old school and the church to join the byway beyond. Go left to rise behind **Kirkbank**, as the road becomes a track. Find a gate/stile after a fenced recess to gain access to the open fell. Ascend the shallow combe, merging with the Seaness path, for a pleasant steady plod on firm turf. When you get to the head of the **Millergill Beck** valley take the opportunity to break right to the tarn, and then veer back right and south over stony ground to reach the plump **cairn** on the south top for the perfect bird's-eye view over the Millom and Barrow district. Backtrack to the fell summit, from where the northward prospect of Lakeland will tantalise.

WALKING THE LAKE DISTRICT FELLS – CONISTON

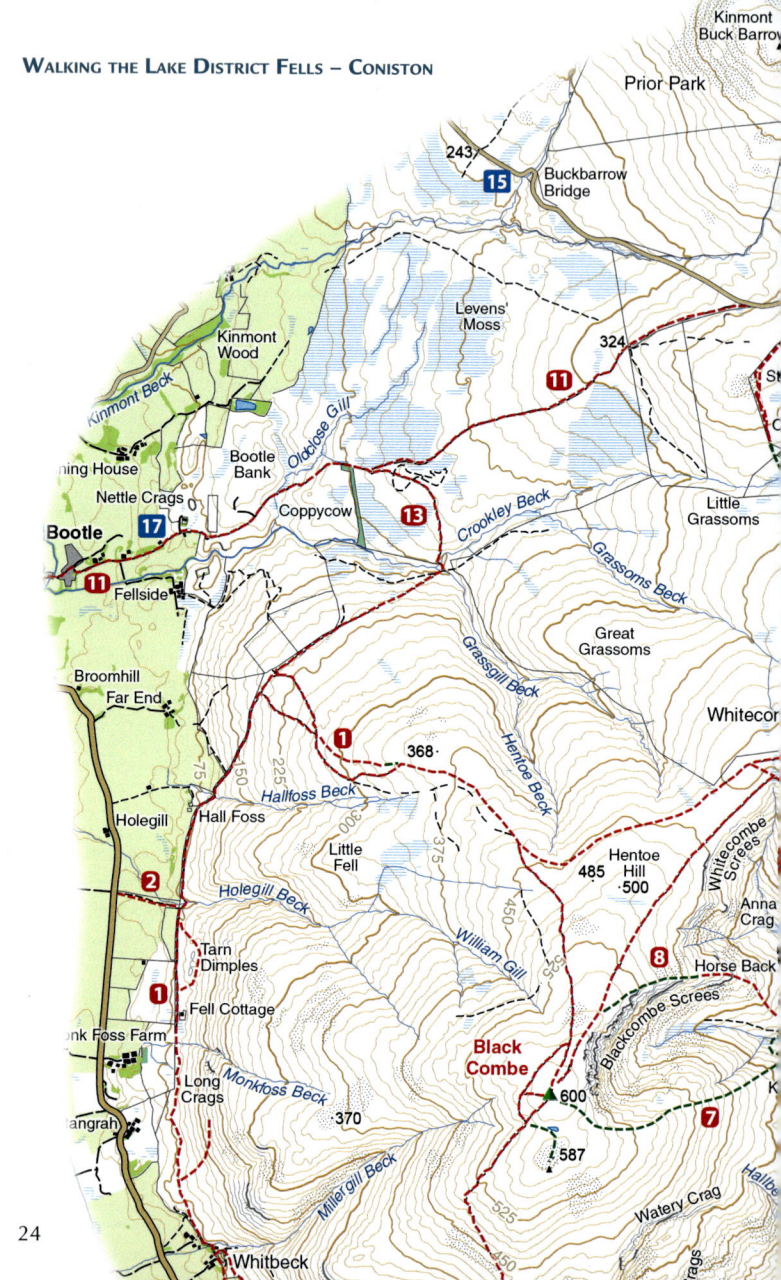

WALKING THE LAKE DISTRICT FELLS – CONISTON

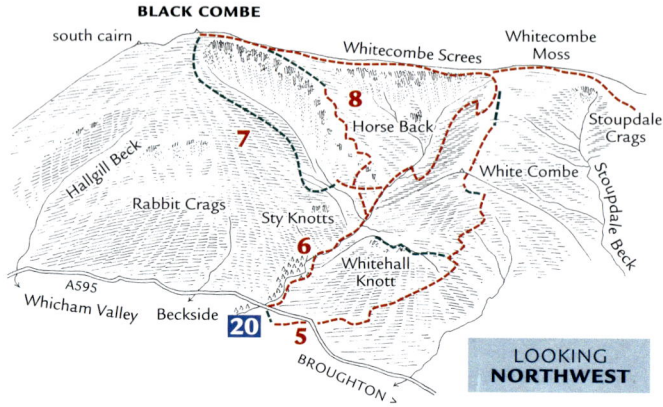

Ascent from Beckside 20

Get right to the dark heart of the fell with these, the most impressive but less-frequented routes.

Via White Combe →*5.6km/3½ miles* ↑*555m/1820ft* ⏲*2hr 15min*

5 From the generous layby close to Beckside Farm head east, taking full advantage of the field-path via Cross Bank to the south of the verge-less main road, newly equipped with hand-gates. As you regain the road take the leafy lane from a gate at the bend above Fox & Goose Cottages. The lane leads to a gate onto the bracken slope of **Whitehall Knott**. Go up left then diagonally across the slope on a grooved track, mounting onto the northern shoulder. (The short ridge of Whitehall Knott is worthy of a detour. It's a fine spot from which to peruse the Whicham valley and consider the fat ridge of Sty Knotts climbing to the top of Black Combe.) As the drove-way continues up by stunted gorse shrubs it gleefully fends off the bracken, but it does not go to the ridge-end summit of **White Combe**. Watch to break left on a path which peters out. The shelter-cairn at the summit is a fine place to halt and delve into your rucksack for a bite to eat, with the great scoured hillsides of Blackcombe and Whitecombe Screes the focus of attention. A narrow ridge path leads purposefully northwest from here, fading as it approaches the junction with

1 BLACK COMBE

the path at the valley head. Curve naturally around the rim and make the final good mile of ascent southwest over easy ground.

Via Whitecombe Beck →*5.2km/3¼ miles* ↑*555m/1820ft* ⏲*2hr 10min*
6 This path starts from the foot of the valley. Follow the gated lane direct from the main road at Beckside. Pass the old farmhouse of **Ralliss**, keeping right to avoid the immediate environs of **Whicham Mill**. As the woodland ends a gate leads into the combe's inner sanctuary. The path skips over a plank footbridge, keeping to the west side of the beck until an obvious switch right over a broader plank footbridge. The path switches left again as it begins to climb up the valley-head slope, zig-zagging towards the end. At the top, turn left to join Route **5** for an easy stroll to the summit.

Two ridges take in Blackcombe Screes; Horse Back (Route 8) is the better climb and Sty Knotts (Route 7) the better descent.

7 To ascend either of the two ridges, follow Route **6** to the ford of Blackcombe Gill, cross, then look left to join the first path that keeps above its north bank. Just after the point where Route **8** breaks right on a faint path, turn left to cross the beck. The **Sty Knotts** route is barely visible on the ground, so the only

Head of the Whitecombe Beck valley

Looking northeast into the heart of Lakeland from Blackcombe Screes

advice is to devise a line that avoids the worst of the bracken to climb south to gain the ridge and then proceed west up to the summit.

8 For the **Horse Back** ridge, start out with Route **7** then seek a faintly evident path mounting above a small fenced area. As the ridge narrows the path threads up through rocks and climbs impressively in steps – exciting situations abound. Curve naturally left, following the brim of **Blackcombe Screes** over pathless ground, to join the path from White Combe (Route **5**) for the final approach to the summit.

Ascent from Hallthwaites 21

Via Graystones →*6.8km/4¼ miles* ↑*615m/2020ft* ⏱*2hr 30min*

A rewarding linear journey

9 From Hallthwaites traverse the intermediate ridge on a footpath served by ladder-stiles via **Bank House**. The view from above **Baystone Bank farm** is a delight. After joining the farm roadway go right at a stile. Follow the lane

1 BLACK COMBE

towards Whirlpippin. Short of the cottage find a footpath signed right. Go through the gate and brief lane opening into a pasture, the invisible path keeping close company with the wall on your left. Towards the end go through a dip, and cross a ditch and then a ladder-stile onto the open fell. For all its best endeavours bracken fails to subsume the path. Slip over the wave-like knoll of Force Knott and keep on along the top of the bank to the east of **Stoupdale Beck**. Marshy ground makes the going soft to begin with but firmer ground eventually arrives and the path rises purposefully onto the western slope of **Graystones**. The facing fellside, known as Leadmine Breast, is a reminder of the days of small-scale prospecting, for copper as well as lead. The path passes by gorse, rising onto the ridge high above Stoupdale. At the dale head a small broken slope bears the ambitious name of **Stoupdale Crags**. The path skirts the top of the gullies and you are rewarded with a fine view down the valley before you head over the peaty plateau of **Whitecombe Moss**, slightly south of west, to meet and follow Route **5**. (In mist, keep within the fence that runs along on the north side of the plateau.)

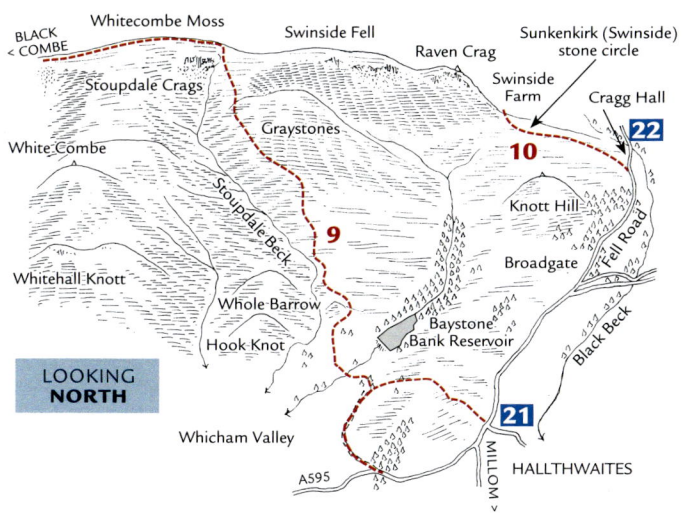

Ascent from Cragg Hall 22

Via Sunkenkirk stone circle →6.6km/4 mile ↑500m/1640ft ⏱2hr 30min

The opening leg for a comprehensive linear traverse of Black Combe

10 Follow the farm access lane (no private cars) to **Swinside Farm**. Close to the farm buildings find the Bronze-Age **stone circle**, comprising some 40 or 50 stones (everyone comes up with a different number). Follow on to the left of the farm buildings via two gates, on a track coming up through a hollow to run close beside a wall. As the track levels find a faint path left; this quickly dissolves on the pasture bank, but an easy ascent ensues, avoiding the bracken, to a cairn on **Raven Crag**. Continue to where a sturdy wall strikes over the fell. Either squeeze through the hogg-hole or carefully use the projecting wall-stile

Long view of Black Combe over Caw, from Brown Pike on Dow Crag

immediately to its left to cross the wall. The grassy ridge of **Swinside Fell** continues, with an opportunity to glance left into the upper Whicham Beck valley. Come up to a stile at a fence junction. Cross and initially follow on with the fence, crossing the brow of **Whitecombe Moss** to be drawn naturally onto the edge path above **Whitecombe Screes** to complete the ascent with Route **5**.

1 BLACK COMBE

Ascent from Bootle 17 or the Corneyfell Road summit 16

Via the Old Road →9.7km/6 miles ↑655m/2150ft ⏲3hr

A grassy byway, useful in creating a circular outing beginning from Whitbeck

11 The Bootle Fell byway gives a grand insight into the style of roads before the advent of tarmac: where feasible it is flanked with neat ditches (or a fosse) to allow run-off and minimise wash-out. After Route **13** has curled up the fell to the right, from a stile/gate the road becomes confined as it progresses to reach the Corneyfell Road, heading on up to the road summit where the fell opens up once more. Here join Route **12**.

From the road summit →5.2km/3¼ miles ↑290m/950ft ⏲2hr

The high start negates much of the ascent, although wet ground may hamper progress.

12 From the summit of the Corneyfell Road join the ridge wall over **Stoneside Hill**, a really good viewpoint for Buckbarrow, and, from the depression beyond, follow the ridge fence onto **Whitecombe Moss**. As a barbed fence intervenes step over the plain fence and keep to the west side of the continuing fence to avoid the even wetter ground on Swinside Fell indicated by the rushes. The semblance of a path descends to cross a tall fence at a fence junction. Follow the fence south-southwest to join Route **9** and advance to the summit.

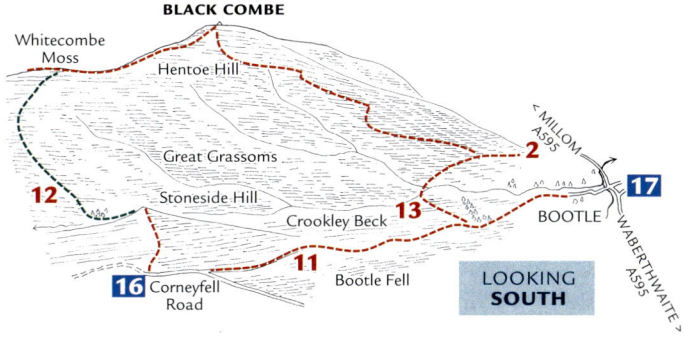

Ascent from Bootle 17

Via Crookley Beck and the north ridge →6.7km/4¼ miles ↑605m/1985ft
⌚2hr 15min

A quiet grassy way

13 Park in the village off the main street opposite the church or, failing that, with due sensitivity, on Fellgreen, above Fell Gate Cottage (SD 116 885). The road running up from the village is a pleasure to tread. From Fellgreen the old Bootle Fell byway proceeds through a gate. Passing **Nettle Crags**, winding up then down through the **Oldclose Gill** dell, spot Gibson's Spout over to the right in Crookley Beck. The old road climbs to pass the top end of **Coppycow**. Immediately beyond the trees find a huge granite erratic known as the Resting Stone. (There is a fat finger-sized hole in the upper south side, presumably an example of Bronze-Age cup-and-ring symbolism. The open fell flanking the byway also has Bronze-Age field systems, but there isn't much to see.)

As the open track bends left take the second green path rising right. This crosses over the bracken bank and slices through a cross-paths to avoid the broad sphagnum marsh. Descend into the **Crookley Beck** valley to ford the beck, passing over the hurdle gate, smartly followed by a concrete culvert of **Grassgill Beck**. Now heading southwest, keep to the higher of the two subsequent green paths slanting across the fellside, duly coming alongside the top of the enclosure wall. As a field-gate is spotted, just before the path begins to descend, take the obvious path left, up the gently rising ridge, with Route **2**.

The summit

Retiring and something of an enigma, the gently domed top of Black Combe ensures that, even from afar, the actual summit is barely perceived and only hoves into view at the last moment of any ascent. Seen from the south, notably from Kirksanton, the portly south cairn pricks the skyline as the sham summit, the convex slope hiding the true top. Coming upon the shallow domed table-top with the wind whistling off the ocean the crude wind shelter is of greater value than usual. The OS column gains permanent benefit from

Black Combe from the Giant's Grave standing stones, Kirksanton

this humble huddle of boulders. The majority of such pillars have become redundant but this one still serves cartographers as a strategic point in the network of the global positioning system.

The view worthiest of admiration lies to the northeast, with the 'Four Threes' (fells over 3000ft) – Scafell, Scafell Pike, Skiddaw and Helvellyn – all in view. Surveyed from the summit the working world of south and west Cumbria displays a historic industrial scene, from the Walney shipyards and the old Millom ironworks, swinging round north beyond the Calder Hall/Sellafield complex to the headland of St Bees, which shields the former marine coalfields of Workington and Whitehaven.

Safe descents

The immediate concern when descending Black Combe is the broken precipice of Blackcombe Screes, which lurks unseen close under the eastern lip of the summit plateau. As the majority of visitors will have come via the Whicham path (**4**) their minds will naturally turn to a straightforward retreat, although many wisely make a circuit upon the continuing bridleway down the broad north ridge (**1**), cutting back S to Whitbeck (and Seaness (**3**), for

Whicham church). Those who have come up the Whitecombe Beck valley may be lured into descending either side of Blackcombe Screes (**7–8**). In mist beware of the fall of the ground.

Ridge route

Buckbarrow →*7km/4¼ miles* ↓*290m/950ft* ↑*230m/755ft* ⏲*2hr 10min*
Follow the emerging path leading NE, watchful to keep a safe distance from the profound declivity overlooking the Whitecombe Beck valley. As the ground levels a narrow peaty trod draws close to a wire fence traversing Whitecombe Moss. As a barbed fence intervenes cross the left of the two stiles over the plain fence and keep to the west side of the continuing, gently descending fence, with little encouragement of a path across the marshy moor. The semblance of a path descends to cross a tall fence at a fence junction. Head straight on, keeping just left of the dwarf-conifer shrubbery, coming up to the netting fence beside the rising wall. Climb to the stony top of Stoneside Hill. Descend, keeping the wall to your left and advancing to the summit of the Corneyfell Road. Cross directly over, keep the wall close left and clamber over Great Paddy Crag before slanting half-right, weaving through boulders and outcrops to reach the summit cairn.

Looking back from Whitecombe Moss

2 BLACK FELL 322M/1056FT

Climb it from	Tom Gill **36**, Tarn Hows **37**, Hawkshead, High Cross **38**, Oxen Fell **35** or Silverthwaite **39**
Character	Coy backdrop to Tarn Hows, clothed in trees and walled allotments
Fell-friendly route	7
Summit grid ref	NY 340 016

Lying within the triangle of Skelwith Bridge, Hawkshead and Coniston, Black Fell forms the northerly backdrop to the comparatively low, intrinsically wild, undulating ridge on which sits the ever-popular Tarn Hows. A perfect embodiment of the picturesque, enhanced by unabashed human intervention, this magical mix of trees, rock and water was the brainchild of James Marshall, a wealthy linen magnate and Leeds MP who moved to Monk Coniston in the 1860s. Today this wonderful place has been made thoroughly accessible for all visitors, from the wheelchair-bound to lively imps. The National Trust has embarked on a programme to recreate James Marshall's original vistas, having acquired the estate thanks to the generosity and farsightedness of Sir Samuel Scott, who purchased it from Beatrix Heelis (née Potter) in 1930.

↑ *Black Fell summit column (photo: Maggie Allan)*

WALKING THE LAKE DISTRICT FELLS – CONISTON

2 BLACK FELL

Evidently the fell name derived from the eastern perspective, which sees afternoon and evening light cast shadows down the steep slopes, clearly visible to patrons tumbling out of the fashionable Drunken Duck Inn about half a mile away to the east.

Walkers enjoying the Cumbria Way, heading north from Coniston, understandably relish their encounter with Tarn Hows, but the majority are unaware of Black Fell. The lack of wear on the one path to the top shows that the actual number of visitors is quite modest. However, this summit is the perfect place to come for a first inspection of this marvellous landscape, the lie of both high land and low land superbly displayed. The fell is usually approached from the Mountain Road (1–6), with options to take in the scenic Tom Gill waterfalls (1) and Tarn Hows (1–4). Two routes from the north (7–8) offer a quick way to the top.

Ascent from Tom Gill 36 or Tarn Hows 37

All the fun of the fell

Via Tom Gill →*0.7km/½ mile* ↑*90m/295ft* ⏲*25min*

Visitors are naturally drawn to park at the main Tarn Hows car park; however, the far more exciting walk sets off from the smaller car park at Tom Gill.

1 There are three paths from the Tom Gill parking area to Tarn Hows. A stepped path climbs in harmony with the north bank of the beck through woodland, particularly revelling in the graceful waterfall of the upper section, below the dam. Of the two paths climbing on the south side, directly from the car park, one in the stony lane joins the one-way road; the other branches left, winding up pasture. Both have their special merit for easy descents. On reaching Tarn Hows, choose from Routes **2** and **3**.

From Tarn Hows →*3.2km/2 miles* ↑*200m/655ft* ⏲*1hr 20min*

Easy scenic strolling on a rightfully popular trail

2 From the Tarn Hows dam a broad path, fit for an urban park, proceeds north. The northern continuation leads on to meet the

Black Crag forming the backdrop to Tarn Hows

fell-crossing lane, known as the Mountain Road, where Black Fell proper begins. Follow this lane right (east), bound for an enclosure (marked as Iron Keld or 'iron well' on OS maps) with two access points. Pass through the enclosure, following the track uphill to exit onto the fell proper, and climb the ridge path, mounting north-northeast to the prominent fell-top pillar.

Via Tom Heights →*4km/2½ miles* ↑*225m/740ft* ⏱*1hr 30min (from the Tarn Hows car park)*

A less-frequented option, perfect for the wandering spirit

3 An alternative option is to venture onto the wonderfully undulating top of Tom Heights. As the path around the western side of Tarn Hows makes the first rise into woodland go sharp left under an ageing larch. An obvious path climbing the bank winds up onto the rising ridge gaily decked with birch, each stepped knoll inevitably marked with a cairn. The cairned summit is a place to pause – perhaps wondering where all the people have gone – and admire the view westward over Holme Fell to Wetherlam and northeastward to Black Fell with the Near Eastern Fells behind. The ridge path threads on down north and then east through the tough growth. Taking damp ground in your stride, pass another prominent cairn to reach the broad path from the tarns at the ladder-stile/gate entry onto the Mountain Road, where you join Route **2**.

Ascent from Hawkshead or High Cross 38

Walkers approaching Black Fell from Hawkshead village can follow a footpath up to Hawkshead Hill (1.6km/1 mile) for either High Cross (left) or the minor road via Borwick Lodge (right) to gain the Mountain Road (Route **5**).

From High Cross via Tarn Hows →*5km/3 miles* ↑*260m/855ft* ⏲*1hr 30min*
4 Bus travellers can alight from the Coniston Rambler service at High Cross at the northern tip of Grizedale Forest (Forestry Commission car park). A well-defined path leads by Wharton Tarn via hand-gates through woodland to reach the road leading north to Tarn Hows. Join the formal trail, passing **Tarn Hows** on whichever side you choose, to enter the Mountain Road at a hand-gate. Turn right for Iron Keld and follow Route **2** to the summit.

From Hawkshead Hill via Borwick Lodge →*5.2km/3¼ miles* ↑*195m/640ft* ⏲*1hr 30min*
5 From the hamlet of Hawkshead Hill follow the minor road to Borwick Lodge, just before **Knipe Fold**. Fork left onto the Mountain Road and walk up the walled lane, taking the first kissing-gate on the right into the enclosure. Keep to the track and then the path, which sweeps up northwest to meet the main track at the kissing-gate at the top of the enclosure. Complete the climb with Route **2**.

Ascent from Oxen Fell 35

A direct approach from the west

Via the Mountain Road →*2.7km/1¾ miles* ↑*165m/540ft* ⏲*1hr 20min*
6 From Oxen Fell High Cross the Mountain Road begins as a proper road, providing access for High Arnside Farm, but quickly turns into a gravel trackway. This is a lovely walk with a succession of scenic turns. Passing the Tarn Hows access gate, the lane winds up and levels under Arnside Intake, advancing to a gate entry, left, into the enclosure. Join Route **2** to proceed to the summit.

Low Arnside

Ascent from High Park road-end or Silverthwaite 39

Direct →2km/1¼ miles ↑190m/625ft ⏲1hr

An excellent 'quick way to the top'

7 From the High Park road-end a footpath commences from a gate, and then leads east via a short wooded lane. This descends momentarily, with a wall to the left, then, where another footpath joins at a gate, climbs the pasture beside the same wall to a gate, coming up to merge with the Park Farm bridleway (Route **8**). Coming up to the top of the enclosure, find the path to the summit branching left.

Via Park Farm →6km/3¾ miles ↑290m/950ft ⏲1hr 30min

8 From Skelwith Bridge and the Brathay Vale, the National Trust Silverthwaite car park is the best starting point. This gives access to the riverbank path heading serenely downstream. Entering woodland, tight by the busy road, the river becomes tumultuous. **Skelwith Force** is a real force to be reckoned with – and to admire. The footpath passes on by the Kirkstone Quarry workshops to cross Skelwith Bridge. Keeping company with the Cumbria Way, head west via

2 BLACK FELL

Park Farm to Low Colwith. Go left up the road to meet the **A593**, then turn left along the main road and branch right after a bus shelter, through a gate, onto the bridleway climbing the northwestern side of **Park Fell**. The open track winds up with excellent views back to Lingmoor Fell and the great swelling heights about Great Langdale. The track passes a sheep-wash fold on the right and winds on by Low Arnside cottage to merge with Route **7**.

9 Walkers wishing to complete an off-road circuit of the fell, having begun at Tom Gill, can follow a footpath after descending Route **7**. It rises, fenced, inside the pasture on the west side of the A593 at the High Park road-end and continues directly over at Oxen Fell High Cross, dipping down into the wooded dell beneath **Holme Fell**. You can then either cross the road at a ladder-stile before **Yew Tree Tarn** to trace the woodland path under **Tom Heights**, or follow the path on the western side of the tarn.

The summit

Black Fell has a conclusive rock summit, adorned with a stone-built OS pillar. Old maps give it the somewhat over-dramatic name Black Crag. The view is an utter joy. The Coniston Fells loom large to the west, with the fells simply crowding into the great northerly arc, Scafell Pike and Great End making sneaky guest appearances either side of Bowfell. Also in view are the Langdale Pikes, Blencathra through the Thirlmere trench, and Helvellyn and Fairfield, Red Screes and the Kentmere Fells leading to a long Pennine skyline beyond Windermere.

Arguably the best views northwards are to be found on the ridge over the ladder-stile, although there is no means of reaching a public road from this northerly enclosure. A prominent viewpoint cairn down on the eastern shoulder of the fell, less than 200 metres from the summit, overlooks the wooded vale towards Windermere.

Safe descents

Take care not to clamber over walls or stray from paths. Woodland thicket and giraffe-high bracken await the wayward wanderer. Simply backtrack to the enclosure then either take the Park Fell bridleway to go north (**7–8**), or pass on down through the enclosure to join the Mountain Road for points east, west or south (**1–6**).

3 BRIM FELL 795M/2608FT

Climb it from	Coniston **32** or Walna Scar Road **31**
Character	A mid-ridge summit, holding all its craggy, watery treasure in the eastern coves
Fell-friendly route	3
Summit grid ref	SD 270 985
Link it with	Coniston Old Man, Dow Crag or Swirl How
Part of	Coniston Triple Treat

Literally the 'brim' of the Coppermines Valley skyline, comprising the lion's share of the Old Man ridge yet subjugated to ancillary rank on grounds of altitude, Brim Fell cradles two wind-whipped tarns, Levers Water and Low Water, on either side of a blunt ridge which ends abruptly at Raven Tor. Below the cliff runs the lateral Boulder Valley, which in its lower portion harbours some extraordinary chunks of rock, the biggest known as the Pudding Stone (it has one easy scrambling ascent for those with the aptitude and inclination). At the head of the Boulder Valley lie fenced clefts associated with possibly the oldest copper mine in the area, Paddy End.

↑ *Brim Fell from Coniston Old Man*

3 BRIM FELL

Viewed from the west, however, Brim Fell has few endearing qualities. Its shattered cliff and scree form a conclusive eastern headwall to the Seathwaite Tarn valley. The unrealistic marking of a footpath into this wild hollow from Levers Hawse is a cruel mystery that Ordnance Survey mapping should rectify for the sake of delicate ankles and necks, lest walkers presume this a safe recourse in hostile conditions – it isn't!

With so much attention focused on the Old Man of Coniston it seems likely that anyone seen climbing Brim Fell is there by mistake. Some walkers clearly reach Low Water and walk over to its outflow, thinking they are on the main path, and then, having crossed the outflow, find that any hint of a path disappears. Instead of backtracking they head on up the inviting grassy slope (4) to the saddle to the rear of Raven Tor and climb Brim Fell, oblivious of their error. In fact, it is a master-stroke, for this is definitely the finest way onto the main ridge. Alternatively, the fell can be accessed from Levers Water via Levers Hawse (1, 3) or from the Walna Scar Road via Goats Hawse (5).

Ascent from Coniston 32

Rewarding choices on less-frequented paths

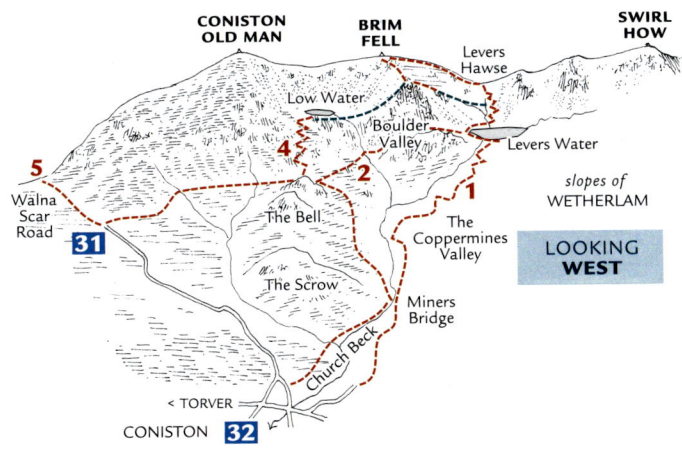

WALKING THE LAKE DISTRICT FELLS – CONISTON

Via Levers Water →5km/3 miles ↑745m/2445ft ⏲2hr 50min

1 Start from the bridge in the centre of the town, beside the Black Bull Hotel and brewery. Follow either the road and open valley access track on the north side of **Church Beck**, or cross the beck and turn right, beginning along the **Walna Scar Road** and turning right after the Sun Hotel, following

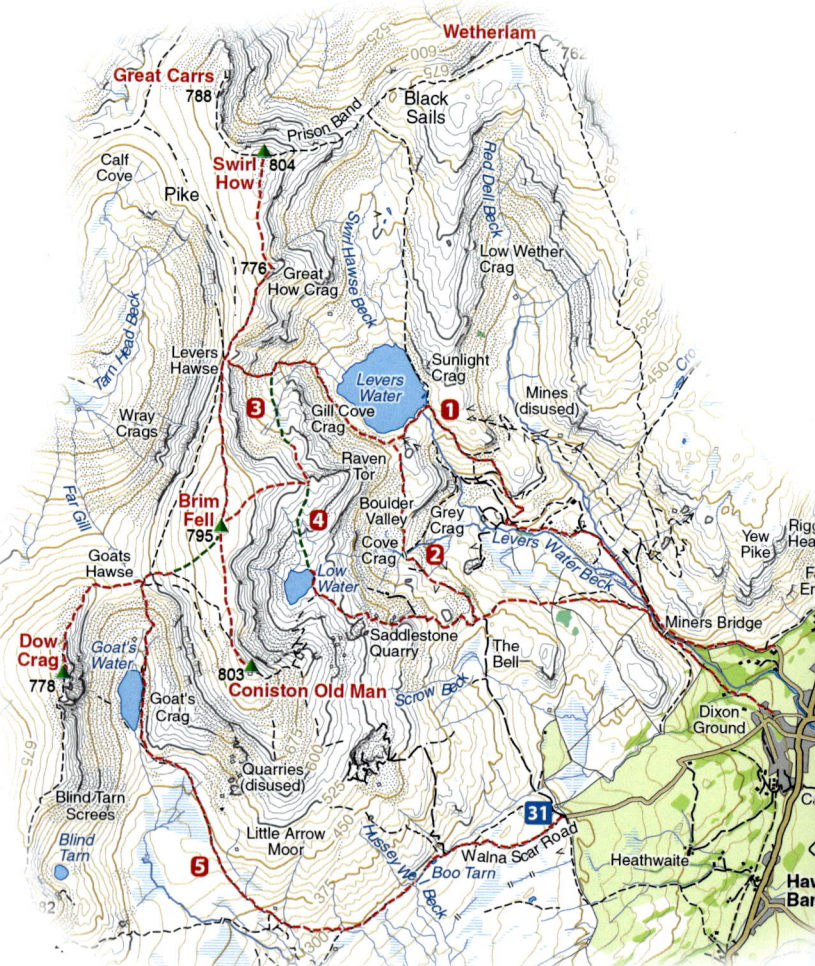

3 BRIM FELL

Mine enthusiast abseiling into the Simon's Nick/Paddy End copper mine, adjacent to Levers Water

a signpost to the 'Old Man' via **Dixon Ground**. Reach **Miners Bridge** by either route and join the main valley track on the north bank of **Levers Water Beck**, which leads on to the Coppermines Youth Hostel. The continuing track winds on up, dominated towards the end by the massive cleft of Simon's Nick, part of the Paddy End copper workings. It finally reaches the outflow and dam of **Levers Water**, cradled in a wild corrie rimmed with crags. Go left along the low dam, skirting the tarn, rising to pass under the fenced mine workings at the back of Simon's Nick. **Be warned:** the mine workings are a death trap and the preserve of well-equipped speleologists only. Here join Route **2** or **3**.

2 A popular path veers left from the southern shore of **Levers Water**, crossing the brow left and wending down the intriguing **Boulder Valley** to pass the Pudding Stone after a plank footbridge. It then joins an old quarrymen's track, leading back to **the Bell** cutting, where you can join Route **4**.

3 Otherwise follow the clear if rough path contouring above the tarn beneath **Raven Tor**. After fording one gill it veers uphill with Cove Gill, steeper sections suitably pitched. Keep to the well-made path as it rises, avoiding the loose scree which appears to offer a more direct route. The ground steepens further, with consistent pitching zig-zagging to **Levers Hawse**, where the main ridge route is joined. Turn left, due south, to reach the summit cairn.

An intriguing alternative branches south before the main stepped section begins and accompanies Cove Gill into the cove recess, slipping over a saddle to find a faint path across a loose section, leading to the skyline col directly behind **Raven Tor** to join Route **4**.

The going is easy all the way, but in mist you should stay with the main path to Levers Hawse.

Via Raven Tor →5.7km/3½ miles ↑780m/2560ft ⏱2hr 45min

A splendid route, predominantly on grass

4 Follow Route **1** to **Miners Bridge**. Keep to the south bank, soon to climb diagonally up the slope through hand-gates, with open views of the extensive spoil and remaining buildings of the Coppermines Valley (including the youth hostel) over to the right. At the saddle between **the Bell** and the main fell join the track coming up from the Walna Scar Road fell-gate. Climb up the main ascending quarrymen's track, passing various features of the **Saddlestone Quarry**, stark reminders of hard toil of another age. Arrival at **Low Water** gives

Raven Tor and the Levers Water dam

a final excuse to pause before you branch right, threading through the large boulders to cross the outflow. Head north up the grassy slope to the saddle to the rear of **Raven Tor**. Make a brief detour up the bank, right, to the cairned top of the tor and look through the notch across the airy gulf to Great How Crags. Back at the saddle aim west. Minor broken outcrops lead onto the plateau. Pass a large cairn among fragmented bedrock en route to the main summit cairn.

Ascent from Walna Scar Road fell-gate 31

Via Goats Hawse →*4.8km/3 miles* ↑*570m/1870ft* ⏲*2hr 25min*

By normal convention this route is used as an easy-on-the-knees descent, ideal for the round trip.

5 Follow the **Walna Scar Road** (an open cart track) west, eventually rising through two rock cuttings to branch right, up steps, onto a clear part-pitched path traversing into the Cove. Continue to **Goat's Water** and up to **Goats Hawse**. Take the main path towards **Coniston Old Man**, curving up from the hawse, but then branch half-left and climb the grass slope direct to the summit.

The summit

Although the fell-top of Brim Fell is gently domed and almost bereft of surface features, the summit cairn, composed of thick wafers of bedrock slate, is a gem, a solid pile far grander than the cairn on Swirl How. The view is only hampered by the extent of the plateau but it is brim-full of detail.

Safe descents

In misty conditions put your faith in either Levers Hawse, due N (**3**), with its well-pitched path leading E down to Levers Water, or Goats Hawse to the SW (**5**), with a steady descent S down by Goat's Water and the Cove to join the Walna Scar Road, in both instances seeking the shelter of Coniston. Goats Hawse also provides a safe line NW into the Seathwaite Tarn valley for the Duddon valley.

Ridge routes

Coniston Old Man →*0.8km/½ mile* ↓*25m/80ft* ↑*30m/100ft* ⏲*20min*
Head S, keeping steep ground several strides' length to the left. An easy stroll leads assuredly to the summit.

Dow Crag →*1.3km/¾ mile* ↓*170m/560ft* ↑*130m/425ft* ⏲*40min*
Descend the grassy slope SW to Goats Hawse, joining the regular path curving round from W to S to the summit bastion.

Swirl How →*2.4km/1½ miles* ↓*110m/360ft* ↑*120m/395ft* ⏲*40min*
Follow the ridge on its steady descent to Levers Hawse (which, like Link Hause on the Fairfield Horseshoe, is not a cross-over pass). The ridge route climbs NNE (don't be drawn left to Fairfield saddle), glancing by the tops of Little How Crag and the more significant Great How Crag. Beyond, weave through the irregular surface outcrops to the summit.

Swirl How from the north ridge

4 BUCKBARROW 549M/1801FT

Climb it from	Corneyfell Road summit **16**, Bootle **17** or Buckbarrow Bridge **15**
Character	The fabulously rocky summit crowning a moor
Fell-friendly route	1
Summit grid ref	SD 152 910
Link it with	Black Combe or Whitfell

Buckbarrow's summit area is an oasis of mountain Lakeland, with three – if not four – rocky tops to explore. It shares with the crest of Stoneside Hill a sense of rugged wildness, a welcome contrast to the sleeker lines of Black Combe and Whitfell.

From the Corneyfell Road rise the uninviting fenced western slopes of Prior Park (the name indicative of medieval monastic deer enclosure). The eastern slopes run down over Plough Fell, angling south over Thwaites Fell to end in the old coppice woodland at the foot of the Duddon valley. Within the woods lies possibly the fell's greatest treasure, the reconstructed remains of Duddon Bridge iron blast furnace, which ran on locally sourced charcoal until 1867, when it

↑ *Looking south from the summit of Buckbarrow*

succumbed to the greater efficiency of coke. A bridleway from the site climbs onto the fell via the subsidiary top, Barrow.

Access to this fell-top could not be easier; a gently rising ridge wall leads from the Corneyfell Road summit straight onto the midriff of the summit mass on Great Paddy Crag (1), but the summit itself is well defended by rocky ground. An alternative 'backdoor' approach follows Buckbarrow Beck up from Buckbarrow Bridge (3). Fellwalkers eyeing linear outings will see the pleasure in a 'Bootle to Boot' connection availing of the Old Road (2), or the 'Black Combe to Devoke Water' ridge route, and in either case Buckbarrow makes a most satisfying early objective.

Ascent from the Corneyfell Road summit 16

A mist-defyingly simple ascent

Direct →2km/1¼ miles ↑150m/490ft ⏱45min

1 Park at the road summit and follow the clear path north in harmony with the ridge wall. As **Great Paddy Crag** rears there is the element of choice. Either slant up right, threading through boulders and outcrops onto the summit, with only spasmodic hints of a path, or bear left, keeping beside the fence under the boulder bank, passing a curious wind-shelter-like object, then head west-northwest to a gateway and mount the easy slope to reach the western scarp-top summit of **Kinmont Buck Barrow**. The cairn here, which rests upon a more ancient predecessor, is a smaller version of one on Whitfell summit, although this top surveys a great sweep of land and ocean. Backtrack to the gateway and slant half-left via a broken wall to reach the main summit of Buckbarrow up the boulder slope.

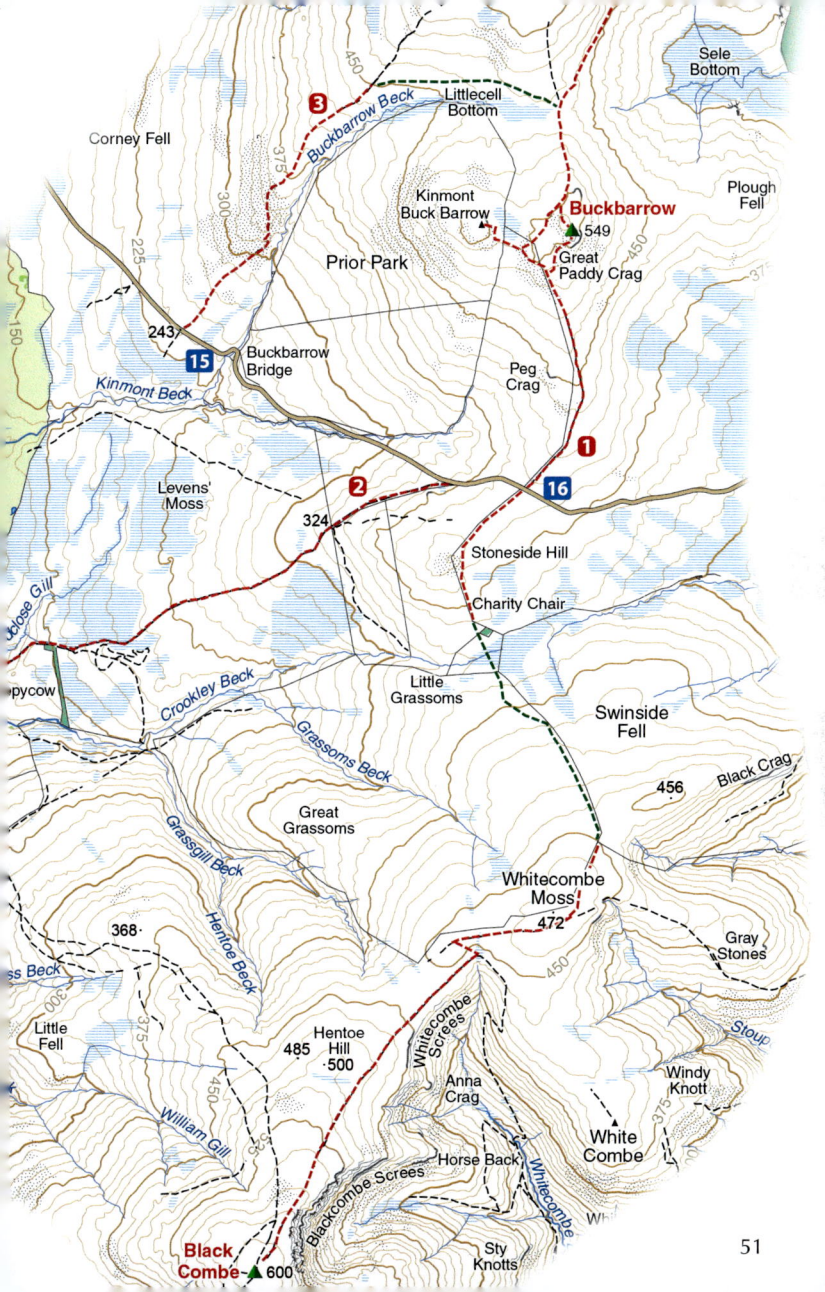

Ascent from Bootle 17

Via the Old Road →8km/5 miles ↑530m/1740ft ⏲3hr

The Old Road is a pleasure to stride along.

2 The honest ascent starts from Bootle, following the Old Road up from Fellgreen. The open byway is a firm green ribbon, winding up into a lane to meet the Corneyfell Road some 250 metres west of the road summit. From the road summit follow Route **1**.

Ascent from Buckbarrow Bridge 15

Via Littlecell Bottom →3.7km/2¼ miles ↑330m/1085ft ⏲2hr

A straightforward ascent, following the line of Buckbarrow Beck

3 Follow the green track, originally made for peat extraction on the plateau of Burn Moor, directly up from the open road. Watch for the shepherds' quad-bike marks forking right off the green-way short of Hare Raise. Contour round the northern side of the **Littlecell Bottom** marsh, linking up with the ridge path coming from the north off Burn Moor. Head south, perhaps keeping among the outcrops for greater interest, up to the summit.

The summit

This rocky crest would not be out of place anywhere in Lakeland. In fact, it is very reminiscent of Cold Pike, but with a rather different view. Take time to savour it, particularly northwards, where Whitfell draws attention to the majesty of the central Lakes.

Safe descent

Follow the ridge wall S off Great Paddy Crag (**1**) to the summit of the Corneyfell Road. The nearest settlement is Bootle, down the Old Road (**2**), which branches into a lane, going WSW, some 200 metres from the road summit.

Buckbarrow from the Old Road above Bootle

Ridge routes

Black Combe →*7km/4¼ miles* ↓*230m/755ft* ↑*290m/950ft* ⏲*2hr 25min*
For much of the way a wall, then a fence, acts as a guide. Although this land is open access there are, as yet, no stiles. Follow the ridge wall off Great Paddy Crag, crossing the Corneyfell Road and mounting onto the rocky hillock of Stoneside Hill. Descend S, looking for a suitable gap through the decrepit wall and netting fence near the sheepfold at Charity Chair. Pass the stunted conifer spinney and skip over the ditch to follow a low bank to a fence junction. Step over this tall obstacle and continue up the rough moorland with the fence to the left. Near the brow step over the plain fence immediately beyond the barbed fence junction and continue over Whitecombe Moss, to join with the path from the Whitecombe Beck valley, which runs above the steep escarpment of Whitecombe Screes and rises SW onto the summit.

Whitfell →*2.4km/1½ miles* ↓*70m/230ft* ↑*95m/310ft* ⏲*40min*
Head N, crossing Littlecell Bottom, and contour across Burn Moor's eastern slopes before rising to the summit.

5 CAW 529M/1736FT

Climb it from	Seathwaite **49**, Water Yeat **28** or Kiln Bank Cross **26**
Character	A great stand-alone fell with plenty to offer the explorer
Fell-friendly route	1
Summit grid ref	SD 230 944
Link it with	Stickle Pike or Walna Scar
Part of	Fox Haw, Caw and Pikes

Viewed from Ulpha, Caw is a real peak, a fell that simply demands to be climbed. Its presence is disproportionate to its size, catching the eye from as far away as the M6. If you stand on its summit you can see its central importance to an appreciation of beautiful Dunnerdale, as the northern slopes fall quickly away beneath your feet, giving a fabulous outlook towards the Scafells.

Caw is defined to the east and west by the Rivers Lickle and Duddon respectively, and there is much rock on all sides, its several subsidiary pikes adding immeasurably to any ascent. Routes 1 and 7 make use of the Park Head Road bridleway, which runs along the western flank; Route 2 sweeps up from

↑ *Caw from Fox Haw*

5 Caw

Dunnerdale to join Routes 3–4 from the Lickle valley, taking the summit from the east via Pikes; Route 5 makes a pathless ascent of the southern slopes and Route 6 offers a handy link with the Park Head Road from the southwest.

Ascent from Seathwaite 49

Via Park Head Road →*2.5km/1½ miles* ↑*425m/1395ft* ⏱*2hr*

A heritage route, the way of former toil, now a pleasing inquisitive trek

1 From the road bend 100 metres east of the Newfield Inn, pass through the gated sheep pen onto the rough cart track of Park Head Road up by a gate, close to **Old Park Beck**, and look for the stone-retained incline branching up left. Stride at ease up the soft turf. The tooling shed and spoil heap mark the end of the original path. The mine level invites a tentative peer – to judge by the quantity of slate in the heap it must run deep into the fell. The hint of a continuing path now mounts the grassy rake above (south-southwest), eventually bending left to the summit.

The Duddon valley from the Caw slate mine

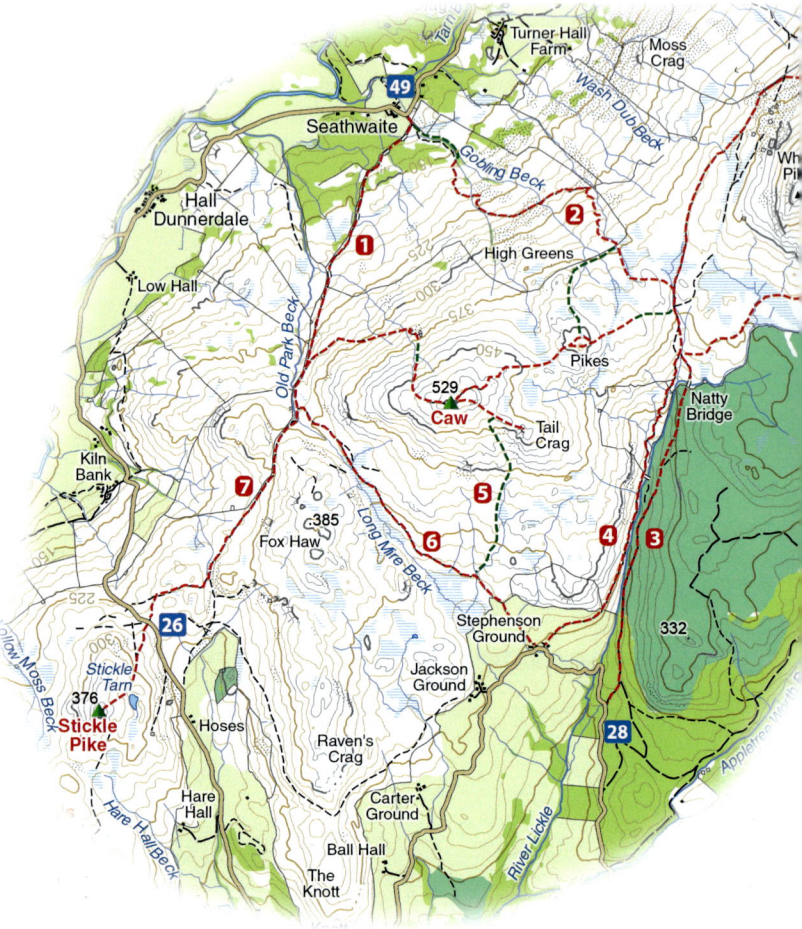

Via Pikes →*3.3km/2 miles* ↑*455m/1495ft* ⏲*2hr 20min*

A route for the solitary wanderer who loves being in wild places

2 From the road bend 100 metres east of the Newfield Inn, pass through the gated sheep pen onto the rough cart track of Park Head Road. A less-than-obvious drove-way branches off the track left, immediately clear of the

5 Caw

sheep pens. Keep **Gobling Beck** to your left as you rise over marshy ground then climb a bracken bank, fording the beck, left, to curve around a rush patch, now onto a far clearer green path. This slips through a gateway and contours northeast, before winding up the enclosure to a hurdle in the boundary wall. Either trend right along the wall then south to clamber over Green Pikes, or keep with the continuing path up Yaud Mire to embark on the easier ridge heading southwest to the summit of **Pikes**. Continuing, a path trends down right, into the hollow, before setting its sights on the main summit. (This path would be unreliable in mist.) The path becomes clearer and then splits momentarily before the steep final pull to the pillar.

Ascent from Water Yeat 28

Via the Lickle valley →*4km/2½ miles* ↑*260m/855ft* ⏱*2hr 10min*

Two valley approaches following the infant River Lickle upstream to tackle the fell from the east

3 From the forest gate 300 metres south of the bridge (SD 239 928) enter the part-cleared plantation beneath **the Knott**, on a clear if infrequently used forest track. The track wends up the valley, nearing the juvenile **Lickle**, with the rough slopes of Caw clearly in view. (As the mature plantation gives way to younger stock you will see a path branching down left which leads to an elegant flag footbridge otherwise hidden from the track. If you take this, you can proceed along the west-bank path to pass through a wall and join the continuation of the forest track on the open fell beyond Natty Bridge.) Keeping with your forest track, pause at the next turning space to admire, to your left, the waterfall spilling from the combe south of Pikes – a prominent summit later in this ascent. Shortly the track ends at a stile just before an attractive ravine. A serviceable wooden bridge has replaced the old stone-arched **Natty Bridge**, now almost entirely washed away, with only a fragment remaining.

The path, whose ultimate destination is the old Walna Scar Quarry, heads on up the damp fell towards a shallow pass. Carry on until you reach a point where a path bears sharply right off the main path, across from a small outcrop on your left. Leave the main path to round the outcrop in a westerly

WALKING THE LAKE DISTRICT FELLS – CONISTON

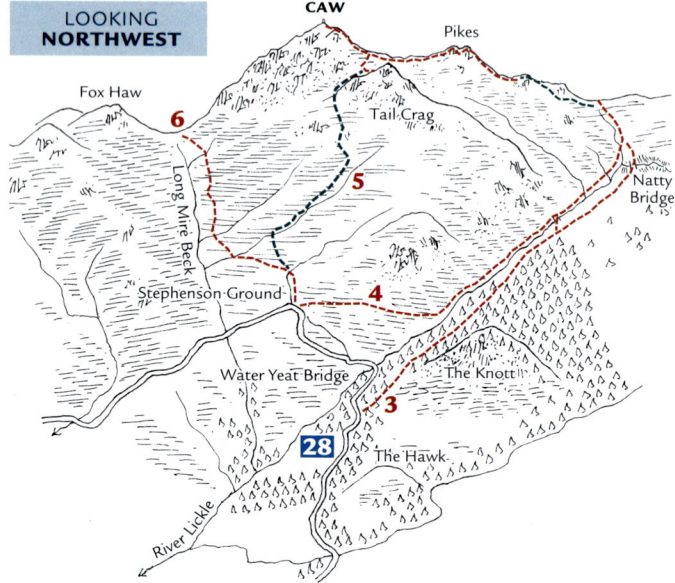

direction, with no hint of a path. Clamber onto the top of the first rise and look northeast to the dominant peak of White Pike, the prow of Walna Scar and southern limit of the principal mountain mass of the Coniston group – a most impressive sight. With only the slightest hint of a path, walk on up the southwesterly trending ridge, passing a lovely pool en route to the rocky peak of **Pikes**. This makes a good intermediate point to rest and consider the Duddon scene. From here join Route **2** to gain the summit.

4 On the far bank of the Lickle an old bridleway, beginning at **Stephenson Ground** (along the road to the northwest), is an excellent alternative upper-valley route, joining Route **3** just beyond Natty Bridge.

Via Tail Crag →2.2km/1¼ miles ↑370m/1215ft ⏲1hr 25min

A pathless line to include the subsidiary top of Tail Crag

5 From the forest-gate parking space walk along the road to cross **Water Yeat Bridge**. The road winds uphill, closing eventually on the farmhouse at

Stephenson Ground. Go through the gate on the right, immediately short of the farmhouse, where two bridleways start, signed 'Walna Scar' and 'Seathwaite'. Take the latter path, passing up by the house to enter a walled lane. After the hand-gate exit the lane. Diverging from the path, aim to follow Broadslack Beck up through the bracken and outcrops onto the ridge between **Tail Crag** and Caw, then detour right for Tail Crag and return northwest to rise to the summit.

Via Long Mire Beck →*3.7km/2¼ miles* ↑*400m/1310ft* ⏱*1hr 50min*

The Long Mire Beck bridleway offers a convenient link-route.

Caw slate-mine incline

6 Follow Route **5** from Water Yeat Bridge to the end of the lane, and then follow **Long Mire Beck** northwest up to the turf trail over the hause to merge with the Park Head Road bridleway, bearing north, then veering off up the quarry incline with Route **1**.

Ascent from Kiln Bank Cross 26

Direct →*3.5km/2¼ miles* ↑*320m/1050ft* ⏱*1hr 40min*

7 A further link approach starts at the Kiln Bank Cross hause at the head of the Dunnerdale Beck valley. Follow the Park Head Road green-way to the Caw slate mine incline and join Route **1**.

The summit

Caw has the perfect summit, but for the imposition of a now-redundant white concrete triangulation pillar – redundant, except when balancing a camera steady for the classic view towards the Scafells.

Safe descents

There are crags on all fronts, the most notable being Goat Crags on the blunt western end, so sticking to a path is important. If heading for the Duddon, aim for Park Head Road (**1**), though look out for your right-hand fork some 50 metres down the north slope. This leads into a grassy rake and down to the slate mine. Bear left here with the incline. The broken southern slope has not a single path, outcrops and, later, bracken hampering progress down by Broadslack Beck to join the Long Mire bridleway (**6**) leading into the green lane and the road at Stephenson Ground.

Ridge routes

Stickle Pike →*3.6km/2¼ miles* ↓*300m/985ft* ↑*150m/490ft* ⏲*1hr 45min*
Heed the advice on descent to Park Head Road via Caw slate mine (see 'Safe descents'), then keep with the track SSW over Brock Barrow hause to the open road at Kiln Bank Cross. Cross the road and continue on a clear path heading up the bank in the same direction, climbing to the compact summit.

Walna Scar →*4km/2½ miles* ↓*75m/245ft* ↑*185m/605ft* ⏲*2hr 15min*
There are two options. Firstly, follow the ridge NE over Pikes to meet the bridleway emerging from the head of the Lickle valley. Then, either follow its continuation N, passing below Walna Scar Quarry to join the Walna Scar Road up to the pass just NE of the summit, or traverse White Maiden by turning right to cross a small flag bridge on Caw Moss and proceeding N on a discernible path towards a gateway in a wall with a tarn beyond, before taking off up the fellside, pathless, keeping the wall close right. From White Maiden, follow the ridge NE to the summit.

6 CONISTON OLD MAN 803M/2635FT

Climb it from	Coniston **32**, Walna Scar Road **31** or Torver **30**
Character	An iconic proud fell inextricably connected to the village and lake
Fell-friendly route	3
Summit grid ref	SD 272 978
Link it with	Brim Fell or Dow Crag
Part of	Coniston Triple Treat

As life turns, fads and fashions change, but not so readily mountains. The old allure lingers and such a distinguished fell as the Old Man of Coniston has laid claim to regular – even daily – visits from time immemorial. The climb up the long slate staircase is always rewarded by a life-enhancing sensation of being on top of a worthier world. An industrial wasteland of mineral and slate extraction fades away as your eyes take in the sumptuous panorama of mountain Lakeland.

Yet this ever-popular summit is only the start of a magnificent line of fells, which reaches its culmination around 3km further north on Swirl How. Walkers are naturally drawn to follow a clockwise horseshoe from Coniston, ending with the descent from Wetherlam back into the Coppermines Valley.

↑ *The summit of Coniston Old Man*

WALKING THE LAKE DISTRICT FELLS – CONISTON

The correct name of the fell is the Old Man of Coniston, although it is colloquially known and labelled on many maps as Coniston Old Man. There are three principal routes to the summit of the Old Man, its position at the end of the ridge giving more scope for tortuous trails than many walkers realise. Invariably, large parties traipse up the fell directly on Routes 1 and 2; the discerning find the best of the fell by starting from the Walna Scar Road and either following Route 3 to wind up the whale-back south ridge above Burstingstone, or approaching from the west by the Cove and Goats Hawse on Route 4. Route 6 offers an approach from Torver.

Ascent from Coniston 32

A recreational hike through a landscape redolent with history

Direct →*4.3km/2½ miles* ↑*755m/2475ft* ⏲*3hr*
1 From the bridge in the middle of the village you have two routes to Miners Bridge. Either take the road past the Black Bull (the Old Man Ale can wait) and turn left by the Ruskin Museum on a road which rises to become an open track, or cross the bridge and

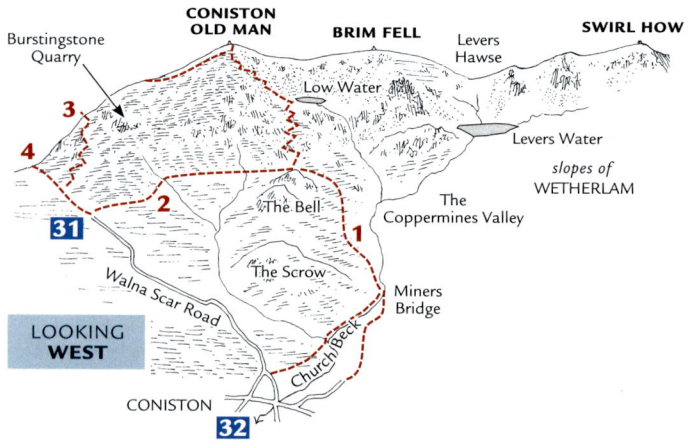

6 Coniston Old Man

WALKING THE LAKE DISTRICT FELLS – CONISTON

The upper zig-zags rising from Low Water

climb the lane, turning right behind the Sun Hotel to a gate at **Dixon Ground** and an open path advancing to a kissing-gate, with **Church Beck** close right. At the gate on **Miners Bridge** the two routes come together. Keep to the south bank, soon to climb diagonally up the slope through hand-gates, with open views of the extensive spoil and remaining buildings of the Coppermines Valley (including the youth hostel) over to the right. At the saddle between **the Bell** and the main fell, join the track coming up from the Walna Scar Road fell-gate (Route **2**).

Climb up the main ascending quarrymen's track, passing various features of the **Saddlestone Quarry**, stark reminders of hard toil of another age. Arrival at **Low Water** gives a final excuse to pause before tackling the final narrow, winding quarry path up the northern slope to the summit. For all the repair work that is done on this popular path, loose slate continues to give discomfort.

6 CONISTON OLD MAN

Ascent from Walna Scar Road fell-gate 31

Two exciting ways to the top

If you leave your car at the bottom of the Walna Scar Road, rather than parking by the fell-gate, you can console yourself that the climb thus far was a good warm-up for the rigours ahead. From the fell-gate car park two options are apparent.

Via the main tourist trail →*3.2km/2 miles* ↑*610m/2000ft* ⏱*2hr 15min*
2 Go right along the open track to link with the direct Route **1**. This gives you an opportunity to visit the top of **the Bell**, a mini-mountain and a superb situation offering an intimate view of the Coppermines Valley, and a modest objective to have under your belt if mist scuppers the rest of the day.

Via Little Arrow Moor →*3.2km/2 miles* ↑*555m/1820ft* ⏱*2hr 20min*
3 Quite the better option follows the **Walna Scar Road** (an open cart track) west. Passing the foot of the Burstingstone Quarry track – the quarry is still occasionally active, hence the metal barrier – notice a footpath sign directing right for the 'Old Man'. This climbs the bank, drifting left onto a shoulder of **Little Arrow Moor**. An older path runs on across the eastern slope above the quarry, but this has fallen from favour and is now rarely used. The popular path comes close to the edge overlooking **the Cove**, then bears up right onto the upper ridge, with no hazards. Proceed up the ridge to the summit.

Via the Cove →*5km/3 miles* ↑*560m/1835ft* ⏱*2hr 50min*

This route is most frequently used as an easy descent for jaded knees.

4 Alternatively, where Route **3** turns off, continue with the **Walna Scar Road** track as it rises through two rock cuttings, then branch right up steps onto a clear part-pitched path traversing into **the Cove**. Follow on over the **Goat Crag** rock-step and along the eastern shore of **Goat's Water**. The pitched path winds up to **Goats Hawse** depression then swings naturally up right to the summit, the path never in doubt. Sadly, the erosion is all too apparent.

5 Follow Route **4** to **the Cove**, from where an old green path can be followed, right, up to a ruin. (This was originally an access route to the old

WALKING THE LAKE DISTRICT FELLS – CONISTON

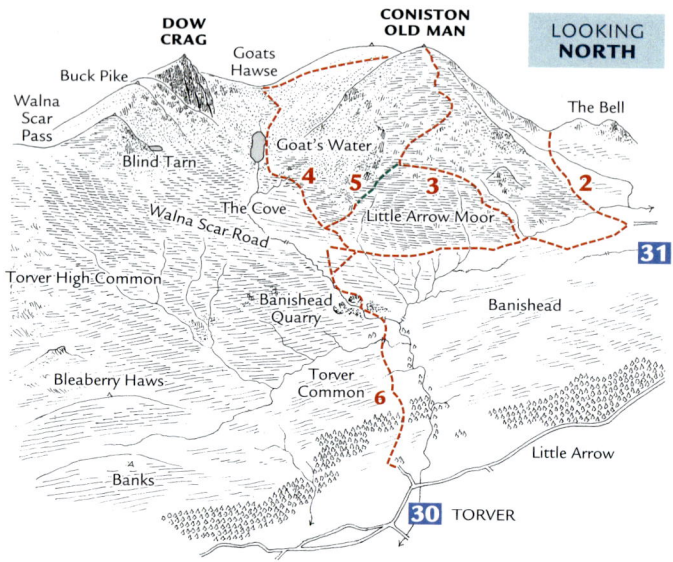

quarries high up on the southwest slope of the Old Man.) When this path bends left at the ruin, carry straight on up the pathless slope to the skyline to join the Little Arrow Moor path (Route **3**) just where it hits the edge.

Ascent from Torver 30

Fascinating quarries add considerably to the interest of this route.

Via Banishead Quarry →6.4km/4 miles ↑695m/2280ft ⏱3hr 30min

6 Park at the church hall at Torver (£1 donation requested) next to St Luke's and the Church House Inn, or at the road-end off the bend of the main road (SD 285 945). Follow the lane up by **Scarr Head**, entering a gated bridle-lane signed to 'Walna Scar'. Pass ruined barns, following another sign to 'Tranearth'. Cross a concrete bridge, with Tranearth Climbers' Hut over to the left. Continue to a hand-gate then through sheep-handling pens to a gate and then over the wooden bridge. Keep to the main track, up through the slate tips, to swing round the fenced **Banishead Quarry**. At the western end Torver

Banishead Quarry with Torver Beck spilling into the pool to soak away mysteriously

Coniston from the Old Man

Beck falls into the pool at the base of the quarry and soaks away through a cave. The route ascends the bracken bank, with several green-ways to choose from, to merge with the Walna Scar Road track (Route **4**).

The summit

The drystone viewing platform and cairn are now depleted (the old cairn was a handsome edifice twice the height of the present one) and in need of a serious facelift. There is also a stone-built OS column, an ideal leaning post while you gaze awestruck, the profound drop beneath your feet into the hanging valley of Low Water making you feel as if you're above the clouds. This is the best view in the Coniston group, across the Coppermines Valley to Wetherlam, backed by ridge after ridge of wonderful fells, with the majestic Scafells appearing half-left. Wander left to look across at the face of Dow Crag. The ridge-edge location gives a sense of isolation and finality, with the fells one way and the wooded lowlands about Coniston Water and the

Safe descents

Wind is always a nuisance and, on occasion, a real danger on the fells. Prevailing southwesterlies encourage walkers to seek the shelter of the popular slate staircase down by Low Water (**1**), heading directly for Church Beck. The most pleasant descent is without question by Goat's Water on the path heading NW from the summit (**4**). This curves down to the broad saddle of Goats Hawse, turns due S down the pitched path to skim the shores of Goat's Water and then ventures on down the Cove to meet the Walna Scar Road. There turn left for Coniston or keep straight on (**6**), by Banishead Quarry, for Torver.

Ridge routes

Brim Fell →*0.8km/½ mile* ↓*30m/100ft* ↑*25m/80ft* ⏲*20min*
The walk to Brim Fell is as easy as falling off a log. The one concern is to keep the steep ground of the corrie a comfortable distance to the right. Take care that you are not drawn down the popular path NW to Goats Hawse. The ridge broadens, as does the path, as it advances N to the large solitary cairn.

Dow Crag →*1.6km/1 mile* ↓*150m/490ft* ↑*145m/475ft* ⏲*40min*
This is an exciting walk, linking two compatriot summits. The clear path leads NW, curving down to Goats Hawse. From here climb naturally round the scarp W, turning S to climb to the magnificent summit bastion.

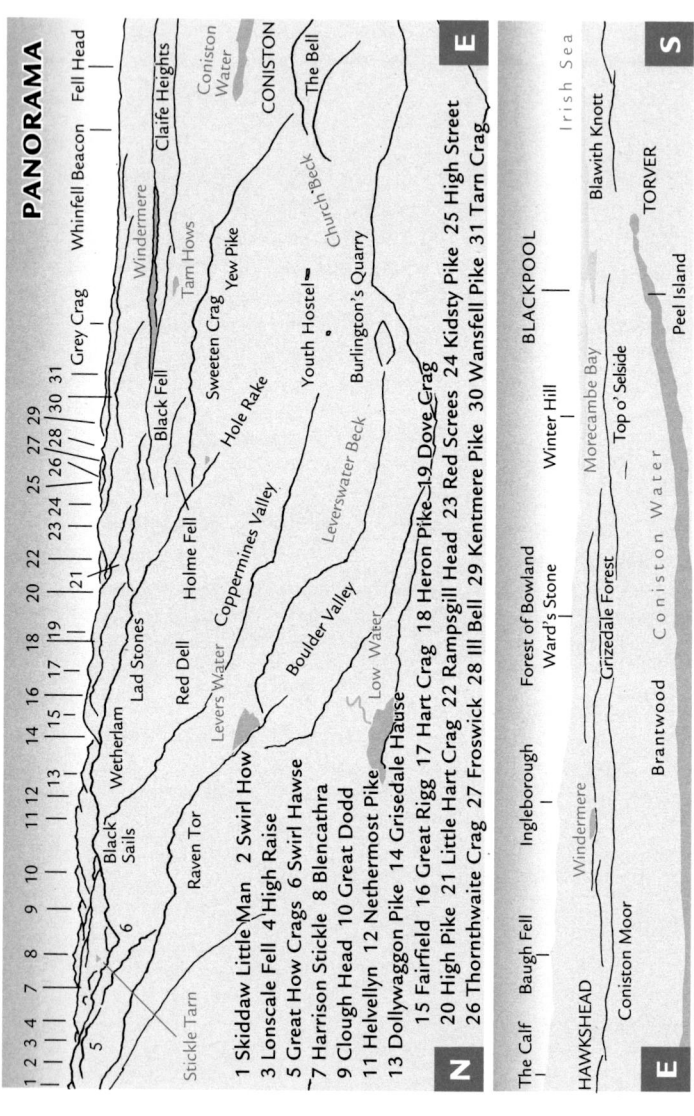

6 Coniston Old Man

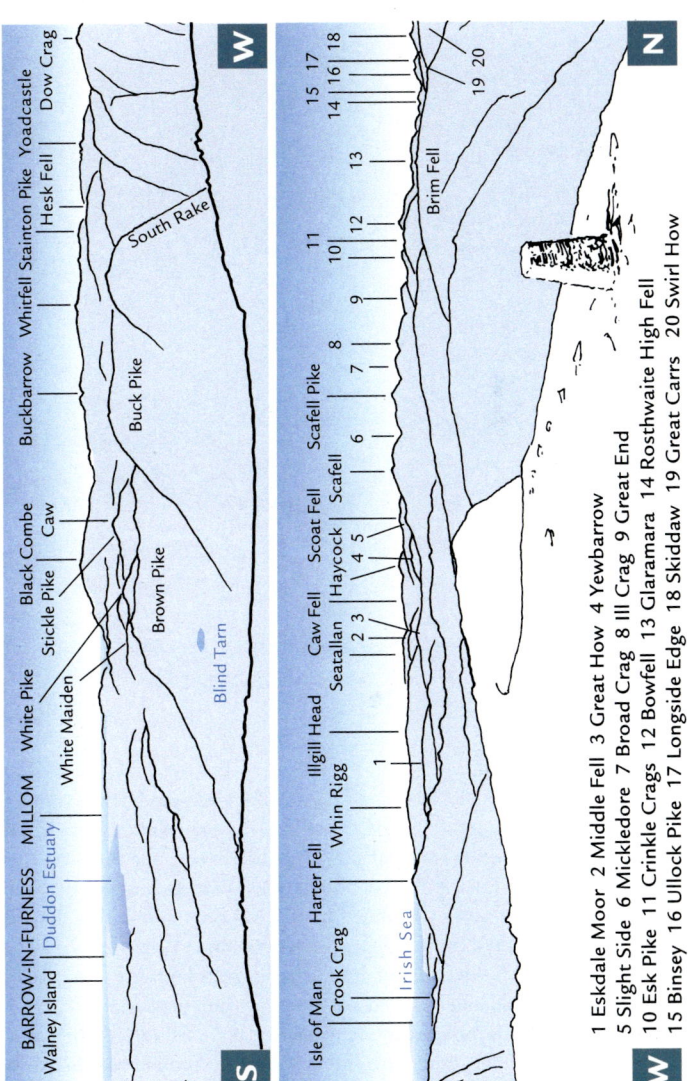

1 Eskdale Moor 2 Middle Fell 3 Great How 4 Yewbarrow
5 Slight Side 6 Mickledore 7 Broad Crag 8 Ill Crag 9 Great End
10 Esk Pike 11 Crinkle Crags 12 Bowfell 13 Glaramara 14 Rosthwaite High Fell
15 Binsey 16 Ullock Pike 17 Longside Edge 18 Skiddaw 19 Great Carrs 20 Swirl How

7 DOW CRAG 778M/2552FT

Climb it from	Walna Scar Road **31**, Torver **30** or Seathwaite **49**
Character	A glorious peak with cliffs to rival any in the district
Fell-friendly route	4
Summit grid ref	SD 262 978
Link it with	Brim Fell, Coniston Old Man or Walna Scar
Part of	Coniston Triple Treat

Dow Crag is one of the finest fells in the Lake District, revered by rock climbers and fellwalkers alike – good to look at, good to stand on, good to wander over and a superb climb whatever your capacity or approach. From the Duddon valley all it offers is bulk, a tantalising peaked summit with no obvious line of direct ascent, but from the east it's a different matter. Whether you are on the Old Man, approaching up the Cove or looking up from Coniston Water, you see a real mountain, dominated by one absolutely massive crag. Its buttresses and gullies, on a par with Scafell, humble the bold and strike awe into the timid.

The South Rake (3), the simplest of scrambles, gives fellwalkers their most intimate view of the cliff; otherwise walkers must be content to admire the wild precipice from a safe distance along its fearsome edge. Dow Crag is most

↑ *Dow Crag from the summit of the Old Man*

7 Dow Crag

commonly approached either across Goats Hawse (2, 8) or from the summit of the Walna Scar Road following the northbound ridge (4, 7), making two impressive steps, over Brown and Buck Pikes, on the way. Cradled beneath the two is Blind Tarn, as lovely a crystal pool as you could imagine, while further north Goat's Water has an altogether darker feel, with crags and scree pressing down upon its steely waters.

Ascent from Walna Scar Road fell-gate 31

Via Goats Hawse →*5.7 km/3½ miles* ↑*550m/1805ft* ⏱*2hr 30min*

An approach of great drama and excitement, hidden and unsuspected at the start, following in the footsteps of pioneering climbers

1 Start from the fell-gate parking area and follow the open track west, passing the tiny rush-filled **Boo Tarn**. To the left swathes of bracken shield the

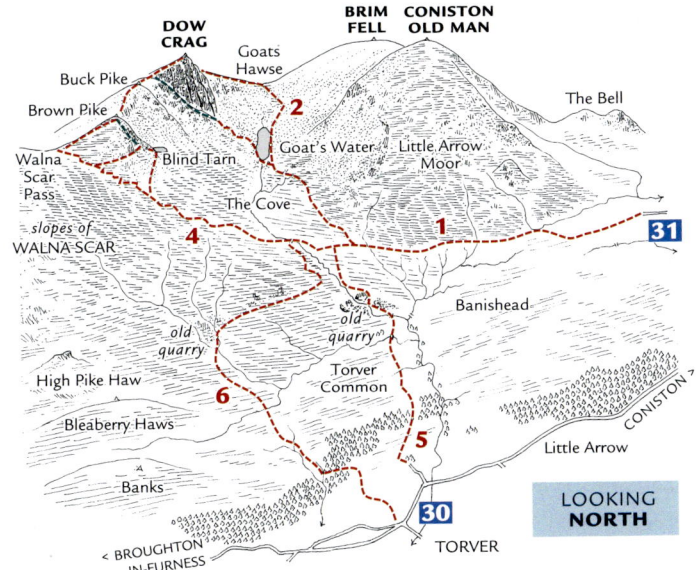

common, dotted with stones left by the Bronze-Age farmers of this upland. The track begins to climb, winding through two rock cuttings.

2 From the Walna Scar Road (Route **1**), take the obvious pitched steps right, leading off the track 200 metres short of Cove Bridge (built to serve the Blind Tarn slate quarry). The path mounts a rock-step beneath Goat Crag and advances to Goat's Water, a wonderfully wild setting. To meet the demands of a regular clientele the path up to Goats Hawse has been pitched, drawing up to the saddle at the head of the combe. At the top go left, turning from west to south as the worn ridge path climbs steadily to the final triumphant summit.

Via the South Rake
→ 5km/3 miles
↑ 590m/1935ft ⏲ 3hr

If the weather is suitable and your energy levels up to it, serious consideration should be given to climbing South Rake. It is the fellwalker's one chance to get really close to Dow Crag.

3 Follow Routes **1** and **2** to Goat's Water. Ford the outflowing beck, passing giant boulders. The scree above is not at all pleasant, but there's no choice. The path climbs up to the foot of Great Gully, where there's a blue stretcher box down to the right. A contouring sheep trod can then be seen going right beneath the crag to Goats Hawse. Enter South Rake by bearing up left. Scramble by the entrance to Easy Gully, onto the rough ledges. The rake is obvious. There is no sense of entering a deep cleft or forbidding gully, just a scrambly open weakness that does have loose stuff but

7 Dow Crag

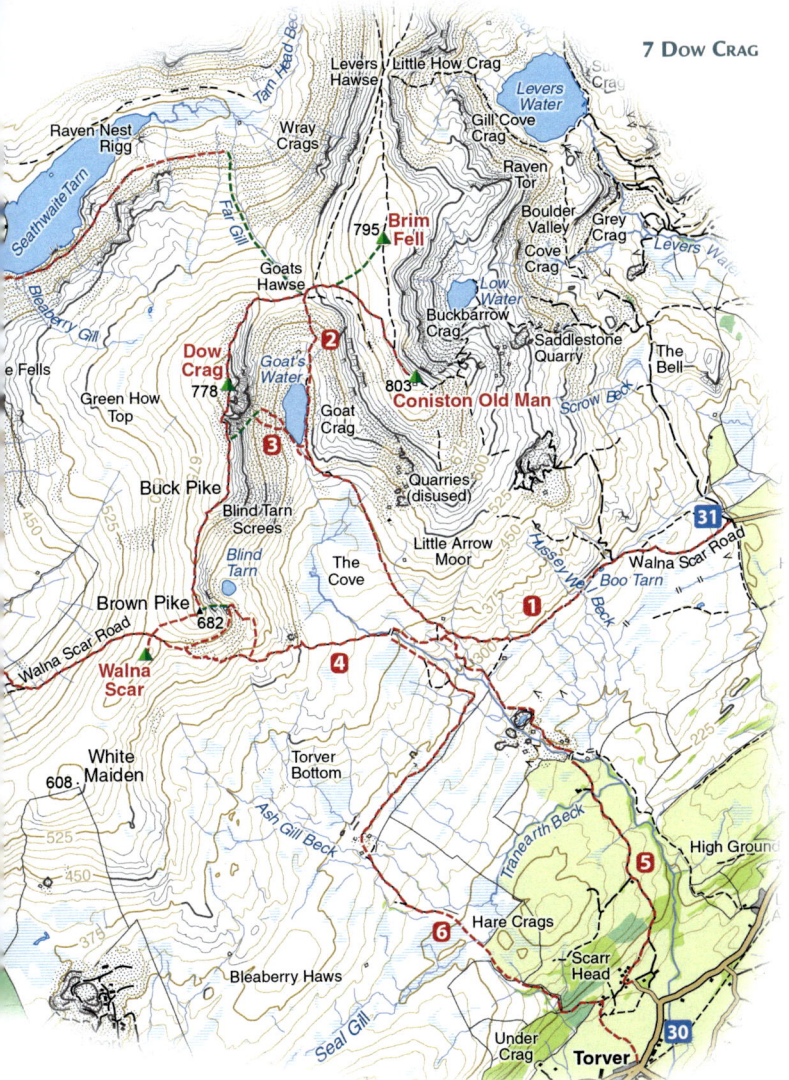

has far more of the firm hand-holds that lend confidence and ensure steady progress. The outward views down to the tarn and across the blank side of the

View up Great Gully

Old Man are fabulous but most impressive are the near buttresses. The top comes sooner than you expect and, chuffed with yourself, you'll relish grappling with the summit when it arrives.

Via Walna Scar Pass →6km/3¾ miles ↑630m/2065ft ⏲2hr 30min

For the simplest ascent stick with the Walna Scar Road.

4 For the simplest ascent stick with the Walna Scar Road (Route **1**) to the top of the pass and bear right onto the rising ridge, passing the cairns on **Brown** and **Buck Pikes**. On the way up a visit to **Blind Tarn** is a delectable addition, using the old quarry green-way which cuts back, right, below the stone shelter. The tarn is a little mysterious, there being only a soakaway pool and no sign of an escaping gill, not even tell-tale rushes. Explore the quarries and then either use the narrow trod traversing from the upper quarry back to the track close to the stone shelter, or scramble straight to the top of Brown Pike direct from the quarry ruins – the outcrops are mild-mannered stuff. Follow the ridge north to the summit.

Ascent from Torver **30**

There are two lines of approach from Torver. On reaching the Walna Scar Road, you can then take your pick of Routes **2**, **3** and **4**.

Via Banishead Quarry →6km/3¾ miles ↑670m/2200ft ⏲3hr 40min

The classic line from Torver, taking in the impressive Banishead Quarry

5 Park at the church hall at Torver (£1 donation requested) next to St Luke's and the Church House Inn, or at the road-end off the bend of the main road (SD 285 945). Follow the lane up by **Scarr Head**, entering a gated bridle-lane signed to 'Walna Scar'. Pass ruined barns, following another sign to 'Tranearth'. Cross a concrete bridge, with Tranearth Climbers' Hut over to the left. Continue to a hand-gate then through sheep-handling pens to a gate, then over the wooden bridge. Keep to the main track, up through the slate tips, to swing round the fenced Banishead Quarry. At the western end Torver Beck falls into the pool at the base of the quarry and soaks away through a cave. The route ascends the bracken bank, with several green-ways to choose from, to merge with the Walna Scar Road track.

Via Ashgill Quarry →6.7km/4¼ miles ↑760m/2495ft ⏲2hr

A damper, more 'off-the-beaten-track' approach, avoiding the crowds

6 Start from the Wilson Arms and follow the footpath/lane rising via High Torver Park, through woodland and up an old trackway onto the fell via gates and stiles, leading to Ashgill Quarry. Traverse right to rise on an old path by Torver Beck to Cove Bridge on the Walna Scar Road.

Ascent from Seathwaite 49

Few choose to ascend from Seathwaite. Routes from the west take the fell unawares, with all the drama reserved for the final stages.

Via the Walna Scar Road →6km/3¾ miles ↑680m/2230ft ⏲2hr 50min

7 The Walna Scar Road climbs out of the Duddon valley, leaving the valley road around 1km north of Seathwaite, tarmac quickly giving way to a rough track at the fell-gate. (There is also the well-marked field-path route via

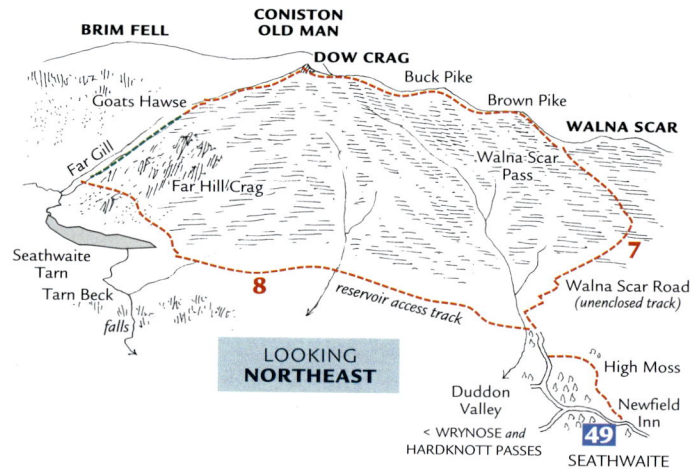

Approaching the summit from the south

Turner Hall and High Moss (Rucksack Club hut), which takes a great slice out of the road walking.) Popular with mountain bikers too, the 'road' provides a straightforward efficient means of getting onto the Dow Crag ridge: turn off left onto Route **4** at the road summit.

Via Seathwaite Tarn →*8km/5 miles* ↑*750m/2460ft* ⏱*3hr 15min*

8 Where the Walna Scar Road track begins (see Route **7**), so too does the gated reservoir access track bound for Seathwaite Tarn, which supplies water to the lower Furness area. The track traverses the lower western slopes and branches right, just short of the dam, to join a path which draws across the fellside, passing a measuring gauge, beneath Near and Far Hill Crags. The path peters out opposite Blake Rigg Crag, at which point turn uphill to follow Far Gill to Goats Hawse, then join Route **2** to advance to the summit.

The summit

There are summits and there are summits: Brim Fell needs a cairn; Dow Crag doesn't. There's no room for one thing. The irregular battlement of the summit bastion, like a Roman altar, has a 'focus', with an easy scramble on and off, north and south, but beware the east! The view down the cliff is utterly breathtaking. There are few summits with quite this sense of the precipitous. Further glimpses down the face from the high brow can be gained along the south edge. Peer down Easy and Great Gullies to marvel at the void.

Safe descents

For all the eastern scarp threatens, especially with a stiff southwesterly blowing, the walker can find safe haven more readily from this top than many another. If you follow the ridge S (**4**), stepping down first from Buck Pike, then Brown Pike, the summit of the Walna Scar Road is sure to be found. From there either go right for Seathwaite in the Duddon valley (**7**), 3.6km away, or left for Coniston (**4**, **1**), 5.2km away. It's a similar story should you trek N (**2**), for the ridge naturally declines to the broad saddle of Goats Hawse, from where a pitched path leads S down by Goat's Water and on via a rock-step at Goat Crag down the Cove, again to meet the Walna Scar Road. This time Coniston is 3.2km away and the Duddon valley uphill and over the pass. The steeper slope N from Goats Hawse (**8**) has no real dangers, but the terrain to the reservoir track is rougher and the distance to Seathwaite just that bit greater at 6.8km.

Ridge routes

Brim Fell → *1.3km/¾ mile* ↓*130m/425ft* ↑*170m/560ft* ⏱*40min*
Climb carefully down the north side of the summit outcrop, then descend with the ridge path to the broad depression of Goats Hawse. The main continuing path curves up with a right-hand bias; for Brim Fell branch off at will up the predominantly grassy slope NE to the chunky summit cairn.

Coniston Old Man → *1.6km/1 mile* ↓*145m/475ft* ↑*150m/490ft* ⏱*40min*
Descend N to Goats Hawse. As the main continuing path curves up right, stick with the trade route to the summit. In mist remember that the steepest ground lies to the east.

Walna Scar → *1.6km/1 mile* ↓*180m/590ft* ↑*20m/65ft* ⏱*30min*
Follow the ridge S, via Buck and Brown Pikes, down to the Walna Scar Road track. The modest summit and cairn lie at the top of the first rise beyond the pass.

8 GREAT CARRS 788M/2585FT

Climb it from	Castle Howe **42**, Little Langdale **40**, Wrynose Pass **43** or Wrynose Bottom **44**
Character	A handsome rising ridge forming a great northern scarp embracing the Greenburn valley
Fell-friendly route	2
Summit grid ref	NY 270 009
Link it with	Grey Friar or Swirl How
Part of	The Swirl Round

A curving crescendo of a ridge rises up from the meadows of Little Langdale and culminates on the peaks of Great Carrs and Swirl How: from Wrynose Pass it steps purposefully up via Rough Crags, Wet Side Edge and Little Carrs, the trajectory of most ascents (1–2).

Walks from Wrynose Pass (4) involve just 395m/1295ft of ascent, but circular route options are limited, Swirl How and Grey Friar being simply out-and-back destinations from the summit. From Wrynose Bottom the fell is guarded by a high rim of crags dominated by Hellgill Pike, which can be climbed by means

↑ *Southern aspect of Great Carrs*

of a tough off-beat clamber up the west side of Hell Gill (5). The lonely upper reaches of the Greenburn Beck valley, a glacial hollow filled with boulders and marsh, afford the least attractive approach (3); most walkers wisely settle for Swirl Hawse and Prison Band rather than slog up the excessively steep grass slope of Broad Slack.

Ascent from Castle Howe 42 or Little Langdale 40 *off map E*
Via Wet Side Edge →*6.5km/4 miles* ↑*670m/2200ft* ⏲*3hr 15min*

The classic ascent via a sweeping ridge

1 There are two ways onto the Wet Side Edge ridge, the shorter of which begins from above Fellfoot Farm. Immediately above Castle Howe find a recessed gate/stile on the left. Follow the track, with a wall on your left, go through the next gate and slip over the facing bank, past a guide cairn, to ford the infant **River Brathay**. Climb the steep bank ahead, between irregular walled enclosures, past the distinctive rocks on Hollin Crag, and turn right, up the easy ridge. As Route **2** joins from the left, either keep with the main path or slant left to follow the true ridge path, climbing more steeply up to Little Carrs, crossing the traversing path for the Fairfield saddle and Grey Friar. Follow the exciting rocky scarp edge to the summit.

2 This lowest section of the ridge can also be gained from the old Greenburn Mine access track. The track can either be joined from Fellfoot via Bridge End or from the vicinity of Slater Bridge via the lane by Low Hall Garth climbing hut. About 2km from Slater Bridge cross a footbridge over **Greenburn Beck**, situated directly right after the gate in the intake wall at NY 295 023. The ridge path angles up the left side of Rough Crags, above Greenburn Tarn, progressing steadily by **Wet Side Edge**. The path from Wrynose (Route **1**) enters from the right at a prominent cairn: continue with Route **1** to the summit.

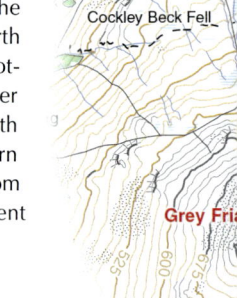

8 Great Carrs

Via Greenburn Beck →6.5km/4 miles ↑675m/2215ft ⏲3hr 30min

Visit the lonely valley of Greenburn before embarking on a steep slog up the valley head.

3 The mine access track (see Route **2**) leads not only to the historically important remains of the old copper mine, but also along the dwindling trod into

the wild corrie beyond Greenburn Tarn, aiming for the saddle between **Swirl How** and Great Carrs. Soggy ground culminates in a painfully steep grass slope, where the sad remains of a Halifax bomber litter the scree. On reaching the saddle turn right for the summit.

Ascent from Wrynose Pass 43

Via Wrynose Pass → *2.2km/1¼ miles* ↑*395m/1295ft* ⏲ *1hr 30min*

The Wrynose Pass ascent is oh so tempting: a high-level walk that can start at 395m/1295ft and involve only the same height-gain again on a simple ridge. As a there-and-back route to the top of Great Carrs it is just fine.

4 There are two parking areas, although the only marked path onto the ridge begins from the higher one at the top of the pass. Note the huge specimen erratic close left as you climb just west of south towards the ridge. A large cairn marks the point of arrival on the ridge-top. Commit its characteristics to memory for your return. Follow the ridge, in harmony with Route **1**, to the summit.

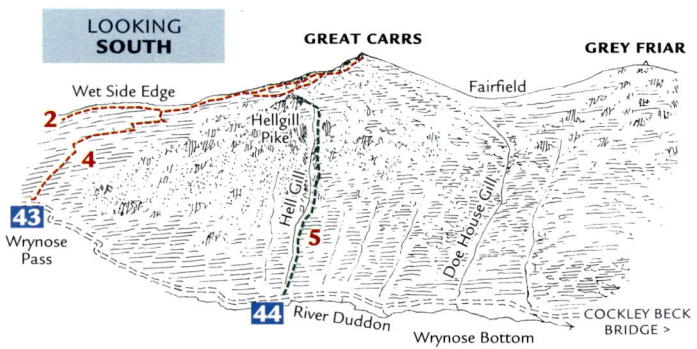

8 Great Carrs

Swirl How and Great Carrs from the cairn on Wet Side Edge

Ascent from Wrynose Bottom 44

Via Hell Gill →*1.8km/1 mile* ↑*525m/1720ft* ⏲*2hr*

The adventurer's route, making a steep, pathless but unproblematic ascent beside Hell Gill

5 Find room to park off the open road, just west of the footpath signed on the north verge. The striking cleft of Hell Gill is not a place to fear, unlike its namesake on Bowfell's Band. Keeping to the west side, ascend above the rowans and enter the upper half of the ravine as it slips through the rock band, passing a small pinnacle. From the higher realms of the gill the views across the valley are quite superb, with Little Stand, Cold Pike and, beyond, a grand array of fine fells, including Scafell. As the slope eases you can comfortably drift half-left to climb Hellgill Pike, sufficiently offset from the main ridge path to enjoy exclusivity for high-level camps, and then cross to join Route **1**.

The summit

Great Carrs boasts a narrow grassy summit ridge above a fine craggy escarpment, culminating in a small rocky top with a bedraggled cairn. It's an impressive spot to rest, peering straight down into the wild hollow of Greenburn. Ahead is Wetherlam and right Swirl How, and to the north, beyond Little Stand, the mighty Scafells.

A memorial cross and cairn are located a few metres down the west slope from the lip of Broad Slack at NY 270 007. Beside them is the undercarriage of the Halifax bomber, a reminder of a tragic accident on a training flight in 1944. The remains of the fuselage lie in the scree over the edge, while the Merlin engine stands outside the Ruskin Museum in Coniston, where a more thorough explanation of the sad event is given.

Safe descents

The main descending ridge (**1**), trending from N to E, offers safe ground towards Wrynose Pass (**4**) in 2km or, taking care over Rough Crags, Slater Bridge in Little Langdale (**2**) in 6.4km.

Ridge routes

Grey Friar →*1.2km/¾ mile* ↓*130m/425ft* ↑*145m/475ft* ⊕*40min*
Descend W, on grassy terrain all the way, crossing the Fairfield saddle, then continue to the summit.

Swirl How →*0.5km/¼ mile* ↓*20m/65ft* ↑*40m/130ft* ⊕*15min*
Follow the ridge the short distance to Swirl How's summit cairn, curving from S to E.

9 GREAT WORM CRAG 427M/1401FT

Climb it from	Birkerfell Road (Devoke Water track-end) **8** or Woodend Bridge **9**
Character	A lovely place to roam off the Birkerfell Road, blessed with spacious views
Fell-friendly route	2
Summit grid ref	SD 193 969
Link it with	Green Crag

Divided into long walled enclosures spreading their tendrils above the meadows and woods of Hall Dunnerdale, the ground swells to the gentle scarp of Great Worm Crag. It is clearly a distinct summit, but for many fellwalkers it is nothing more than an intermediate halt, a means to an end, on the approach march to Green Crag from the Birkerfell Road. However, there are enough who appreciate its situation as an end in itself; they know a good view when they see one and, most of all, value the ease with which it may be achieved.

There are three natural routes to the top. All ascents involve some pathless terrain and wet ground is difficult to avoid. The most direct options are from the Birkerfell Road (1–2), whereas the longer Route 3 offers a little more interest in the form of Birkerthwaite and Great Crag.

↑ *Great Worm Crag from Caw*

WALKING THE LAKE DISTRICT FELLS – CONISTON

Ascent from the Birkerfell Road (Woodend Bridge) 9

Via Freeze Beck → *1.2km/¾ mile* ↑*195m/640ft* ⏲*1hr*

The direct line, following the rise of the land

1 From the point where **Freeze Beck** flows under the open road a path ascends. After a positive start it falters over marshy ground then resumes more confidently, past a large heap of anciently gathered stones, rising to the sky-line summit cairn, a far more modest assemblage.

Via the southern slopes → *1.6km/1 mile* ↑*195m/640ft* ⏲*1hr 10min*

2 From the cattle grid, where the road emerges onto the open fell, ascend to the left of the wall. As the ridge becomes more apparent trend left away from

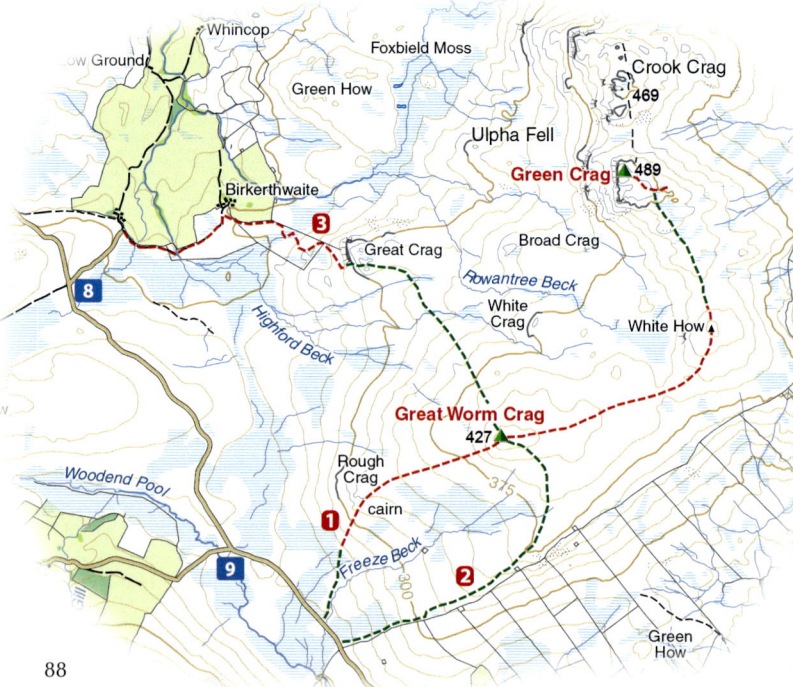

the wall, passing above a sheepfold with a fine view towards Caw, and angle across the shallow combe to the summit cairn.

Ascent from the Birkerfell Road (Devoke Water track-end) 8

Via Birkerthwaite →3km/1¾ miles ↑215m/705ft ⏲1hr 30min

The longer approach adds a little more variety and interest.

3 From the parking area go east, down the open road, to High Ground. Bear right, with the wall on your left, on the gated track signposted to Birkerthwaite. At the white-walled Ganny House Cottage branch off right to the gate in the paddock corner. Pass through the sheep pen, now with a wall on your left. Ignore the wall-stile by the next gate and gently rise to a broken stile/gate in the fence. A grass path slants on below Great Crag towards the modest saddle. Where the remains of an old wall abut the crag you can scramble up a steep ramp, or skirt round the crag altogether and climb the summit from the east. From here make a beeline southeast up to the summit of Great Worm Crag.

Great Worm Crag summit (photo: Karl Holden)

The summit

A small cairn on a grassy rise marks an otherwise bland summit. The outlook is spacious. Attention is inevitably drawn north towards Green Crag. Either side of this rocky eminence are the distant Pillar and the Scafells to its left and Bowfell immediately over its right shoulder.

Safe descents

All routes are safe (if soggy) in reverse – though take care around Great Crag. The wall-line to the south (2) would offer the greatest security in mist.

Ridge route

Green Crag →*2.4km/1½ miles* ↓*90m/295ft* ↑*40m/130ft* ⏲*30min*
Follow a good path ENE, skirting marsh, to the top of White How and then bear NNW, following an intermittent path up the broad ridge to the rocky top.

From near Broad Crag and Meeting Hill; Devoke Water can be seen in the distance (photo: Don Dawber)

10 GREEN CRAG 489M/1604FT

Climb it from	Woolpack Inn **6**, Stanley Ghyll **7**, Birkerfell Road (Devoke Water track-end) **8**, Fickle Steps **48** or Seathwaite **49**
Character	A set of exciting knobbly tops set invitingly above Eskdale
Fell-friendly route	1
Summit grid ref	SD 200 983
Link it with	Great Worm Crag or Harter Fell

Wainwright took the view that this was the last bit of decent fellwalking south of Eskdale. The many excursions in this guide prove him wrong but there is no denying the extra special qualities of Green Crag. It has something of the Northern Highlands about it: shapely craggy knots elevated from a bleak boggy moorland. But what makes it different and so superb is dear wooded Eskdale. Only a surly soul could deny that Eskdale is the most exquisite of valleys and, coupled with Green Crag as the high point of a day's walk from the valley bottom, life can offer little better.

While many are content to stroll up Stanley Ghyll via graded paths and stout footbridges to stand before the plunge pool of shady Stanley Force, the fellwalker will revel in the savage beauty of Birker Force (1, 4), spilling from a rim of craggy

↑ *Green Crag summit cairn (photo: Maggie Allan)*

WALKING THE LAKE DISTRICT FELLS – CONISTON

10 GREEN CRAG

ground fringing the upland pastures. It is worth wrenching yourself away from the verdant tracks and paths of the Duddon (6–8) and Esk (1–4) to gain the solitude of lesser-known paths. The approach from Birkerthwaite over Great Crag (5) best conveys the fell's qualities and character, and can be incorporated into a circular expedition including Great Worm Crag for some lovely lonely fellwandering.

Ascent from the Woolpack Inn 6

Whether starting from the youth hostel or the Woolpack Inn, begin by walking west along the valley road to the lane signed to Penny Hill farm. Cross the picturesque **River Esk** at **Doctor's Bridge**. There are now two options.

Via Low Birker →*4km/2½ miles*
↑*410m/1345ft* ⏱*2hr*

The more direct route

1 Go right, following the lane and track to **Low Birker**. Immediately past the house bear up left on the path, climbing through the bracken. An early fork right, through a hand-gate, gives access to the rough fellside and a view of the cascading Birker Gill from below, but this is not a sane route to the scarp top. Keep with the main path, which, higher up, passes through dense juniper, to a hand-gate in the enclosure

WALKING THE LAKE DISTRICT FELLS – CONISTON

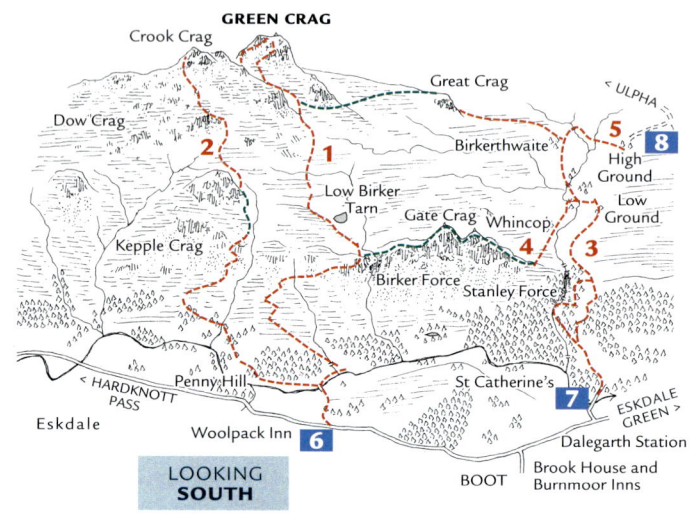

Eskdale from the ruined peat hut (photo: Maggie Allan)

corner. The peat road now begins a quick sequence of zig-zags and then levels to pass a roofless peat store. The track then broaches the moor, missing the best view of Birker Force, so make a point of bearing right to have a proper look – also a good place for a refreshment break. Your route now becomes altogether bleaker, skirting marshy ground and rising across the shoulder of a knoll above Low Birker Tarn. A brief descent leads to a long southward-slanting traverse before a solitary thorn promises firmer ground up ahead. Keep on the path all the way through the light bracken, making for the damp slope that rises to the saddle between Crook Crag and Green Crag. Turn right for the summit.

Via Kepple Crag →*4km/2½ miles* ↑*430m/1410ft* ⏲*2hr*

2 Follow the hedged lane ahead towards Penny Hill farm. A permissive path has been created to avoid unnecessary disturbance to the farmyard, so you are ushered right and left through gates, rejoining the open track leading to another gate and a lonesome pine. The track then forks. Keep right, rising to a gate, then slant left up to a wall and go right to a gate by an old pen. Rising with the wall on your left, ignore the 'Harter Fell' sign directing left and keep right on the winding track, passing three ruined peat stores as you round Kepple Crag. Then, slipping over a low saddle between damp combes, head south, straight up the fell, without a path. Keep to the right of the prominent outcrops to find a fresh path, which glances by the lateral ridge-top of Crook Crag en route to the main saddle, past a unique boundary stone, and carries on straight up to the summit.

Ascent from Stanley Ghyll 7

Low Ground via Stanley Force →*2km/1¼ miles* ↑*120m/395ft* ⏲*1hr 25min*

Ascend through attractive woodland to visit the striking Stanley Force en route to the fell plateau.

3 From the car park a lane leads south from the river, crossing the line of the Eskdale Trail – recommended as a means of completing circular walks at scenic dale-floor level. There are two options: either remain with the rising gated lane and subsequent track, or visit the luxuriant environs of Stanley Ghyll, linking back to the open track above the woodland. To

Birker Force

10 GREEN CRAG

visit the waterfall, enter the wooded National Park Access Area through a gate. The popular path leads upstream, crossing three footbridges in the darkly shaded ravine en route to the plunge pool of 12m **Stanley Force**, the spray making paths and woodwork slippery. Visitors are warned not to venture beyond, as there is no route through to the open fell. Having enjoyed the waterfall, backtrack and take the stepped path beside a tiny gill from between the second and third footbridges. The path bends right to descend, with a lovely view ahead of Scafell framed by the foreground woodland, but at this point take the path, left, to emerge from the wood at a gate and rejoin the original track. Go left, shortly passing through a gate, and keep on the green track to the lonely retreat of **Low Ground**. Cross the stile beside the white-washed cottage and turn left down its access lane to a fork. From here Route **4** leads off on the left fork to **Whincop**, but there are two other tracks leading off from the right fork, each a useful link to Route **5**. The main track leads to **High Ground**, still a working farm, and eventually meets the road, but turning left on a footpath at the conifer spinney leads you directly to and through **Birkerthwaite**.

Via Gate Crag →*4.5km/2¾ miles* ↑*350m/1150ft* ⏱*1hr 50min*

The Gate Crag brink affords great views across Eskdale.

4 At the end of Route **3** take the left fork and, at the first gate left in a dip, enter an enclosure containing young deciduous trees. Cross the stone bridge and follow the track to **Whincop**. Pass through the environs of this old steading. Pass to the left of the house down a short lane to a ladder-stile and flag bridge, keeping the wall to your left, amid bracken. Ignore the next ladder-stile, which is defended by a damp patch of ground, and instead skirt right, intent on the prominent rising scarp ridge. Ford the tiny gill and make up the rock spine on an evident path, enjoying charming views into Eskdale. The ridge culminates at the cairned top of **Hartley Crag**. Continue, dipping to cross the broken wall short of **Gate Crag**, the next rise in the ridge. Another cairn marks the top of this higher crest, which also offers much for the eyes and camera. There is no path to the head of **Birker Force** from here, but the terrain, although damp, is simple and your course is east. Join Route **1** to proceed across the combe to the summit.

Ascent from the Birkerfell Road (Devoke Water track-end) 8

Via Great Crag →*4km/2½ miles* ↑*285m/935ft* ⏱*2hr 10min*

A highly pleasurable approach, taking in the excellent viewpoint on Great Crag

5 From the parking area go east, down the open road to High Ground. Bear right, with the wall on your left, on the gated track signposted to Birkerthwaite. At the white-walled Ganny House Cottage branch off right to the gate in the paddock corner. Pass through the sheep pen, now with a wall on your left. Ignore the wall-stile by the next gate and gently rise to a broken stile/gate in the fence. A grass path slants on below Great Crag towards the modest saddle. Where the remains of an old wall abut the crag you can scramble up a steep ramp, or skirt round the crag altogether and climb the summit from the east. There are two cairned tops, both excellent viewpoints. From here there is no path across the rough fell, but your route is in a northeasterly direction, bound for the saddle northwest of the Green Crag stack. Turn right on Route **1** and find a ramp, high on the north side, which gives access to the summit.

Ascent from the Duddon valley (Fickle Steps or Seathwaite) 48 & 49

Approaches from the east contrast the delightful sylvan environs of the Duddon with the wilder expanse of fell above.

Via Wallowbarrow Crag →*5.2km/3¼ miles* ↑*380m/1245ft* ⏱*2hr 30min*

6 Two paths converge on the memorial footbridge. One begins opposite the Newfield Inn, while the second begins at the school house, both crossing Tarn Beck on footbridges. From the memorial footbridge follow the path ahead into pasture and through gates to reach High Wallowbarrow farm. Turn right before the house, climbing through more gates up to the saddle beside Wallowbarrow Crag. This is a popular venue for climbers. An open track pursues a northerly course through deer gates in the tall fence and enters a lane flanked by massive drystone walls. The views hereabouts are quite delightful. Approaching Grassguards itself, use the permissive path avoiding the farmyard and skirt around the garden hedge through hand-gates to reach Grassguards Gill and join Route **8**.

10 GREEN CRAG

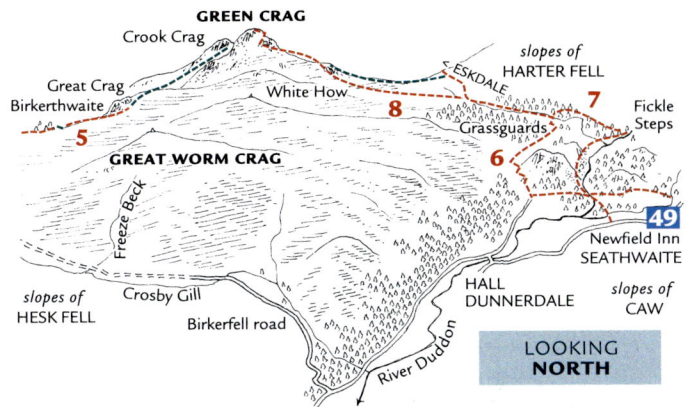

Via Wallowbarrow Gorge →5.5km/3½ miles ↑390m/1280ft ⏲2hr 45min

Wallowbarrow Gorge shows the Duddon at its best and makes a charming opening to this ascent.

7 Grassguards can also be reached on a footpath ascending the gill from Fickle Steps. The stepping-stones are fickle indeed (except in drought conditions) and difficult to cross, despite the metal cable. The better approach is to walk up **Wallowbarrow Gorge** from the memorial footbridge (see Route **6**), the large boulder scree a startling feature and the river tightly hemmed in by the trees.
    8 From Grassguards the path is clearly marked, with gates and planks. Watch for the left turn at the top; the footpath to Eskdale veers right through the broken wall but your path bears left. Cross a ladder-stile over the wall onto the open fell, a narrow sheep track pursuing a rather serpentine course west-southwest towards Green Crag. The summit is attained by rounding an outcrop, right then left.

Low-level circuit →4.8km/3 miles ⏲1hr 30min

If the fells are concealed in mist and itchy feet can't be resisted then do this three-miler, but, like everything else, it's even better in sunshine.

WALKING THE LAKE DISTRICT FELLS – CONISTON

From Birks Bridge down through the Wallowbarrow Gorge the River Duddon is at its most impressive. The circuit from the Newfield Inn up **Wallowbarrow Gorge** from the memorial footbridge to Fickle Steps, rising to **Grassguards** and

Old boundary stone beneath Green Crag

turning back south on the track to **High Wallowbarrow**, is one of Lakeland's most cherished dale walks.

The summit

The greatest crags on Green Crag face west. The summit is ringed by rock walls, which can be efficiently penetrated either via a ramp from the north or a small step from the east. Being a fell-top frequented only by the more discerning walker, the small summit cairn is little disturbed and looks old. The views are long, the string of tops to Black Combe outshone by the major summits of the Western and Mid-Western groups and the Coniston Fells to the right of the nearby peaked summit of Harter Fell.

Safe descents

Care is needed right from the start, particularly in mist. Backtrack along whichever of the two lines you arrived by, so that you are retracing familiar ground. Then aim N down to the broad grassy saddle. Find the embedded stone boundary marker in the middle of the saddle and take a bearing NE, crossing the featureless, peaty, tussocky moor. Cross a fence-stile at the corner of forestry and join the Eskdale–Duddon path (left for Eskdale, right for the Duddon).

Ridge routes

Great Worm Crag → *2.4km/1½ miles ↓40m/130ft ↑90m/295ft ⏲45min*
An intermittent path holds to the broad ridge SE, with some marsh to skirt and one nice top to stand on, White How, at which point the ridge switches SW to cross another shallow dip and gain the summit plateau.

Harter Fell → *3.2km/2 miles ↓145m/475ft ↑310m/1015ft ⏲1hr 45min*
Head down to the broad saddle N of the summit. Locate the boundary stone and take a bearing NE across the moor. Cross the fence-stile at the northwestern end of the largely felled forestry. A clear path climbs, initially with a tall fence on the right, continuing ENE to the summit.

11 GREY FRIAR 772M/2533FT

Climb it from	Wrynose Bottom **44**, Cockley Beck Bridge **45**, Troutal **47**, Fickle Steps **48** or Seathwaite **49**
Character	Integral to the Coniston group, this sturdy fell, bearing over Seathwaite Tarn, is beautifully set apart.
Fell-friendly route	7
Summit grid ref	NY 259 004
Link it with	Great Carrs

The Franciscan Grey Friars were renowned for their grey attire. Perhaps Grey Friar has some lost connection with itinerant monks, because this fell is no more grey than any other Lakeland peak. In fact, from a distance it seems to lack any distinction. Even from Hardnott Pass it looks bulky, featureless and none too inviting.

Whatever the long view, as a climb it is pleasurable, especially for its northern outlook, which shows the Scafells in true proportion for once. Another attraction is that, lying west of the main Coniston ridge, it does not attract many wandering visitors, but only those who make the extra effort to cross the hause and rest beside either of the twin summit cairns.

↑ *Grey Friar from Goat's Hawse*

11 GREY FRIAR

The map shows how nature has bequeathed an apparently dour fell a curious long, low toe-hold in verdant Seathwaite and the dramatic Wallowbarrow Gorge. Of the watercourses most closely identified with the fell, Tarn Beck merits special mention as it tumbles west from the hanging valley cradling Seathwaite Tarn, bounding excitedly over great boulders. Seathwaite Tarn, an austere reservoir, may lack the more obvious charm of many a Lakeland corrie tarn but the craggy slopes give it a wild dignity. Beneath Great Blake Rigg, a little further up the combe, are ruins and spoil from three small-scale copper-mine levels.

The most direct approaches are from the Wrynose road to the north (1–2). Other routes rise westwards from the Duddon valley (3–6), converging on Seathwaite Tarn dam to either mount the long southwestern ridge of Troutal Fell (7–8), or proceed across rough terrain to the combe head (9), thence taking the summit from the east.

Ascent from Wrynose Bottom 44 or Cockley Beck Bridge 45

Via Troughton Beck →*2km/1¼ miles* ↑*520m/1705ft* ⏲*1hr 20min*

The direct ascent is steep and unrelenting.

WALKING THE LAKE DISTRICT FELLS – CONISTON

1 You can start a direct ascent of Grey Friar from immediately before where the open road running down-dale from Wrynose Pass crosses a cattle grid at NY 256 019. Climb the initially steep grass-and-boulder slope between Troughton Gill and the fence (no path). Rise to the top of the fenced enclosure on your right.

Go round to the left of the outcrop, following small cairns, and climb quite steeply on a southerly course, dodging intermittent outcrops, to reach the north top on the skyline.

Via Great Intake →2.5km/1½ miles ↑550m/1805ft ⏲1hr 40min

2 The enclosure on Route **1** can also be reached from Cockley Beck Bridge, where there is better casual parking available. Immediately south of the house find a stile guiding a footpath along the edge of a paddock to a wall-stile. Go right, over damp ground, to join a track emerging from behind the farm buildings. Follow this, winding uphill past the remains of an old copper mine (right) to a stile/gate. The track leads onto the broad marshy shoulder. Bear south-southeast, rising to a stile in the fence to meet and join the direct ascent (Route **1**).

Ascent from the Duddon valley (Troutal, Fickle Steps or Seathwaite) 47–49

A cluster of attractive approach routes begin from lower down the valley, Seathwaite Tarn dam the principal mid-point objective.

Via Troutal Fell →4.2km/2½ miles ↑580m/1905ft ⏲2hr 15min

3 An efficient path starts from Troutal, following the gated approach track to Browside. Go left from the gate near the isolated house, on a track, through a further gate, soon switching back uphill to a gateway in the top wall. Three paths could be followed from this point, but the best, a nice turf trod, is signposted right. This curves around the right side of an outcrop and comes back left. Watch for waymark posts guiding round marshy ground as you head on towards the dam, where you can choose from Routes **7–9**.

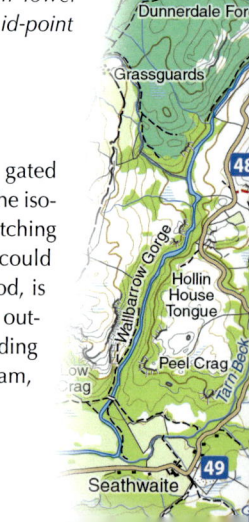

11 Grey Friar

WALKING THE LAKE DISTRICT FELLS – CONISTON

Via Tarn Beck →5.5km/3½ miles ↑620m/2035ft ⏱2hr 50min

A superb second option homing in on this tract of fell explores the delights of the Tarn Beck valley either from Seathwaite (road walk via Hollin House to Tongue House) or the common above Fickle Steps.

4 From the common trace the footpath east, down through bracken and woodland, behind a barn, into pasture at a stile, and then either continue to **Tongue House** and go left, or go left by Thrang Cottage and on to a hand-gate to cross a small footbridge over **Tarn Beck**. A footpath now accompanies the beck upstream, avoiding wet ground as best it can and heading for a wooden footbridge at the bottom of the Tarn Beck cascades. The footpath continues over a ladder-stile and through a gate to link up with Route **3**. (On the way you can visit the top of Troutal Tongue to your left, over a stile at the ridge-end – a superb viewpoint for Harter Fell.)

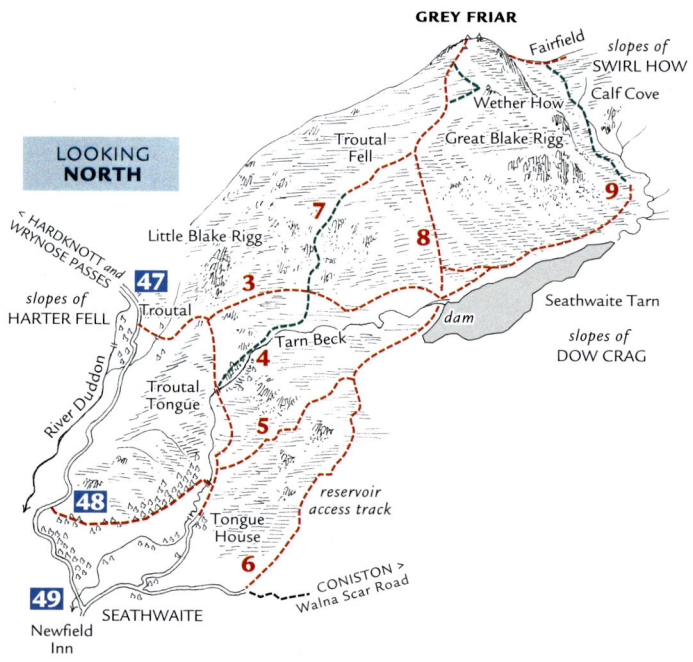

Looking to Great Blake Crag from the south shore of Seathwaite Tarn

The really exciting choice, however, branches off up the rough north bank through the bracken, climbing through the breach where the wall meets the falls, scrambling easily up the sequence of great boulder steps beside the amazing fuming falls. Once on the level wet moor, bear left from the old sheepfold to join the contouring path (Route **3**), or proceed straight up the slope ahead with Route **7**.

5 A well-used footpath also winds up the rough pastures from **Tongue House** to meet the reservoir access track (Route **6**).

Via Calf Cove →*9.2km/5¾ miles* ↑*660m/2165ft* ⏱*3hr 20min*

The Walna Scar Road and reservoir access track offer the easiest approach to Seathwaite Tarn. You can then choose between an elevated ridge-walk (Routes 7–8) or a trailblazing, pathless ascent of the wild upper reaches of the combe (Route 9).

6 For greatest ease follow the **Walna Scar Road** up from Seathwaite. There is also the well-marked path through the fields via **Turner Hall** and **High Moss** (the Manchester-based Rucksack Club hut), which takes a significant slice out of the road-walking. As the road turns into a track at a gate take the left branch through another gate, this being the access track to the dam. Cross the dam-wall footway and choose from Routes **7–9**.

7 From the Seathwaite Tarn dam (see Routes **4–6**) cross the tarn's outflow and take the path forking left. After passing scree and outcropping on your right, turn right and climb pathless straight up the fellside, aiming for the notch in the skyline, onto **Troutal Fell**, a narrow path emerging as you reach the ridge. In the closing stages a brief deviation right will take in the cairn on the prominent pike of Wether How, high above Great Blake Rigg. Returning to the path, the summit plateau is shortly reached at a guide cairn.

8 From the dam (see Routes **4–6**) a direct ascent heads straight ahead up the obvious rigg, slightly east of north, onto **Troutal Fell**, with a clear path underfoot. This is a very pleasant approach. The summit dome seems distant for much of the way. On reaching the skyline turn right up the ridge, joining Route **7**.

9 Reach **Seathwaite Tarn** by your pick of Routes **4–6**. The path that leads along the northern shore is rather more likely to be used as a return leg, but venturing to the headstream via Calf Cove is an interesting expedition. Beyond the reservoir the path passes an area of copper-mining activity, crossing a spoil apron. Pass ruined miners' dens on a dwindling path, which contours by two further blocked mine levels with associated spoil tongues and ruined stone huts. Follow the western and then the eastern bank of **Tarn Head Beck**, climbing steadily into **Calf Cove**, passing successive perched erratics, and climb without a path to **Fairfield** hause. Go left (west), now with the clear ridge path, to the summit.

The summit

A gentle dome, informally interspersed with low outcrops, and two parallel ribs some 40 metres apart, each surmounted by a cairn, define the highest ground. The summit faces the less flattering aspect of Brim Fell, Coniston Old Man and Dow Crag, but the view to the north is excellent. The northern cairn, though frequently overlooked, fully merits a visit.

Safe descents

In mist a plateau top like this can be troublesome, especially with craggy slopes tucked directly under the broad southeastern and northwestern edges, the

Matterhorn Rock near the summit of Grey Friar

southeastern being the more treacherous. Cautious walkers can thread down through the broken northwestern slopes en route to Cockley Beck Bridge (**2**). However, it is far better to take a bearing SW onto Troutal Fell (**7**) and seek the easier slopes leading to the Seathwaite Tarn dam (**8**). Although more long-winded, the slopes leading into Calf Cove from Fairfield hause (**9**) are also quite benign. Walk ENE to the grassy col and then slip down pathless into the hollow, keeping with Tarn Head Beck and avoiding the valley marshes by traversing above Seathwaite Tarn. The two routes converge at the dam. You can then either follow the open path to the north of the outflowing beck (**3**) to reach Troutal via Browside, or, having crossed the dam, join the assured track (**6**) to the metalled Walna Scar Road, which leads to Seathwaite… and an inn!

Ridge route

Great Carrs →*1.2km/¾ mile* ↓*145m/475ft* ↑*130m/425ft* ⏱*40min*
If only all ridge routes were this simple… but guidance may be necessary in mist. From the summit cairn aim NE, pass the Matterhorn Rock (a miniature of its namesake) and descend with the ridge path to arrive at a three-way fork on Fairfield hause. Take the middle course, ENE, up the largely grassy slope to the summit.

12 HARD KNOTT 552M/1811FT

Climb it from	Hardknott Pass **2**, Mosedale **1**, Hardknott Castle **3** or Brotherilkeld **5**
Character	A rocky wedge of fell, commanding an ancient pass and the very best views of the Scafells
Fell-friendly route	4
Summit grid ref	NY 232 023

Climb the Hardknott Pass from Brotherilkeld and Border End looms, a hard nut to crack indeed. In fact, Hard Knott is not that hard at all. The western scarp is steep and rimmed with crags, with little succour for man or beast, but standing tall amid this broken frontage, the Steeple or Eskdale Needle – an exquisite piece of natural architecture – does give inquisitive walkers cause to explore. The summit is a place of exaltation, offering unrivalled views of the grand parade of fells encircling the head of Eskdale.

Perched on the southwest spur is a fully-fledged Roman fort. Contemporary with the construction of Hadrian's Wall, it was part of the native Celt-calming infrastructure of the time. An inscribed stone, discovered in 1964 near the southeast gate, recorded that the fort was erected 'for the Emperor Caesar Trajan Hadrian Augustus' by the Fourth Cohort of Dalmatians. Coin finds suggest the fort was occupied 120–138AD and again 160–197AD.

↑ *Hard Knott summit cairn (photo: Maggie Allan)*

12 Hard Knott

The curtain wall has been restored sufficiently high as to give a real sense of the structure, with the outline of the key internal buildings revealed: the headquarters in the centre, flanked by the commandant's house and granaries. Closer to the road lies a bath-house with three rooms: a *caldarium* to open the skin's pores, a *tepidarium* for scraping the grime from the skin and a *frigidarium* to cool off. When the fort was vacated it is thought that this was adapted and used as a wayside hostelry; the Roman road from the port of Glannoventa (Ravenglass) to Galava (Ambleside) will have remained an active highway throughout succeeding centuries. To the east of the fort is a large level parade ground. The Romans cleared the stones, no doubt tipping them over the nearby scarp. For contemporary eyes the setting is quite magnificent, and imagination can help bridge the lost centuries and lend romance to an all-too-fleeting visit.

A varied selection of routes is available, taking in the fell's various points of interest: the subsidiary top of Border End (1, 4), an excellent viewpoint for lower Eskdale and, specifically, the Roman fort (4–5), displayed on the flat ridge directly below; the Steeple (5–6); and Dod Pike (2), offering a different perspective over wild Mosedale (3) to the east.

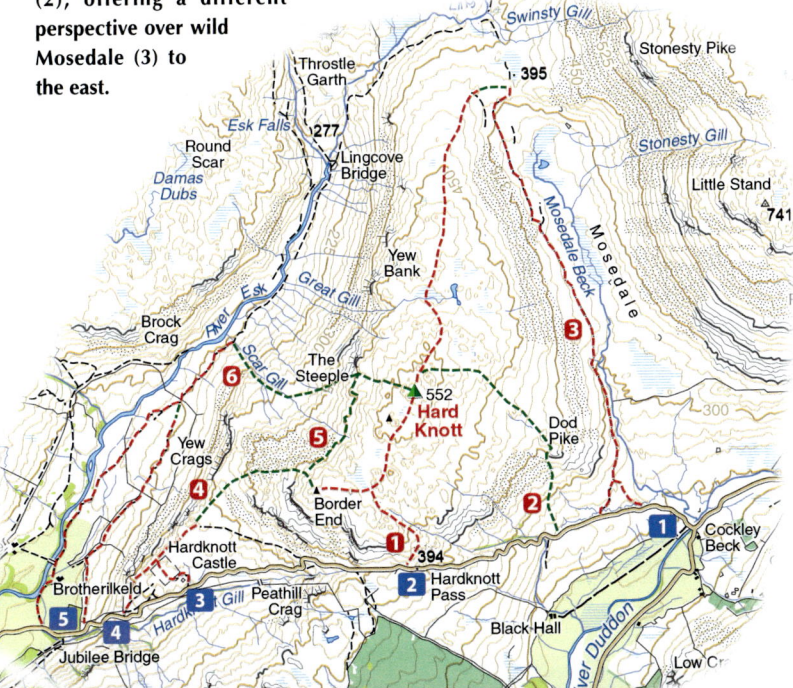

WALKING THE LAKE DISTRICT FELLS – CONISTON

Ascent from Hardknott Pass 2

Direct including Border End →*1km/½ mile* ↑*170m/560ft* ⏱*45min*

It would be a shame to miss the spectacular viewpoint of Border End. It adds little extra walking to the direct ascent from the road pass.

1 There is less scope for casual parking at the top of Hardknott than there is on Wrynose Pass. From the one good layby, east of the cattle grid and summit cairn, you can make a swift unhindered start to a climb. Follow the clear easy grass trod leading up above the headstream of an east-flowing gill to reach a boggy ridge-top hollow, resplendent with cotton grass. Paths branch to left and right. A left turn puts you on course for a cairned top, from which a further cairn is espied. Advance 150 metres to reach this, the summit of **Border End**. What a superb viewpoint! Backtrack to cross the boggy hollow. Follow the ridge, slightly east of north, via further shallow damp hollows and knolls, to reach the prominent summit cairn.

Ascent from Mosedale 1

Via Dod Pike →*2km/1¼ miles* ↑*310m/1015ft* ⏱*1hr 45min*

2 A matter of 40 metres further down the road from the final steep incline at the foot of Hardknott Pass a short rough track indicates a suitable point to embark on the ascent of Dod Pike. The slope, dogged by bracken, is soon beaten. En route inspect the striking rock-wall corner in the lowest outcrop before clambering up and round to top the main outcrop for a novel view of the Duddon

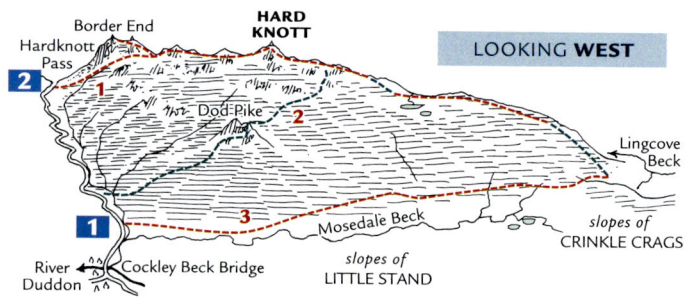

12 Hard Knott

valley, with Little Stand and Grey Friar prominent. Traverse the moorland ridge, aiming northwest; several steps are taken to reach a large pool on a broad shelf, with specimen peat groughs (isolated patches of eroding peat) close by. Continue to reach the ridge path, turning back south to reach the summit.

Via Mosedale →*4.5km/2¾ miles* ↑*315m/1035ft* ⏱*2hr 20min*

Lonely Mosedale offers a longer (and wetter) back-door approach.

3 A bridleway is signposted into Mosedale off the open road (NY 243 017), though some walkers start 100 metres further west; both routes ford a small gill. The bridleway shows evidence of old pitching where it runs close to the beck. Within Mosedale proper soggy ground has to be tackled. Two old cairns are passed en route to the watershed rigg. Turn left, southwest, and the ridge rises at a gentle angle and, as a rocky knot is passed, encounter a great marshy bowl. The path negotiates this to the right, avoiding the really miresome mire, and soon rises towards the summit by some really rather impressive outcrops, the tilted slabs providing tempting camera angles for the Scafells.

Ascent from Hardknott Castle 3

Via Border End and the Steeple →*3.2km/2 miles* ↑*335m/1100ft* ⏱*2hr*

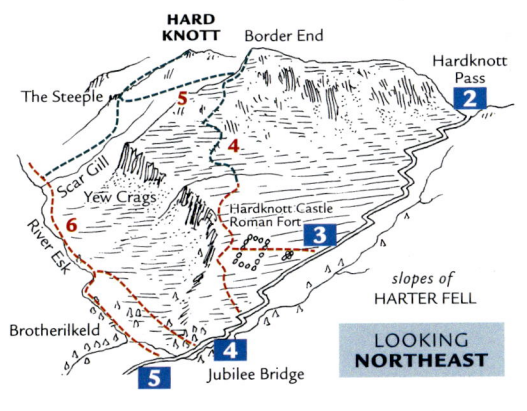

This is a really fine expedition for liberated walkers who love to grasp the nettle and need no evidence of preceding footprints to win their summits.

4 Use the upper of the two laybys specifically created to service visitors to

Hardknott Castle Roman fort from Horseshow Crags (photo: Maggie Allan)

the Roman fort. Wander up to and through the main south gate of **Hardknott Castle**. Pass through to the north gate and turn right, following the path clinging to the scarp, thus avoiding the parade ground. This footpath makes an exaggerated sweep up the fell, ultimately joining an upper hairpin of the modern road. But the more exciting action lies in weaving up the irregular west ridge, dexterously avoiding rocks to gain the cairn on **Border End**. Take time to soak up the stunning view before heading off on Route **5**.

5 Continuing the theme of quest, the Steeple, otherwise known as Eskdale Needle, merits a visit. This is achieved by descending north from the top of **Border End** (see Route **1** or Route **4**). Grassy ground can easily be found as you drift down and across the slope, keeping an eye out for the handsome pinnacle. **The Steeple** makes a superb foreground to a view of the Scafells. Inspect from both sides, then aim directly up the fell onto the summit knoll.

Ascent from Brotherilkeld 5

Via Scar Gill →3.2km/2 miles ↑460m/1510ft ⏲2hr 20min

It is unusual to contemplate climbing Hard Knott from the west, but on a direct ascent to the summit there is a sound easy line which can include the Steeple.

12 Hard Knott

6 Your route follows Scar Gill, clearly identifiable beyond the gate in the intake wall as the rough re-entrant ford situated opposite Heron Crag, on the popular path beside the Esk from Brotherilkeld to Lingcove Bridge. Bracken and rough ground are not an issue and, being pathless, route-finding is only a matter of personal intrepid choice, the ascent linking with Route **5** in the vicinity of the Steeple.

The summit

The summit is marked by a small cairn set upon a rock. This is a marvellous place from which to enjoy the great circle of fells about the head of Eskdale. Double your delight by visiting the furthest cairn on Border End for its amazing view down Eskdale.

Safe descent

In fog the narrow ridge trod is clear enough heading S (**1**). At the third and narrowest marshy hollow bear left, descending to meet the road at the top of Hardknott Pass; head down W for Eskdale and the nearest phone box/hostelry.

Eskdale Needle (photo: Maggie Allan)

13 HARTER FELL 653M/2142FT

Climb it from	Hardknott Pass **2**, Birks Bridge **46**, Fickle Steps **48**, Seathwaite **49**, Jubilee Bridge **4** or Woolpack Inn **6**
Character	A peak in every sense, aloof from the trees at the head of the Duddon
Fell-friendly route	1
Summit grid ref	SD 218 997
Link it with	Green Crag
Part of	Two Hard Knotts

Harter Fell is every inch a fellwalker's fell, its summit a playground for scramblers and a viewpoint for dreamers. Its craggy top catches the traveller's eye from the Duddon at Cockley Beck Bridge and from Hardknott Pass, but the best view of all is from Eskdale, where it is seen to rise from the woods and meadows to a majestic peak. Even better, the conifers of Hardknott Forest, which have dominated the fell's lower slopes, have now come of age and great swathes have been felled, with plans afoot for more diverse woodland to grace the Duddon valley.

↑ *Harter Fell from Muncaster Fell*

13 HARTER FELL

Climb Harter from Eskdale (7–9) and sense for yourself the wonderful setting, or alternatively, make a circuit from the Duddon to the east (2–6), perhaps taking in the exquisite environs of Wallowbarrow Gorge (6). An ascent from Hardknott Pass (1) cuts out some of the climb, though may leave you with wet feet!

Ascent from Hardknott Pass 2

Via Demming Crag →*2.5km/1½ miles* ↑*260m/855ft* ⏲*1hr 10min*

A steady and easy-to-follow approach

1 From the top of the pass cross the cattle grid and descend with the road on the west side, to where a bridleway is signposted left. Follow this path south. Ignore the electric fence-stile and cross another fence-stile to the right of the broken wall corner. The continuing path traverses an undulating marshy tract of fell. With the upper fringe of forestry close left, drift right to cross a further fence-stile. A clear path climbs steadily over heathery ground, pitching through a gully, home to the headstream of Castlehow Beck, and rising to join the path from Birks Bridge as the summit tors are met. Approach the summit from the east through a natural breach.

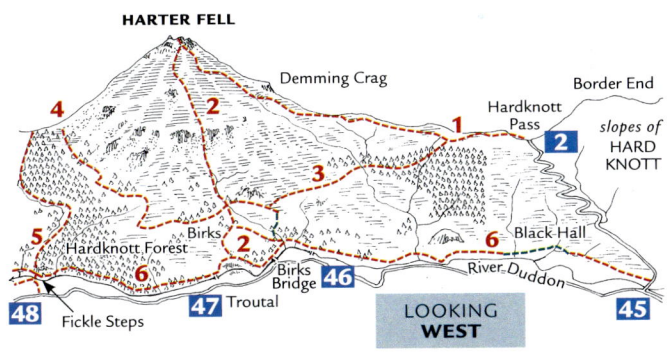

117

Ascent from Birks Bridge 46

Direct →*2km/1¼ miles* ↑*465m/1525ft* ⏲*1hr 50min*
2 From the picturesque environs of Birks Bridge follow a waymarked bridleway up through the oaks of Great Wood and by the Shropshire outdoor centre at **Birks** onto a track leading to an east–west forest track. Follow the low waymark posts defining a path up beside old walled enclosures, past a felled hollow and up the steep bank due west, climbing beside the stony gill onto the heather banks until you reach a fence-stile. Cross the stile and pass an outcrop with the romantic name Maiden Castle. Soon grass replaces ling as the summit rock bluffs draw near.

Via Dunnerdale Forest →*4km/2½ miles* ↑*465m/1525ft* ⏲*2hr 10min*

A conifer-shaded link-route, connecting with Route 1

3 Start out with Route **2**. A seldom-trod footpath runs across the fellside almost due north from the forest track from the outdoor centre. This crosses a further forest track to complete the climb through the residual conifers and reach a hand-gate onto the open fell, joining the path from Hardknott Pass (Route **1**).

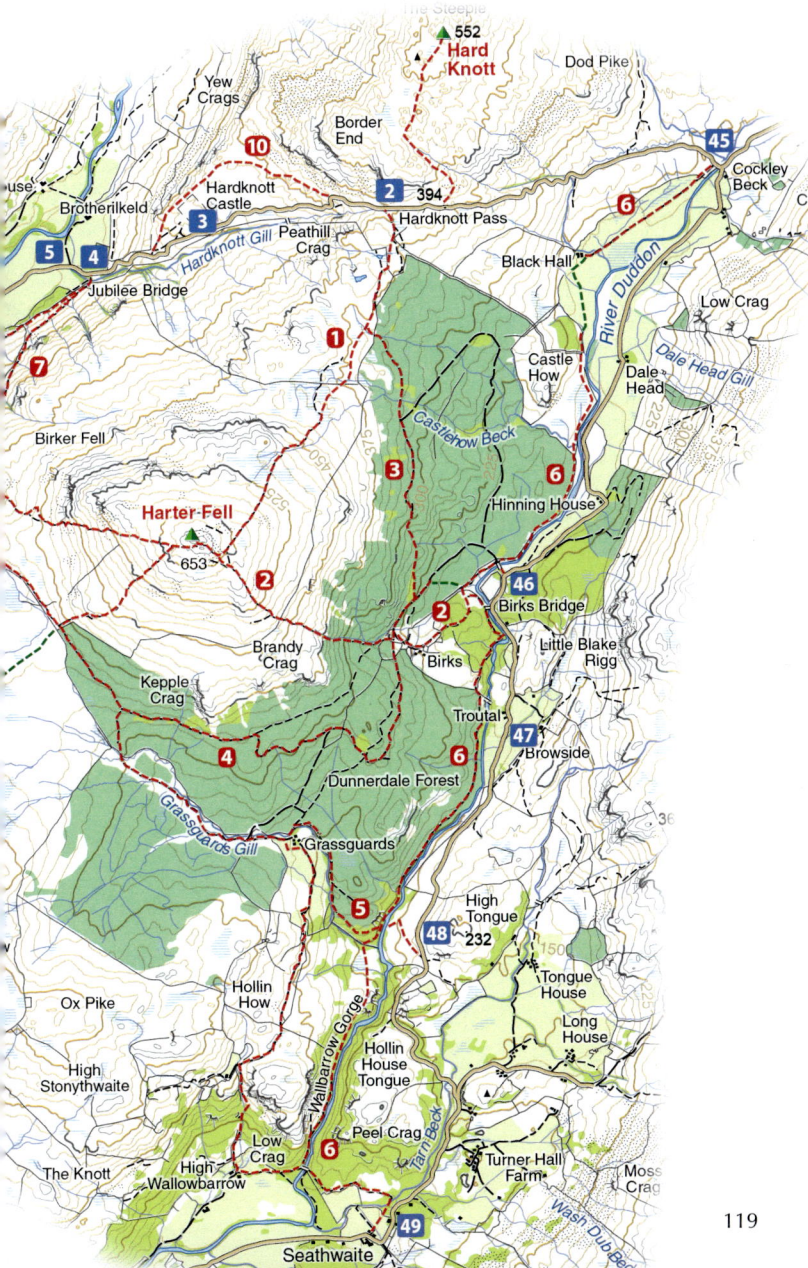

Ascent from the Duddon valley (Birks Bridge, Fickle Steps or Seathwaite) 46, 48 & 49

Via Dunnerdale Forest →*4.4km/2¾ miles* ↑*490m/1610ft* ⏱*2hr 30min*

The Duddon–Eskdale bridleway makes a useful springboard for ascents from either valley.

4 Forest tracks from Birks converge to rise across the southern slopes of Harter Fell, joining the ancient pedestrian pass leading into Eskdale. Cross through a broken wall to the right as the Green Crag path branches left, and then exit the forest at a hand-gate in the fence. Once out of the forest turn sharp right, climbing first with the tall fence then on open fell, on a good path, to the top.

Via Grassguards →*4km/2½ miles* ↑*480m/1575ft* ⏱*2hr 20min*

An attractive walk-in combining fell and forest

5 This old trail emanates from Grassguards, which can be reached from Fickle Steps direct or from Seathwaite by the track from High Wallowbarrow (SD 220 963) – either route an attractive walk. The path follows Grassguards Gill through a gate and then over a plank footbridge, with young conifers to the left, mature ones to the right, in an open tract, to merge with Route **4**.

Duddon valley path

Cockley Beck Bridge 45 to High Wallowbarrow via Fickle Steps 48
→*4.8km/3 miles* ⏱*1hr 30min*

A perfect walk for a wet or windy day, this valley path from Cockley Beck Bridge is a journey of great contrasts and can be followed all the way down to High Wallowbarrow, keeping close to the river most of the way. It can also be used to link the ascents from the Duddon for a circular route.

6 The route begins on a farm track thought to lie on top of the Roman road which once switched up to Hardknott from Black Hall. Still crossing meadows and bending south, the path joins the river beneath Castle How and

13 HARTER FELL

heads on by **Birks Bridge**, now enveloped in woodland and rising and falling on rocky bluffs behind **Troutal**. After a short, densely forested stretch to Fickle Steps, you cross **Grassguards Gill** footbridge and, after a brief climb, reach the grand finale: the verdant confines of the **Wallowbarrow Gorge**, with its massive boulder scree. Quite superb.

Ascent from Eskdale (Jubilee Bridge or Woolpack Inn) 4 & 6

Via Jubilee Bridge →*3.2km/2 miles* ↑*560m/1835ft* ⏱*2hr 20min*

A satisfying circular walk can be made by combining this ascent of Harter Fell with a visit to the Roman Fort on the rigg overlooking the upper Eskdale gorge on the way down (via Routes 1 and 10) and offers scenic moments galore.

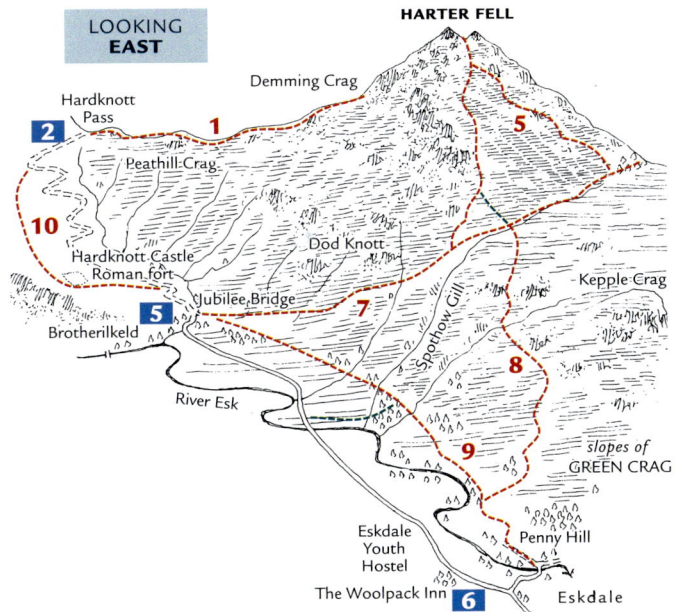

Brotherilkeld from the path beneath Dod Knott

Harter Fell from Penny Hill

7 Begin by crossing the little stone footbridge, built in 1977 to commemorate Queen Elizabeth II's silver jubilee. Pass through successive kissing-gates and be sure to take the peat road, the more obvious made track, ahead. This green-way duly begins to rise and the view back into upper Eskdale is a scene to savour. Climb on through the bracken through two hand-gates. As the path from Boot (Route **8**) merges from the right, bear away left from the notoriously marshy path which runs on beside the fence to Grassguards and take a clear ascending path after a lone rowan. The path has two variants, that closer to the impressive mass of Wallhead Crag being the rougher, with some pitching, while the more comfortable line keeps right, crossing the line of two tumbled walls before rising more assertively to join forces with the path from the forest edge (Route **4**) beneath a classic volcanic outcrop, to find the gap between the summit battlements.

Via Penny Hill →*4km/2½ miles* ↑*580m/1905ft* ⏱*2hr 40min*

Beautiful Eskdale merits all the time you can give it.

8 From Boot either follow the Eskdale Trail to **Doctor's Bridge** or start from the **Woolpack Inn**, following the road west to the lane signed 'Penny Hill',

Eskdale from the summit (photo: Maggie Allan)

which leads over the bridge – a lovely spot to look into the cool clear waters of the Esk. Go straight ahead along the hedged then walled lane towards **Penny Hill farm**. A permissive path, through gates, ushers walkers right and then left, avoiding the farmyard. Rejoin the track east of the farm, go through a gate and, as the track forks, go right, rising to a gate. Through the gate the path veers up left to a wall. Angle right to a gate by old sheep pens and continue up the turf peat-road. At the right-hand bend follow a wooden signpost pointing left to 'Harter Fell'. The path traverses, with the intake wall to the left and below, slipping through a re-entrant gill then aiming diagonally up the facing slope and a gap in the rocks to ford **Spothow Gill** and reach a stile in the fence. Join the path from Jubilee Bridge (Route **7**).

Eskdale valley path

Jubilee Bridge to Doctor Bridge → *2.5km/1½ miles* ⏲ *35min*

9 The Eskdale Trail crops up from time to time in this guide. A particularly choice passage leads down from **Jubilee Bridge**. It's largely a meadow-way which offers a pleasing end to a day's walk over Harter Fell.

13 Harter Fell

Descent from Hardknott Pass via Hardknott Castle →*2km/1¼ miles* ⏲*30min*
10 A bridleway leaves the Hardknott Pass road at the top hairpin. This leads down past the Roman parade ground and along the scarp by Hardknott Castle Roman fort to rejoin the road just above Jubilee Bridge.

The summit

The summit is unmistakable, but whether you choose to clamber onto it is another matter! The more modest situation of the Ordnance Survey column suffices for many visitors. The view is the real pleasure: a grand panorama, with the Scafells and the head of Eskdale perfectly presented.

Summit outcrop and OS column

Safe descents

The first rule of thumb when leaving the summit of Harter Fell is that if there is a path underfoot, you can be confident that it takes you to safety – E to Birks (**2**), W to Boot (**7–8**) and N to the top of Hardknott Pass (**1**).

Ridge route

Green Crag →*3.2km/2 miles* ↓*310m/1015ft* ↑*145m/475ft* ⏲*1hr 10min*
Follow the regular path descending WSW. Take the left fork below the volcanic outcrop. This path leads down to the edge of the forestry. Glance by the tall fence and ignore the path that crosses the fence-stile in the corner. Take a bearing SW across the rough peaty moor to reach the broad grassy saddle between Crook and Green Crags. Climb the bank S and gain the summit from the east.

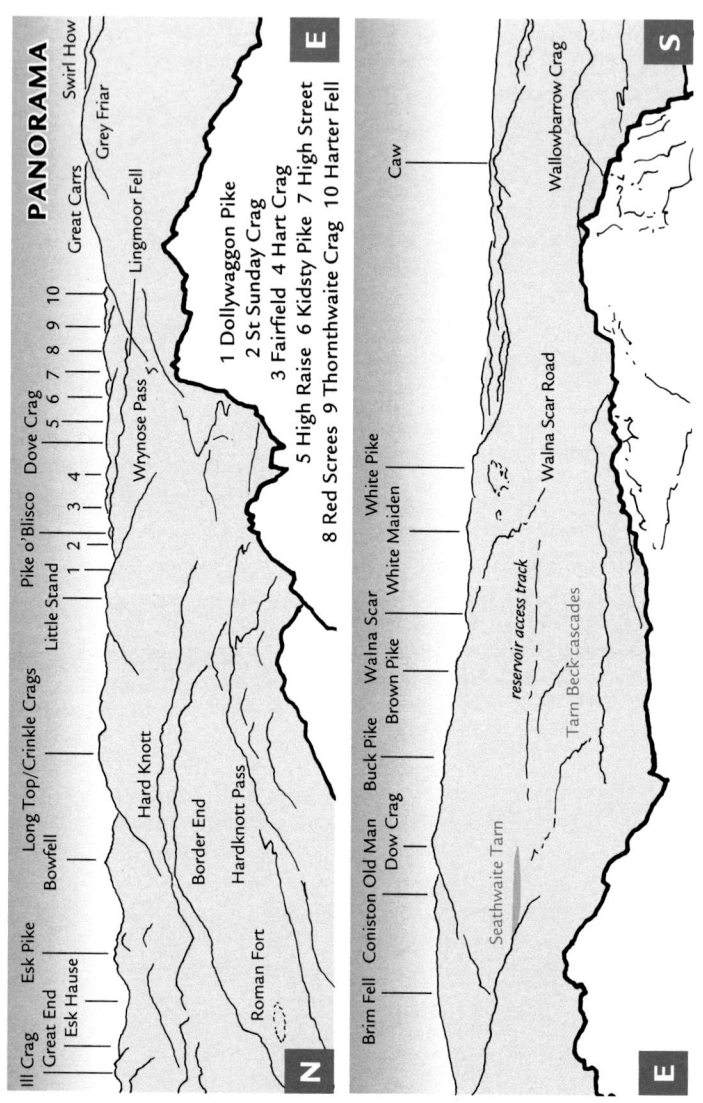

13 HARTER FELL

14 HESK FELL 476M/1562FT

Climb it from	Woodend Bridge **9** or Bobbinmill Bridge **24**
Character	A simple fell that reserves all its glory for its spur top, the Pike, above Rainsborrow Wood
Fell-friendly route	1
Summit grid ref	SD 176 946
Link it with	Yoadcastle

Let's not be too hasty. Puddings (and pudding-shaped fells) can be sweet. Hesk Fell may look like a Pennine outcast but it has interesting historic features to seek out, including the remains of a copper mine and a large Viking enclosure, and with the Pike it makes a striking connection with the Duddon. To the west of the fell lies the vast upland bowl of Storthes, a wilderness wherein even the sheep may look lonely.

The main body of the fell is presently partitioned by electric fencing but the wanderer has been suitably acknowledged and accommodated, with strategic stiles. The summit can be tackled from the north (1), southeast (2) or southwest (5) over pathless terrain. Rainsborrow Wood, presently undergoing a programme to reinvigorate its deciduous diversity, offers attractive approaches from Bobbinmill Bridge, perhaps including a visit to the Pike.

↑ *Hesk Fell from the Pike (photo: Richard Edwards)*

14 HESK FELL

Ascent from the Birkerfell Road (Woodend Bridge) 9

Direct →*2.4km/1½ miles* ↑*240m/785ft* ⏲*1hr*

Two quick routes to the top, taking advantage of a high start from the Birkerfell Road

1 Woodend Bridge, off the Birkerfell Road, is a common starting point for this fell despite the fact that it lacks an attractive return route. Walk to the road-gate, which gives access into the walled enclosures leading to Woodend Farm, but turn left before it and follow up the pasture left, keeping the wall to the right until confronted by the electric fencing. Cross the stile. Ascend the featureless ridge, coming alongside a second fence which almost traverses the fell-top. A few stones have been gathered to form a summit cairn on the south side of the fence, necessitating a nifty step-over.

2 About 1.6km down the road from Woodend Bridge a bridleway leaves the Birkerfell Road south of the entrance to **Crosbythwaite Farm**. After a series of gates it reaches the ridge wall, passing close to the remnants of a D-shaped Viking stock enclosure, over an acre in size. For the summit leave the bridleway right, following the wall up to and over a ladder-stile, and climb the facing slope to the top, or alternatively, go west on Route **5** or take Route **6** to visit the subsidiary top, the Pike.

Ascent from Bobbinmill Bridge 24

Rainsborrow and the Pike have all the fell's scenic aces.

Via Rainsbarrow Wood →*5.2km/3¼ miles* ↑*375m/1230ft* ⏲*2hr 30min*

3 From Bobbinmill Bridge take the rising footpath to the left into partially felled woodland. Footpaths then diverge. The first goes through **Rainsbarrow Wood**, via kissing-gates and ladder-stiles, and then turns sharp left onto a permissive path at **Pike Side Farm**, going west and then north round **the Pike** to gain the ridge at the same point as the bridleway from Crosbythwaite (Route **2**).

4 The second path from the junction (see Route **3**) – the footpath through the top of **Rainsbarrow** – is a special treat. It swings round under the eastern scarp of **the Pike** anti-clockwise and leads into a narrow lateral enclosure. At its end it links to an old mine path climbing left up to the same ridge junction from Baskell Farm. By either route join Route **2** for the final climb to the summit.

Via the old copper mine →*3.2km/2 miles* ↑*280m/920ft* ⏱*1hr 40min*
5 From the point where Route **2** breaks pathless up the slope from the wall south of the summit (SD 182 943), an interesting variant path, a miners' trod, contours left from the ladder-stile to inspect the enigmatic remains of the early 19th-century **copper mine**. Past the mine climb up the open fellside, north, to gain the summit.

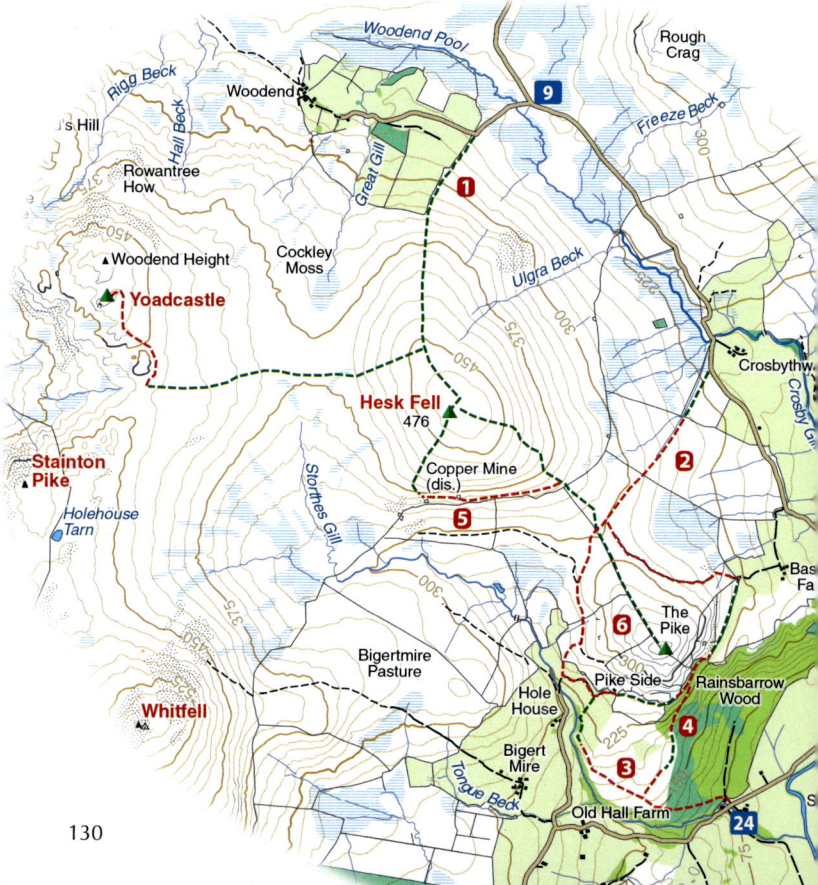

14 Hesk Fell

Remains of the Hesk Fell copper mine, with the shapely profile of the Pike beyond

The Pike →1km/½ miles ↑65m/215ft ⏱20min

6 To revel in the special view from **the Pike** turn left at the Viking enclosure (see Route **2**) and keep the ridge wall close right, via a stile. Heed the notice on the summit: it's not worth even thinking about an eastward descent.

The summit

The featureless fell-top lacks any hint of a cairn or cause to break one's stride. However, instinctively you will want to mark your own visit, standing to stare, with happy satisfaction, at a grand panorama of familiar fells, seen only perhaps this once from a novel station.

Safe descents

All of the ascents described pose no issues in descent.

Ridge route

Yoadcastle →2.4km/1½ miles ↓100m/330ft ↑120m/395ft ⏱1hr

This is not an endeavour to relish on a misty day. The saving grace (while it remains) is the hefting fence, which acts as a guide down to the head of the barren Storthes Gill basin. Leave the summit NW and descend to a stile over the electric fence. Follow on with the fence to the right and, where it bears right, continue W up the rough moor onto the broad and comparatively dry saddle, where a narrow path is gleefully joined. The summit bastion is your obvious target on the near right.

15 HOLME FELL 317M/1040FT

Climb it from	Little Langdale **40**, Cathedral Quarry **41**, Oxen Fell **35**, Tilberthwaite **33**, Hodge Close **34** or Tom Gill **36**
Character	A rugged entertaining little fell, shielded by crags and bound by woodland and quarries
Fell-friendly route	7
Summit grid ref	NY 315 006

Due south of the hamlet of Little Langdale rises a wooded ridge, which reaches its full height above Yewdale's lovely parkland. One of the great little fells of Lakeland, Holme Fell boasts a southernmost facade of rocky ribs, which jut through a dense cover of native trees to give it an air of impregnability. Within its woods and upland pastures lurks a wide variety of plant and wildlife, including – before the bracken runs riot – swathes of bluebells among the birch trees. The dust and noise of slate quarrying has largely died away although some tell-tale signs remain.

The fell offers far more than a clutch of circular strolls through wooded glens and a good ridge-walk (5), with Tilberthwaite (6) and the extraordinary quarried hollows at Hodge Close (4, 8) making very worthwhile quests. Why not take the time to explore the charming environs of Little Langdale (1–4) on your way?

↑ *Wetherlam from the summit of Holme Fell (photo: Maggie Allan)*

15 HOLME FELL

Approaches to High Oxen Fell, Oxen Fell High Cross 35 and Hodge Close 34 from Little Langdale 40 and Cathedral Quarry 41

Direct →2.7km/1¾ miles ↑220m/720ft ⏲1hr 30min

Hiding behind a mantle of trees, Holme Fell is largely obscured from the Little Langdale valley, but a choice of four routes enables you to begin to unravel its secrets.

133

1 The Cumbria Way climbs out of the woods, having casually inspected the thunderous **Colwith Force**, to emerge through hand-gates at **High Park**. Follow the road west to a footpath, signed left, short of Stang End. This leads over a stile across the wet marsh of Little Fell close by **Great How** to enter woodland at a gate. Join the Stang End/Hodge Close track and proceed to the small community of **Hodge Close**.

2 Another woodland path, missing the falls, heads up southwards to join the High Park road at its junction with the Coniston road. From here you can follow either a fenced roadside path leading to Oxen Fell High Cross or a quiet by-road leading directly to **High Oxen Fell** farm.

3 A footpath leaves the road directly from the community of Little Langdale at a kissing-gate 300 metres east of Wilson Place at NY 318 033. Descending the pasture, cross a footbridge, a lovely spot to enjoy the sparkling beck, and walk on to a lane leading to Stang End. Follow the track south to reach **Hodge Close**.

4 From the **Three Shires Inn** go 100 metres west to the minor road junction and take the descending lane, winding down by several handsomely sited houses to the ford and raised footbridge. (At this point there is a discreet car park, accessed via the High Park lane off the Coniston road.) Continue south along the track leading through a valley glade – ultimate destination High Tilberthwaite Farm – and, after the high spoil of **Moss Rigg Quarry**, watch for a leftward-branching track in woodland, leading to **Hodge Close**.

Ascent from Oxen Fell High Cross 35

Direct →*2.5km/1½ miles* ↑*200m/655ft* ⏱*1hr 20min*

Trace the undulating ridge from the Oxen Fell track.

5 From Oxen Fell High Cross you can contentedly follow the road to and through **High Oxen Fell farm** to **Hodge Close** – a useful connection when orbiting the entire fell. To get directly onto the Holme Fell ridge, walk up to the top of the first rise in this by-road, where a recessed gate on the left gives access onto the fell, beside power lines. A definite path passes a pool as it heads onto the emerging ridge. The path mounts a prominent knoll then follows a metal fence, past a patch of bluebells (in season). Note an old cairn, prominent well to the west of the ridge path. The path crosses a stile as the

Typical ridge-top scene (photo: Maggie Allan)

fence straddles the ridge and descends among the heather. As the fence bears right ignore the carpet-wrapped stile and keep left to follow an undulating path, through rocky knots and by a solitary larch, to arrive at the **Uskdale Gap** cairn. **Ivy Crag** rises ahead, surmounted by the fell's largest cairn. Climb direct to this prominent shoulder, a very good viewpoint for Tom Heights and Black Fell. The summit is attained by skirting right, by a marsh, with a worn path stepping up the right-hand edge.

Ascent from Low Tilberthwaite 33 or Hodge Close 34

The saddle of Uskdale Gap is the focus of all but one of these ascents, accessed from the footpath which crosses the ridge from southeast to northwest.

Via Holme Ground → *3km/1¾ miles* ↑*200m/655ft* ⏲*1hr 30min*
6 From Low Tilberthwaite follow the road almost to **High Tilberthwaite** and take the gated footpath on the right, passing through fields and woodland to the Hodge Close access road. Turn left on it to Holme Ground, where you have a choice between Routes **7** and **8**.

7 Follow Route **6** to Holme Ground. Pass through the facing gate on the right and rise to join the lateral bridleway. Turn left (northeast). After just over

Deep dark pool in Hodge Close Quarry (photo: Maggie Allan)

250 metres a path branches right, up through the light birchwood, onto the open slope, heading south-southeast direct to the summit.

8 Alternatively, having followed Route **6** to Holme Ground, where Route **7** branches off right continue with the bridleway a further 250 metres to a path, again on the right, passing up by evidence of small-scale slate quarrying, which leads to a dam holding a charming stretch of water. The path passes to the right and climbs easily to reach Uskdale Gap, from where Route **5** can be followed to the summit.

This approach can also begin from the car park adjacent to Hodge Close Quarry via the road. Before heading off up the fell take hold of your courage and inspect the two monumental quarry holes from within. Follow the road north through the cluster of dwellings. After Hodge Close cottage find a track on the right. This leads to High Oxen Fell farm, but, before you reach the gate, take the inviting path down into the tree-shaded quarry on your right.

15 Holme Fell

Clamber over a chaos of boulders into the quarry depths to see an awe-inspiring cavern supported by a stout pillar, and get a view into the 'blue lagoon' of Hodge Close Quarry.

Circuit from Tom Gill 36

→ *10km/6¼ miles* ⏲ *3hr 30min*

9 If you want to walk right around the fell on tracks and quiet roads, the gated meadow-way from Shepherd's Bridge to **Yewtree Farm** is a useful link.

10 The dale-floor path tracks the Skelwith–Coniston road to High Oxen Fell Cross. (To make the natural link with neighbouring Black Fell follow the lovely Mountain Road east from here.)

The summit

Holme Fell's highest ground is a proud ridge with a short cliff to the east and cairns at either end, though the summit outcrop itself has no cairn. For the best view of Yewdale go a little further south to the cairn on the spur-top of Raven Crag.

Safe descents

Uskdale Gap is the answer. Refrain from rambling about on the rough plateau as there is no way down the east, south or west slopes. The nastiest trap lurks on the south side, with Calf and Raven Crags posing serious problems. Neither is there access into the valley pastures along these fronts. Retreat to Uskdale Gap (**5**), then either go right for Yew Tree Tarn or left (**8**) for Low Tilberthwaite (**6**).

16 MUNCASTER FELL 231M/758FT

Climb it from	Ravenglass **12** or Eskdale Green **10**
Character	A long low fell meriting the full traverse in harmony with La'al Ratty
Fell-friendly route	6
Summit grid ref	SD 112 983

While Black Combe is often considered the seaboard fell, no other fell in the Lake District better serves to show the link between land and sea than Muncaster Fell. On either side of this narrow fell are lush valleys, drained by the rivers Esk and Mite, isolating the fell from any natural bond with any of the other fells. These rivers, with the addition of the Irt (from Wasdale), recoil at the point of entry into the sea, halted by the massive sand bars at the fell's western tip, with almost all the rain from the high Scafells brought together here. The dune landscapes of Drigg and Eskmeals are also high-value wildlife habitats and unique in Cumbria.

This low elongated ridge of wet moorland will have been a bridgehead of another kind. Whether marauding or colonising, over many millennia people have made their first footfall into the Cumbrian hinterland along this ridge, coming

↑ *Eastern end of the Muncaster Fell ridge path, short of Silver Knott*

16 MUNCASTER FELL

up from the ancient harbour at Ravenglass. Bronze-Age and later relics abound, from Swinside stone circle to Barnscar 'city'. The Romans certainly valued it, establishing Glannoventa (Ravenglass) as an important west-coast approach to their northern frontier. Later settlers, most notably the Vikings from the Isle of Man and Ireland, landed here and quickly headed for the hills, establishing their own style of farming. So the walker, wandering alone on the wild and wet of Muncaster Fell, may sense an ancient footfall in every stride.

Three man-made features make Muncaster Fell irresistible: Ravenglass village, a special conservation area; Muncaster Castle, with its magnificent gardens; and La'al Ratty, the miniature railway which, with its distinctive dry hoot, brings back the joy of gentle travel through the loveliest of landscapes. A natural combination of ride and stride, travelling out with the train and walking back upon the fell, or vice versa, makes for the perfect summer's day outing. Indeed, there are four fell-foot stations to choose from: Ravenglass, Muncaster Mill, Irton Road and the Green.

Three approaches are described from Ravenglass (1–3). Routes converge on the main ridge path (9) from both the southwest (4–6) and the northeast (7–8), with Route 10 offering a low-level alternative useful in creating circular routes.

Black Combe from the triple-river confluence at Ravenglass

WALKING THE LAKE DISTRICT FELLS – CONISTON

Approaches from Ravenglass 12

Direct along the road →*4km/2½ miles* ↑*240m/785ft* ⏲*1hr 30min*

The shortest route from Ravenglass involves a considerable amount of road walking.

1 Walkers in a hurry to reach the fell (or backtracking after the ridge-route traverse from Eskdale Green) can follow a footway up from the village by the war memorial to the junction with the **A595**, continuing on, past the public entrance to Muncaster Castle

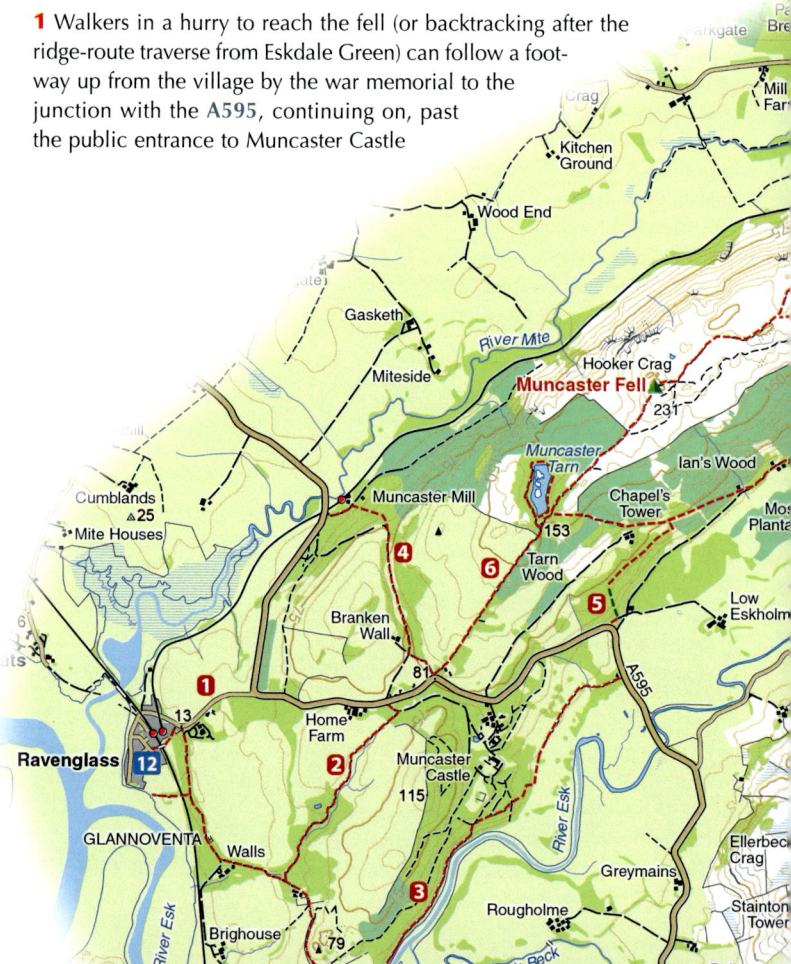

16 Muncaster Fell

grounds, to the sharp right-hand bend. Here the bridleway onto the ridge, Fell Lane (Route **6**), begins.

Via Walls castle and the Esk →*4.5km/2¾ miles* ↑*230m/755ft* ⏲*1hr 50min*

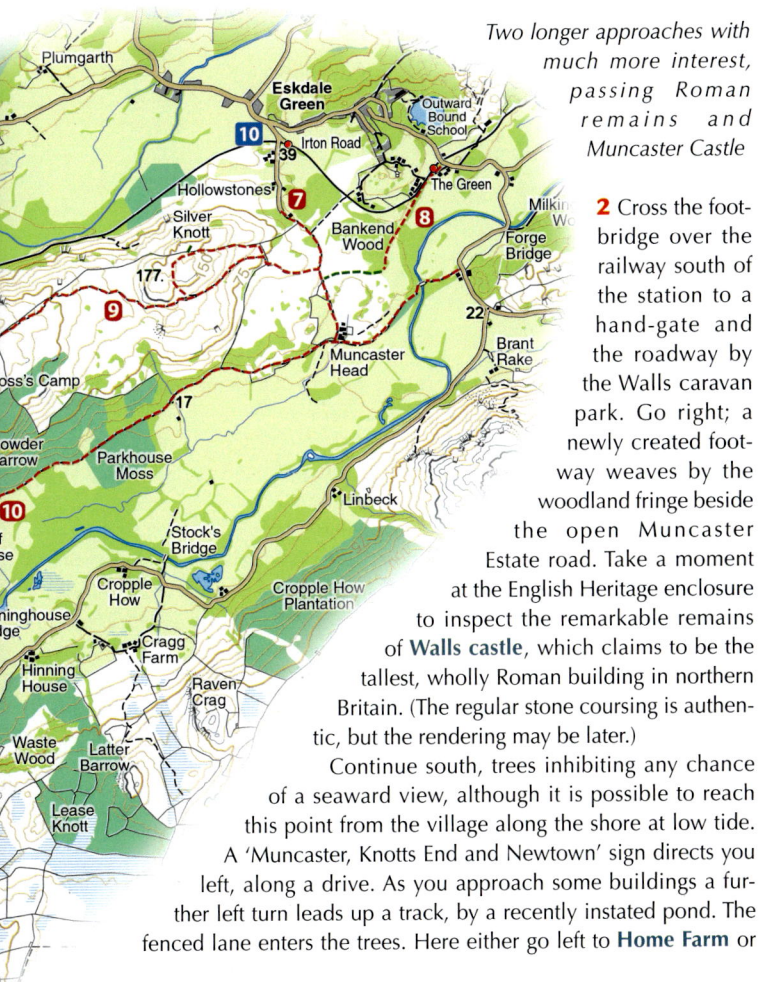

Two longer approaches with much more interest, passing Roman remains and Muncaster Castle

2 Cross the footbridge over the railway south of the station to a hand-gate and the roadway by the Walls caravan park. Go right; a newly created footway weaves by the woodland fringe beside the open Muncaster Estate road. Take a moment at the English Heritage enclosure to inspect the remarkable remains of **Walls castle**, which claims to be the tallest, wholly Roman building in northern Britain. (The regular stone coursing is authentic, but the rendering may be later.)

Continue south, trees inhibiting any chance of a seaward view, although it is possible to reach this point from the village along the shore at low tide. A 'Muncaster, Knotts End and Newtown' sign directs you left, along a drive. As you approach some buildings a further left turn leads up a track, by a recently instated pond. The fenced lane enters the trees. Here either go left to **Home Farm** or

Muncaster Castle with owner Peter Frost-Pennington

continue into the Castle grounds beside the circular Muncaster Interactive building and the Sino-Himalayan garden and turn left to leave through the crenellated gateway (locked at 5.30pm) onto the A595. In either case, go right, along the roadside, to the sharp right-hand bend to enter Fell Lane (Route **6**).

3 An intriguing and pleasant alternative is to start out with Route **2** but then continue straight on on the footpath from Walls castle, signed 'Cumbria Coastal Way', through Newtown Farm and then beneath Newtown Knott, which is surmounted by an old navigation tower. Crossing pasture, enter woodland at a hand-gate, coming close to the bridleway along the Esk shore, almost opposite the Hall Waberthwaite ford. Go left, upstream, on a permissive path, to enter Croft Coppice, and beneath the tree-screened Muncaster Castle, ancient home of the Penningtons, onto the drive across Hirst Park to Hirst Lodge and the A595. Here join Route **5**.

From Muncaster Mill →3.6km/2¼ miles ↑260m/855ft ⏱1hr 15min

Spare a little time to visit the historic Muncaster Mill before embarking on your ascent.

4 A delightful bridleway ascends from the **Muncaster Mill station**, within woodland, joining the access track from **Branken Wall farm** to meet the **A595** at the foot of Fell Lane (Route **6**).

Ascent from Ravenglass 12

Via Chapel's Tower →*9km/5½ miles* ↑*440m/1445ft* ⏲*2hr 45min*
5 Turning left at Hirst Lodge (see Route **3**), follow the **A595** and take the second right (bridleway sign), at the tight left-hand bend, and, after 40 metres, arrive at decking on your left. A permissive path up the wooded bank reaches a lateral woodland track near a grand old spreading oak. Go right. (This track is prone to dampness.) Pass beneath **Chapel's Tower**. As a gateway in a wall nears the path is ushered left to a ladder-stile onto the rising path from Eskholme to **Muncaster Tarn**. At the tarn, join Route **6** to continue.

Direct via Fell Lane →*4km/2½ miles* ↑*160m/525ft* ⏲*1hr 35min*

Fell Lane is the focus of ascents from the west. Routes 1, 2 and 4 all lead to its start and Routes 5 and 10 draw up to join forces with it at Muncaster Tarn.

6 The lane begins from the **A595** road bend. There is a gate halfway up but otherwise it's plain sailing to the rhododendron canopy close to the tarn. Make a point of visiting this secret pool and indulge yourself on the circuit path to sample its 'far from the madding crowd' tranquillity. Lilies grow in the southwestern corner and in a wet season the tarn overflows at both ends.

The track heads up by a gate onto the undulating fell, passing gorse bushes. It forks at the forest corner. The right-hand path avoids the summit altogether – and much of the damper ground for that matter – but the summit is irresistible. The stronger path steps up the short bank to the left and heads for Hooker Crag (the fell summit).

Ascent from Eskdale Green 10

A smart move for summer Ratty riders is to park in Ravenglass, enjoy the ride all the way to Dalegarth, perhaps taking lunch there, and, returning, alight at either the Green or Irton Road station for a fine traverse of the scenic Muncaster Fell ridge.

Via Irton Road and the Green stations →3.5km/2¼ miles ↑150m/490ft
⏱1hr 40min

7 The ridge path is most easily and swiftly gained from **Irton Road station** (SD 137 999). Cross the railway bridge and follow the 'no-through-road', with its pleasing views into Eskdale, to end at Forest How. The green bridleway skirts the garden hedge to the right to slip through a gate onto a track, with dense gorse to the right. The ridge path (Route **9**) branches right from here, just short of a stile/gate.

8 The Green station (SD 145 998) makes for a neat country-walk approach. A narrow path leads west directly from the platform to a stile by a ford (with stepping-stones). Rise on a firm path, holding to the wall, beside woodland. From its right-hand corner, which can be muddied by cattle, traverse the pasture, with the short bank close left, to meet up with the bridleway from Muncaster Head at the stile/gate mentioned above. Follow Route **9** along the ridge to reach the summit.

9 Follow Route **7** or **8** to reach the stile/gate. The ridge-walk begins here, with the path hugging the gorse (not as painful as it sounds) to reach a kissing-gate. A few paces further on the path swings left on a steady stone-edged rise, with something like an outmoded television aerial prominent on the headland up to the right. To take fullest benefit of the ravishing eastern view into Eskdale, stay on the lesser path straight up through the bracken, keeping close to the ridge wall. At the top the briefest of breaches in this wall permits access to the **Silver Knott** bluff. A sheep trod leads south, away from the wall, just missing the highest ground. Descend the bracken bank by a large holly tree to join the incline ridge path. The main path heads west round the headland and dips down an incline to traverse a birch-dappled hollow, before rising to come close to the ridge wall, over much damp ground. The gateway in the wall corner does not spell an end of soggy going, sadly. The path is immediately forced to make an exaggerated leftward sweep around a marsh. Some walkers head on (bound for the summit), climbing the prominent bank, while others angle on left to come past the collapsing stable stone inscribed '**Ross's Camp** 1883', installed to mark the favourite viewpoint of John Ross, agent of the Muncaster Estate. The situation is splendid – a feast for the eyes! The continuing path is firm but has one drawback: it misses the summit completely! However, the path that mounts the bank, passing a large prominent boulder, snakes irresistibly along the ridge and skirts the few knolls flanking Hooker Moss to climb solidly onto Hooker Crag, the summit.

16 Muncaster Fell

Eskdale from the eastern end of the ridge near Ross's Camp

Valley path via High Eskholme ➔ *3.7km/2¼ miles* ⏲ *1hr 15min*

At present there is no continuous path along the shady scarp-base beside La'al Ratty; however, the valley path allows walkers the opportunity to complete their walk in circular fashion, on foot rather than by train.

10 A bridleway leading along the sunny southern foot of the fell, via **Muncaster Head** and High Eskholme (**golf course**), provides the perfect contrast to the moorland traverse. It is wooded for much of the way and interrupted by just one gate (at High Eskholme itself). Immediately west of High Eskholme the right of way splits, forsaking the metalled roadway. The more useful option draws up right by some sheds, a steady well-graded path mounting the slope, to be joined at a ladder-stile by the permissive path out of Chapel Wood (Route **4**). Passing within sight of **Chapel's Tower** and going through a hand-gate en route, it meets the top of Fell Lane at the dam of **Muncaster Tarn**. From here Route **6** leads east to the summit.

The summit

A fine stone-built OS pillar, constructed in the distinctive Eskdale granite, graces the top of Hooker Crag. There is ample scope to sit and glory in a wonderful panorama, a heady cocktail of the mountain and maritime. This is the closest Lakeland fell summit to the Isle of Man, which lies to the west in the middle of the Irish Sea.

Ordnance Survey column on Hooker Crag

Safe descents

There is no way N or S off the ridge from the open fell. Steep pathless scarp, most richly wooded on the south side, offers no appropriate links with recognised paths in either direction. There are, in effect, two ridge paths. That W from the summit (**6**) is obvious enough, but the trail E (**9**) weaves more laboriously towards the valley base of Eskdale Green. The westbound path quickly leads to the shelter and security of woodland, via Muncaster Tarn and Fell Lane, en route to the village of Ravenglass (**1–2**), only 4km distant from the summit.

17 STAINTON PIKE 498M/1634FT

Climb it from	Dyke **13** or Corneyfell Road (Fell Lane) **14**
Character	A fine off-the-beaten-track objective, between Whitfell and Yoadcastle
Fell-friendly route	1
Summit grid ref	SD 152 942
Link it with	Whitfell or Yoadcastle

Stainton Pike nestles into the eastern skyline of the southwestern fells alongside Yoadcastle; from the A595 you sense the two summits as one fell mass. To pick out Stainton Pike as a solitary objective, you need to view it from the Corneyfell Road, above the junction with the A595 at Millgate. The Whitrow Beck approach (1) shows the fell's cleanest profile, emphasised further on the walk-in via the homestead site. But from most other vantage points it has little distinctive form, merging into the vast moorland bowl of Storthes to the east.

Apart from the summit, interest lies in the fragmentary remains of early settlement, the impressive gorge of Rowantree Force and the shining Holehouse Tarn. To judge by the ridge path, walkers traversing from Whitfell to Woodend Height tend to ignore Stainton Pike – most remiss! There are just two lines of direct ascent, both from the west, both more than a bit wet!

↑ *Stainton Pike from the ridge south of Holehouse Tarn*

WALKING THE LAKE DISTRICT FELLS – CONISTON

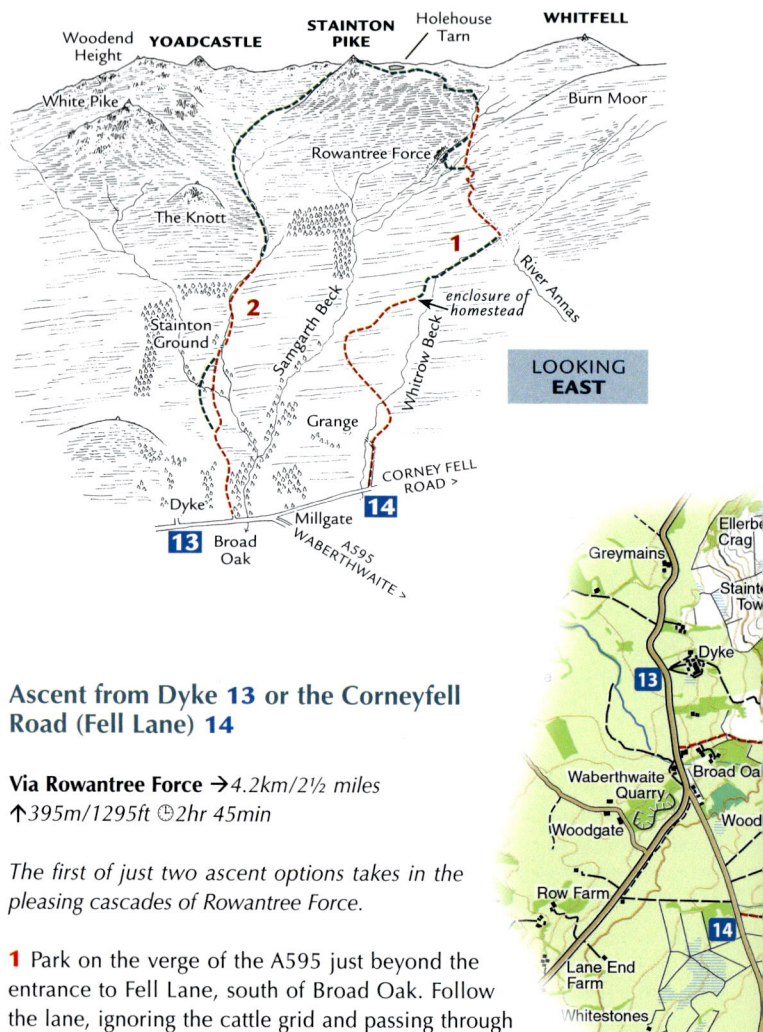

LOOKING EAST

Ascent from Dyke 13 or the Corneyfell Road (Fell Lane) 14

Via Rowantree Force →4.2km/2½ miles
↑395m/1295ft ⊕2hr 45min

The first of just two ascent options takes in the pleasing cascades of Rowantree Force.

1 Park on the verge of the A595 just beyond the entrance to Fell Lane, south of Broad Oak. Follow the lane, ignoring the cattle grid and passing through the facing gate. The bridle-track embarks on a winding course across a rough pasture of rushes and gorse,

17 STAINTON PIKE

no more than an intermittent path after the ford, sometimes in doubt, but continuing eastward between **Samgarth** and **Whitrow Becks**. Finding drier ground, draw alongside Whitrow Beck and wander through the intriguing **homestead enclosure**. A more certain path now angles right, following on up the gullies at the foot of **Red Gill**. A cairn then indicates the start of a grooved path left, partially lined with boulders, which zig-zags as the ground steepens. To visit **Rowantree Force** slip through the adjacent bouldery hollow on your left, passing a small ruined fold, and venture into the ravine. Follow the ravine edge a little way upstream and regain the bridleway, already indistinct as it skirts the Withe Bottom mire. For ease of walking, keep up left and follow the fence, crossing over Sergeant Crag. As the fell levels out cross the fence near **Holehouse Tarn** and follow a spidery path northwest to the summit knoll.

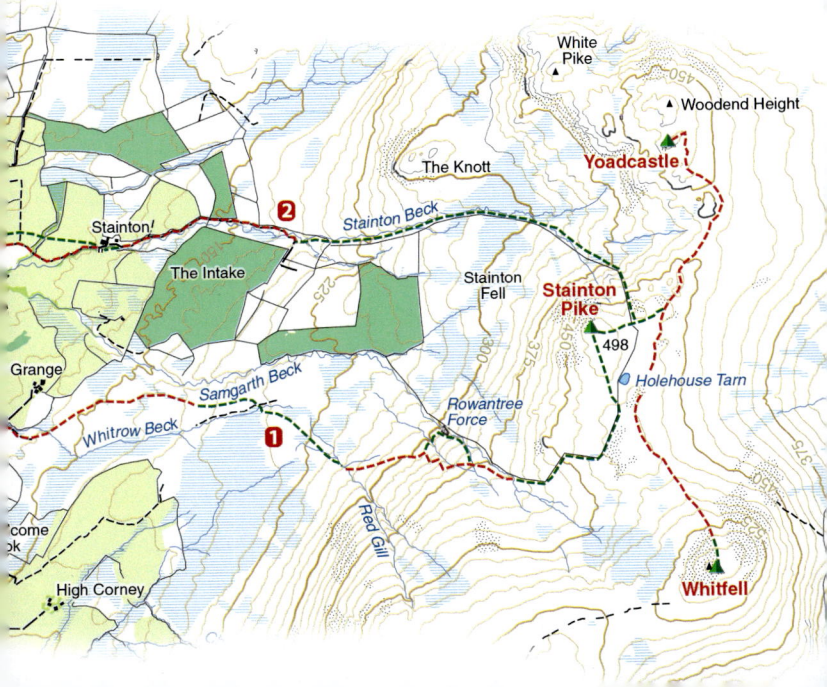

Looking west to the Cumbrian coast over the Rowantree Force ravine

17 STAINTON PIKE

Via Stainton Ground →4km/2½ miles ↑470m/1540ft ⏲2hr 15min

This route along Stainton Beck makes a natural descent on a round trip.

2 Park by the telephone kiosk opposite Broad Oak Farm, cross the cattle grid and follow the farm access track to Stainton Ground. Although there is a footpath, complete with stiles, it is preferable to follow the farm track, unless you wish to wade through the knee-high water at the Black Beck ford. Cross a ladder-stile, right, and an unusually broad footbridge, immediately before the farmyard gate. Embark on a footpath that hugs **Stainton Beck**, via two fence-stiles, pass **Stainton Ground** and continue through gorse and marshy ground. Reach the open fell via two ladder-stiles and an intermediary low fence-stile. Beat a way through the bracken, without a path. Keep the fence close right as you climb to a saddle just east of the summit, finally crossing the fence to reach the cairn.

The summit

A broad north–south ridge culminates with a splendid flourish of rock on a modest outcrop northwest of Holehouse Tarn. It is surmounted by a neat edifice befitting a pike. Make sure you take time to linger and enjoy your visit.

Safe descents

With a fence straddling the plateau just below the summit you have some reassurance in mist, but only if you want to head W. The footpath by Stainton Beck (**2**) is invisible and painfully rough in places but the way is clear at all times.

Ridge routes

Whitfell →1.5km/1 mile ↓5m/15ft ↑100m/330ft ⏲25min
The hint of a grass trod leads S to cross the plain fence just beyond Holehouse Tarn. After the ambitiously named Fox Crags, cross the old bridleway, climbing SE to the substantial cairn.

Yoadcastle →2km/1¼ miles ↓65m/215ft ↑60m/195ft ⏲35min
Cross the plain fence (E) again to join the narrow ridge path to the east of Holehouse Tarn. Go N to Yoadcastle.

18 STICKLE PIKE 376M/1234FT

Climb it from	Kiln Bank Cross **26**, Broughton Mills **27** or Ulpha **25**
Character	A mountain in miniature between the Duddon and Dunnerdale Beck
Fell-friendly route	2
Summit grid ref	SD 212 927
Link it with	Caw

The Dunnerdale Fells are defined as the southwestern slopes of Stickle Pike, a shapely presence between two beautiful valleys: the main Duddon valley and the side valley containing Dunnerdale Beck, which flows into the River Lickle at Broughton Mills. The parallel ridge, enclosing Dunnerdale Beck to the right, actually contains a higher summit, Fox Haw, superior by just under 10m.

Most visitors are content to pick off the fell blithely from the open road summit at Kiln Bank Cross (1–2), but there is a good deal more to appreciate. Why not create a longer skyline route, taking in neighbouring Fox Haw (3) or Great Stickle (5)? A full circuit of the fell is also made possible by footpaths and bridleways to the north (7), east (4) and south (6), with access from Kiln Bank Cross, Broughton Mills and the Duddon valley.

↑ *Stickle Pike summit cairn*

18 STICKLE PIKE

Ascent from Kiln Bank Cross 26

Direct →*0.5km/¼ mile* ↑*115m/375ft* ⏲*30min*

This ascent is a brief one.

1 Park at Kiln Bank Cross and follow the beaten path, curving up the shallow combe from south to southwest. The ground steepens and **Stickle Tarn** does its level best to hide, but seek it out to enjoy a moment's

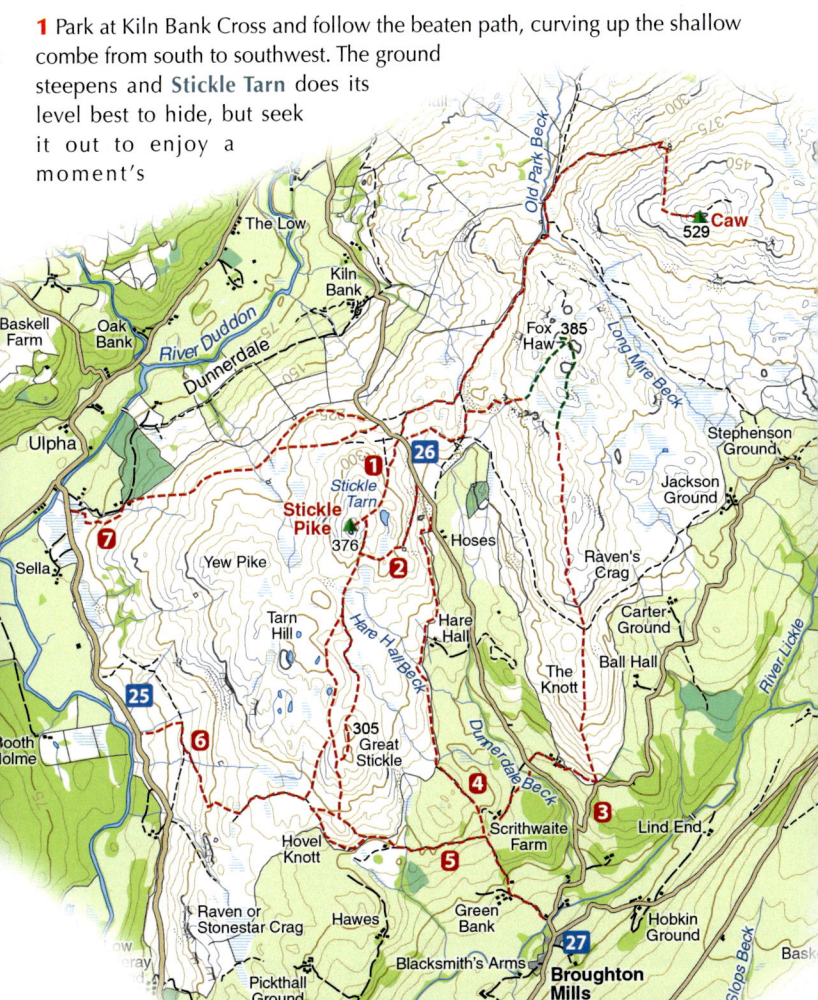

quiet contemplation at this little oasis. The eroded path, strewn with loose stone, inhibits a flowing stride to the top.

2 An interesting variant begins 250 metres down the road, where a slate miners' incline bears right, slanting up the bracken bank to a mine level. Pass up right by a workshop ruin to join the ridge path emanating from Great Stickle. Cut up right to link with the direct route (Route **1**) at a high saddle and go left for the summit.

Ascent from Broughton Mills 27

Via Fox Haw →*5.2km/3¼ miles* ↑*425m/1395ft* ⏲*2hr 15min*

The fell has obvious circular-route potential, the best option being the horseshoe 'Dunnerdale Beck skyline' walk, anti-clockwise from the welcoming Blacksmith's Arms, taking in the neighbouring tops of the Knott and Fox Haw.

3 Either follow the road, crossing the Lickle, and then take the next two right forks to reach the ladder-stile on the left at the foot of **the Knott** ridge or, just

Caw and Fox Haw from Stickle Tarn

18 STICKLE PIKE

over the river, fork left to **Green Bank** then right through rustic **Scrithwaite**, crossing the clapper footbridge and then the dale road. Cross into the lane approach to and through Knott End, through gates, to reach that ladder-stile.

A clear path leads up the ridge, through the bracken, onto the brow of the Knott, with a cairn on almost the highest point. Follow the ridge path north, crossing a broken wall and the bridleway at the saddle. This droveway contours left directly to Kiln Bank Cross but skyliners keep up the broken edge ahead, drawing by a rock-girt pool onto **Raven's Crag**. Strategically sited cairns mark good viewpoints overlooking the white-washed Hoses, with Stickle Pike beyond. The ridge path dwindles at a depression and the route onto the raised headland of **Fox Haw** is undefined. Again the summit rock rib has a cairn with views to merit the effort. Descend the southern slopes southwest to join an old quarry track. Join the Park Head Road green-way, a useful approach route to Stickle Pike from Seathwaite, and after 100 metres branch up right, leaving the track as it goes down to the road-gate at Hoses. Pass a slate-mine level and reach the open parking space at Kiln Bank Cross, where you can choose from Routes **1** and **2**.

Path to Kiln Bank Cross via Hare Hall →*3.2km/2 miles* ⏱*1hr 15min*

4 The **Green Bank** route passes a cottage as it enters woodland and soon emerges again at a hand-gate. It rises to a wooden picnic bench with the most favoured of views down the Lickle valley to the coast. Follow the footpath, rising north along a broken-walled lane, entering the fell enclosure at a gate and then accompanying the intake wall, brushing through bracken above **Hare Hall** to join the road at **Hoses**. Go north for Kiln Bank Cross and Routes **1** and **2**.

Via Great Stickle →*2.7km/1¾ miles* ↑*370m/1215ft* ⏱*1hr 30min*

Another elevated walk, making a more thorough exploration of the fell plateau

5 The skyline route starts out with Route **4** but bears left from the bench, the walled lane rising and dipping to a gate, with stone stoups adjacent. The trackway passes a stone barn and rises to a gate. The continuing green track sweeps around **Hovel Knott** but the prime route branches up through the bracken on a clear path. Aim for the saddle to the right of Hovel Knott, a lovely little viewpoint in its own right. Bear up right from the narrow col. A path weaves over Little Stickle to the fading white-washed OS pillar on **Great Stickle** – a handsome viewpoint for the lower Duddon and Lickle valleys. The northward connection to Stickle Pike has two basic variations: either forge swiftly on on the slightly lower, level path, crossing the marshy hollow, or hold to the ridge (to the left), passing the various attractive pools and puddles that characterise **Tarn Hill**.

Ascent from Ulpha 25

Two paths make effective connections with the spine of the ridge, both fending off the all-too-evident bracken with unexpected ease, and they can be combined to make a really good scenic circular walk.

Via Tarn Hill →*3km/1¾ miles* ↑*360m/1180ft* ⏂*1hr 10min*

6 A signed path steps off the road at SD 201 917 by a small bridge and weaves up the fellside, drifting right. As the climb eases skirt a hollow and angle left into the ridge-top saddle, just north of Great Stickle, to join Route **5**.

Via Low Birks →*2.5km/1½ miles* ↑*310m/1015ft* ⏂*1hr 10min*

7 Less than a mile up the main road, at Ulpha bridge, a strip of tarmac leads from the valley road, close to the old school, and rises to the attractively located cottage at Low Birks. There are two bridleways. The one on the open fell, setting off for Kiln Bank Cross, shows off the Duddon valley to its best. Follow this to mount the bank by the water tank, with the wall on your left. Veer away from the wall to negotiate damp ground, the path briefly indistinct. Pass a large quartz-streaked outcrop and soon after ford a headstream amid juniper bushes. The path splits indistinctly, the clearer path joining the wall on the left to meet the road above the cattle grid sign, just on the Duddon side of the road pass. Turn right along the road and right again with Route **1** to complete the ascent.

The summit

No wonder people race up from the road pass. Stickle Pike has a lovely little summit, with two tops and a view that would cheer the most despondent.

18 STICKLE PIKE

Stickle Pike from the Knott

Safe descent

Cheered as you may be, don't treat the descent with frivolity. Keep tight to the one way up as it is the one way down, especially to the first shoulder.

Ridge route

Caw →*3.6km/2¼ miles* ↓*150m/490ft* ↑*300m/985ft* ⏱*1hr 45min*
Follow the popular path N to the open road at Kiln Bank Cross. Head straight across and take one of two green paths leading NE down to the Park Head Road bridleway. After about 800 metres you come alongside a wall and the bridleway from Long Mire merges from the right. Watch for the obvious Caw Quarry slate miners' incline branching right. Ascend to the mine and climb the rake directly above to reach the OS pillar on the summit.

19 SWIRL HOW 804M/2638FT

Climb it from	Coniston **32**, Little Langdale **40** or Wrynose Pass **43**
Character	Without the kudos of the Old Man, but far more the mountain – and it's a metre higher!
Fell-friendly route	5
Summit grid ref	NY 273 005
Link it with	Brim Fell, Great Carrs, Grey Friar or Wetherlam
Part of	The Swirl Round

The Old Man gets the plaudits and crowds; Swirl How gets the genuine fellwalker – and the nod in height, by a mere metre. (Ordnance Survey maps contradict the HARVEY map and show Coniston Old Man 803m and Swirl How 802m; this guide is consistent with HARVEY maps.)

This is the focal summit of the Coniston group, out from which three major ridges swirl. The ridge that climbs out of Little Langdale (5–6) may be generally considered part of Great Carrs, but in truth its ultimate goal is Swirl How. To the south another ridge runs steadily down to Levers Hawse (2), en route to Brim Fell and the Old Man. Prison Band (3) stretches eastward, an exhilarating rock group.

↑ *Prison Band on Swirl How from east of Swirl Hawse*

19 SWIRL HOW

While Wetherlam dominates northeastern perspectives, Swirl How makes a graceful culmination to the Greenburn valley (4). To the south of the summit, Great and Little How Crags are the exclusive preserve of rock climbers, hence the white-painted notice on the east side of Great How's crest, warning walkers against attempting a descent. The wanderer, however, will enjoy the quest for the goose bield (fox trap) located tight under these crags which can be safely conducted from the climbers' approach path above Levers Water.

Ascent from Coniston 32 *off map SE*

Via the Coppermines Valley →*5km/3 miles* ↑*745m/2445ft* ⏱*2hr 45min*

Having followed the clear track and ensuing path to Levers Water, two straightforward ascent options present themselves. Although steep in parts, both are less fearsome than they might first appear.

1 The regular track, still used by Burlington's slate lorries and United Utilities' vehicles heading for the Paddy End waterworks, advances up the Church Beck valley from Coniston. The approach is level up to the superbly sited Coppermines Youth Hostel then makes a brief steady rise, and then, after the concrete mass of the waterworks, zig-zags up to the outflow of **Levers Water**.

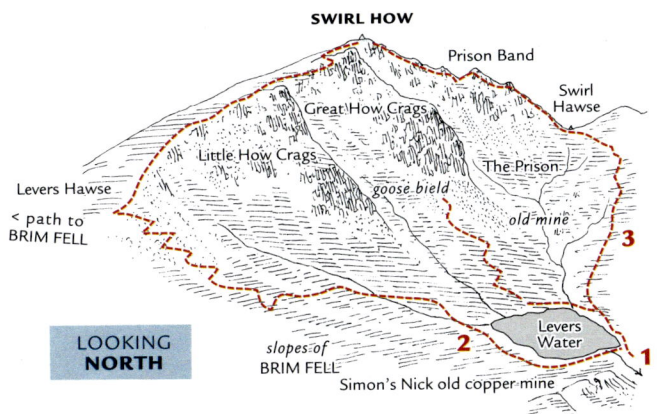

WALKING THE LAKE DISTRICT FELLS – CONISTON

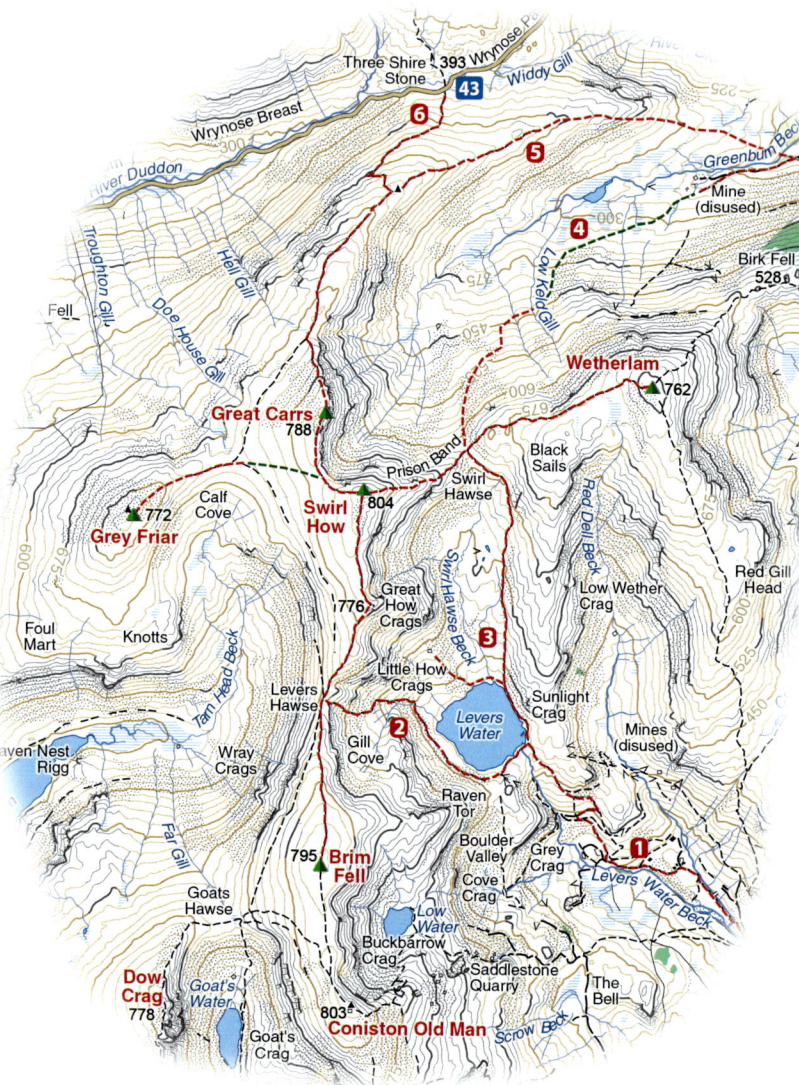

19 Swirl How

Two routes to the summit are at once available: Routes **2** and **3**. Both have their merits and they make a worthy round trip if combined.

2 Follow Route **1** to **Levers Water**. Bear left, crossing the dam causeway, to cross the broken ground associated with the old **Simon's Nick** copper-mine workings. The Boulder Valley path merges from the left as the rough path contours round, well above the southern and western shore of Levers Water. Ford Cove Beck and follow the cairns on a well-maintained path which climbs steadily towards Levers Hawse. The path towards **Gill Cove** is intermittently pitched, more so the higher you get. Avoid the stony gully to the right and keep to the solid footing. When you eventually reach **Levers Hawse** saddle turn right (north). Two paths head northwards. Follow the ridge path proper for the better views back, notably the fabulous view of Brim Fell. The summit lies a little over 1km to the north.

3 Follow Route **1** to **Levers Water**. The path to **Swirl Hawse** has grown in popularity over the years. It can be damp but it is a good route.

Swirl Hawse

Those of a wandering inclination might be tempted to venture up the slope of Great How Crags to inspect the goose bield situated on a shelf beneath the large boulders. It is reached via the left-hand side of a shallow rigg, the climbers' approach to the crag. The tiny pen would have had a cantilever plank, bated with a goose at its tip; the fox would walk the plank, fall into the pen and starve.

Alternatively, you might be tempted to trek upstream with Swirl Hawse Beck, visiting the adjacent rigg with its pools and mine, and the coarse *roche moutonée*, pock-marked and banded with layers of volcanic rock.

The upper cove is thoroughly hemmed in by crags. The miners called it the Prison with good reason, which is how the enclosing rocky ridge rising steeply from Swirl Hawse became known as the Prison Band. There is only the most modest amount of scrambling required in the ascent and, by and large, it's fun. And the summit is a fitting reward for your efforts.

Ascent from Little Langdale 40 *off map NE*

Via Greenburn Beck →5.2km/3¼ miles ↑680m/2230ft ⏲3hr

The more direct of two prime routes out of the Brathay valley

4 From the hamlet of Little Langdale begin by visiting Slater Bridge. It's a work of art which has stood the test of time: a visual and tactile exhibition of the beauty of local slate. Having crossed the bridge, turn right to follow the walled lane by Low and High Hall Garths and then the subsequent open track leading to the old Greenburn copper mine, the site of which is now a protected monument. Thereafter walkers take differing lines up the valley. A feeble path only emerges well up the valley side after crossing High Keld Gill, bound for Swirl Hawse and the Prison Band ridge (Route **3**).

Via Wet Side Edge →6km/3¾ miles ↑685m/2245ft ⏲3hr 15min

A classic ridge-walk

5 Start from Fellfoot via Bridge End and the Greenburn track, crossing a footbridge after the gate in the intake wall to clamber onto the low ridge heading for Rough Crags and Wet Side Edge. Alternatively, immediately above Castle

19 Swirl How

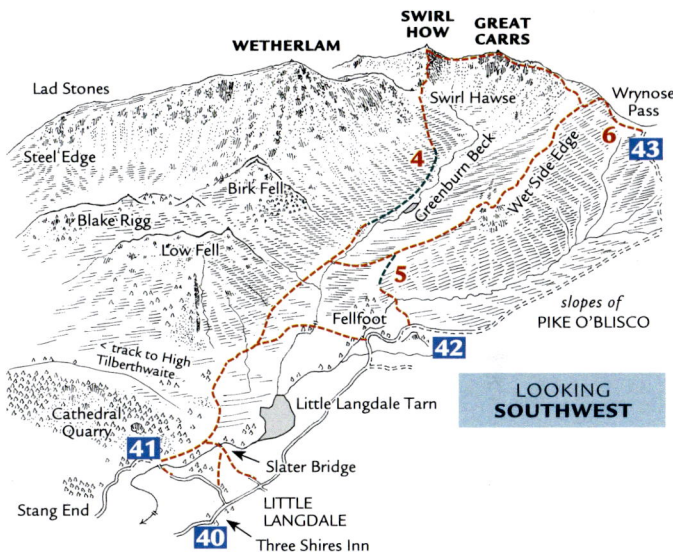

Howe find a recessed gate/stile on the left. Follow the track, with a wall on your left, go through the next gate and slip over the facing bank, past a guide cairn, to ford the infant River Brathay. Climb the steep bank ahead, between irregular walled enclosures, past the distinctive rocks on Hollin Crag, and turn right, up the easy ridge. Follow the ridge to the summit, passing the summit cairn of **Great Carrs** on the opposite side of Broad Slack.

Ascent from Wrynose Pass 43

Direct →*2.5km/1½ miles* ↑*410m/1345ft* ⏱*1hr 30min*

Use whatever horse-power is at your disposal to save your legs and reduce the ascent by starting from the top of Wrynose Pass. The one disadvantage is that it does limit your choice of circular walks.

6 There are two parking areas, although the only marked path onto the ridge begins from the higher one at the top of the pass. Note the huge erratic close left as you climb just west of south towards the ridge. A large cairn marks the point of arrival on the ridge-top. Commit its characteristics to memory for your return. Follow on with Route **5** to the summit.

The summit

The place of congregation at the top of Swirl How is a small flat plateau. Most visitors bounding up in a skyline walk from Coniston are pleased to have made it to the highest point on their round and are ready to face either the Old Man or Wetherlam. Swirl How's rugged cairn, built close to the northern edge plunging into the depths of the Greenburn valley, provides a navigational fix and a place for happy relaxation after the strenuous climb. The view over Wetherlam and across Great Carrs to the Scafells gives a great sense of space. (From here the Isle of Man sits precisely on top of Grey Friar.)

Safe descents

The Prison Band (**3**) is steep, but unless conditions are icy it is a secure route to Coniston, turning right at Swirl Hawse for Levers Water. The ridge path S (**2**) leads to the Levers Hawse depression and is another good route to Coniston. The ridge N (**5**), curving round by Great Carrs, is a straightforward descent along Wet Side Edge for Wrynose Pass (**6**) or into Little Langdale.

Ridge routes

Brim Fell →*2.4km/1½ miles* ↓*120m/395ft* ↑*110m/360ft* ⏲*40min*
Follow the broad ridge S, climbing to the summit from the depression of Levers Hawse.

Great Carrs →*0.5km/¼ mile* ↓*40m/130ft* ↑*20m/65ft* ⏲*15min*
Go downhill W from the summit, curving N round the rim of Broad Slack to reach the summit cairn.

19 SWIRL HOW

Wetherlam from Prison Band

Grey Friar →*1.6km/1 mile* ↓*110m/360ft* ↑*80m/260ft* ⏲*35min*
Descend W on grass into the broad Fairfield saddle, joining the ridge path which rises SW onto the summit plateau, passing the Matterhorn Rock (a miniature of its namesake).

Wetherlam →*2km/1¼ miles* ↓*190m/625ft* ↑*145m/475ft* ⏲*50min*
Take care right from the start. Descend E down the rocky Prison Band ridge. It is straightforward but requires care in wet, windy or icy conditions. A large cairn marks Swirl Hawse, from where the ridge path climbs easily NE, avoiding the top of Black Sails, then E to the top.

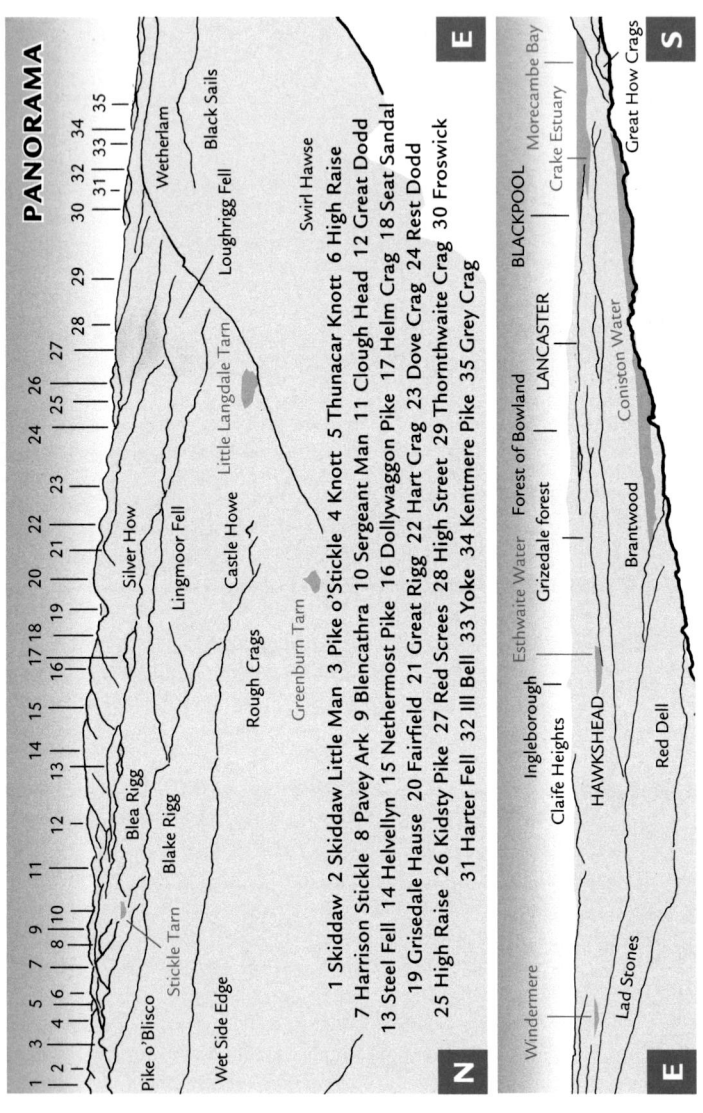

19 Swirl How

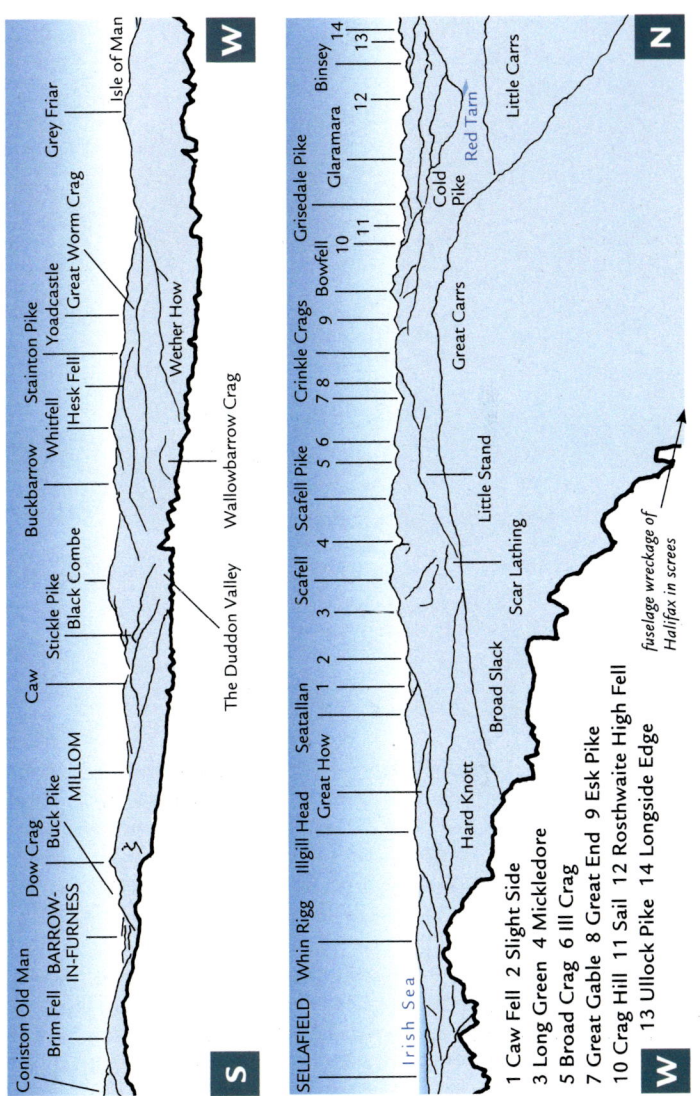

20 WALLOWBARROW CRAG 292M/958FT

Climb it from	Seathwaite **49** or Fickle Steps **48**
Character	The seldom-visited crown of a popular south-facing crag beside a gorgeous wooded ravine
Fell-friendly route	4
Summit grid ref	SD 222 968

Wallowbarrow Crag is a heather-capped, wood-shawled, little craggy eminence. This harmony of crag and gorge brings to the Duddon something of the drama and magic normally accorded exclusively to Castle Crag and the Jaws of Borrowdale. Greatly appreciated by rock climbers for its sunny – and therefore quick-drying – easily accessed crags, it is largely unknown to fellwalkers. However, the massive fist of magma, the remnant plug of an ancient volcano vent, is, in fact, the Duddon's focal viewpoint.

Access onto its rough top is confined to one narrow trod (4) and one heather-choked gully (5), both rising from the bridleway as it draws up to the low saddle on its west side. But why not ramble round through the gorge to Fickle Steps (3), ascend to Grassguards and track back along the bridleway, only then to step onto the crag and appreciate its unique Duddon credentials.

↑ *Wallowbarrow Crag*

20 Wallowbarrow Crag

Ascent from Seathwaite 49

Circuitous route via Wallowbarrow Gorge →*3.7km/2½ miles* ↑*230m/755ft*
⏱*2hr*

It would be a shame to miss out on the scenic delights of Wallowbarrow Gorge.

1 Opposite the Newfield Inn a footpath leads through gates to a small footbridge spanning **Tarn Beck**. The path passes a small weir, skirts a marsh and comes alongside a wall, before arriving at the memorial footbridge to join Route **3**.

2 The memorial bridge can also be reached via a footpath that leaves the valley road opposite the old school house, again crossing a **Tarn Beck** footbridge and weaving through woodland, passing the Duddon/Tarn Beck confluence on the way. At the memorial bridge join Route **3** to continue.

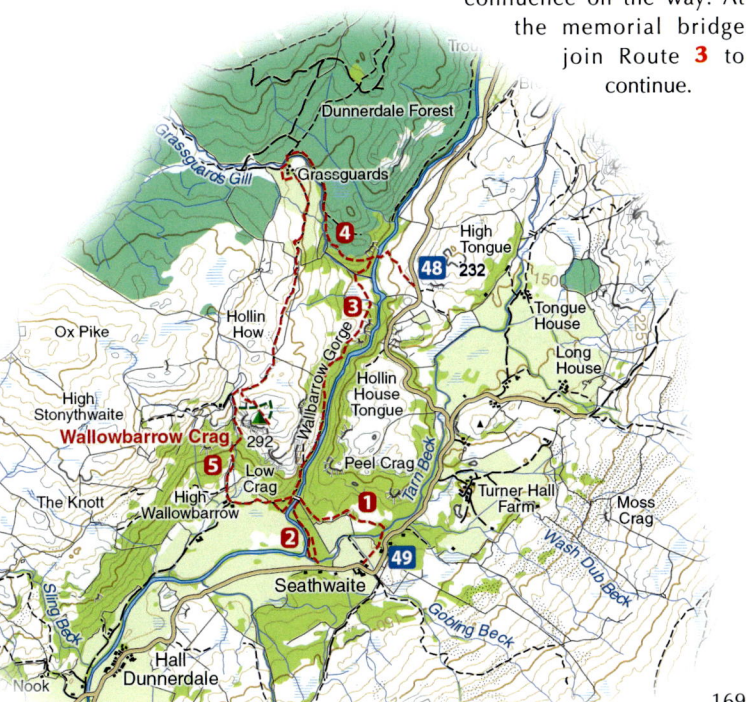

3 Follow Route **1** or **2** to the memorial bridge. From here venture up **Wallowbarrow Gorge** to your right. Progress through a fantasy world of rock and native woodland, over stiles. The boulder scree spilling from the high crag is particularly impressive. The path climbs then dips to a wooden footbridge over **Grassguards Gill** and advances to Fickle Steps. Here join Route **4** to ascend to the summit.

Ascent from Fickle Steps 48

The back-door approach

4 A path from the open common descends to cross the Fickle Steps stepping-stones (not always easy, as they are prone to submersion). On the far bank another path angles up the woodland half-left to rock steps then through a

The Duddon from the Grassguards track

hand-gate, following the gill to the forest-track access to Grassguards. Cross the footbridge to the left. A permissive path orbits the farmhouse and buildings on the right through hand-gates. Follow the bridleway beside a short thick-walled lane and an enclosure protected by deer gates until you reach the faint path leading left, onto the top.

Direct from High Wallowbarrow farm → *1km/½ mile* ↑*185m/605ft* ⏱*45min*

Slip around the crag for the swiftest ascent.

5 Reach the memorial bridge via Route **1** or **2** and head directly for High Wallowbarrow farm by wood and meadow. Follow the bridleway right from the barn-end and ascend through gates. Climbing up from beneath the mighty crag, veer left to come alongside a wall. As this nears the top either look for the weakness up a gully to the right (no path) or, higher up, find a thin path onto the top... and feel exulted!

The summit

A mix of heather and bedrock characterises the cairnless summit. The outlook is sumptuously intimate, with the Duddon valley down-dale beyond Ulpha, and, to the north, Harter Fell and Bowfell, with Seathwaite Tarn sparkling below Grey Friar.

Safe descents

It is imperative that you leave the top of Wallowbarrow Crag on a NNW bias down to the bridle-track (**4–5**). No other line of descent is remotely tenable, nor safe!

21 WALNA SCAR 621M/2037FT

Climb it from	Coniston **32**, Walna Scar Road **31**, Torver **30**, Hummer Lane **29**, Water Yeat **28** or Seathwaite **49**
Character	The abrupt southern terminus of the Dow Crag ridge, with two fine viewpoint tops and a remarkable quarry to peer into
Fell-friendly route	1
Summit grid ref	SD 258 963
Link it with	Caw or Dow Crag

Off to climb Walna Scar…? The rough road that crosses the high pass between Coniston and Seathwaite? No, the fell! Walna Scar completes the Dow Crag ridge to the south, although its highest point, a grassy hummock, is bettered as a summit by both White Maiden and White Pike further south.

Stand in the bar at the Newfield Inn at Seathwaite and look down at the regular, striated dark-and-light, slate-flag floor. This tells of another side of Walna Scar's more recent history, as a source for excellent building stone. Gaping quarries (visited on Route 6) could be said to 'scar' the western slope of the fell.

Although it can be easily 'bagged' from the old road (1–2, 7), the fell has excellent approaches over wild country (3–6, 8) to suit the fellwandering connoisseur, with Routes 3 and 5 taking in White Maiden and Route 6 visiting White Pike.

↑ *Looking down on the Walna Scar Pass cross-ways*

21 WALNA SCAR

Ascent from Coniston 32 *off map E* or Walna Scar Road fell-gate 31

Via the Walna Scar Road →*3.2km/2 miles* ↑*390m/1280ft* ⏲*1hr 50min*

The Walna Scar Road track allows for a free-flowing stride almost all the way to the top.

1 The **Walna Scar Road** springs from the centre of Coniston (1.6km and 170m ascent from the fell-gate). Climb on an initially steep gradient, past the old station. The toil eventually abates – thank goodness – and progress becomes more leisurely in the country lane, rising to the fell-gate onto the common, where most car-borne walkers park and embark. (A minority of 4x4 drivers park beyond **Boo Tarn**.) The track climbs through two stone cuttings, crosses Cove Bridge and mounts the steep flank of **Brown Pike**. The ingenious sentry-box shelter gives a moment's pause prior to reaching the saddle. Turn left (south) at the saddle and climb onto the gentle apex of the fell.

Brown Pike from the marsh below High Pike Haw

WALKING THE LAKE DISTRICT FELLS – CONISTON

21 WALNA SCAR

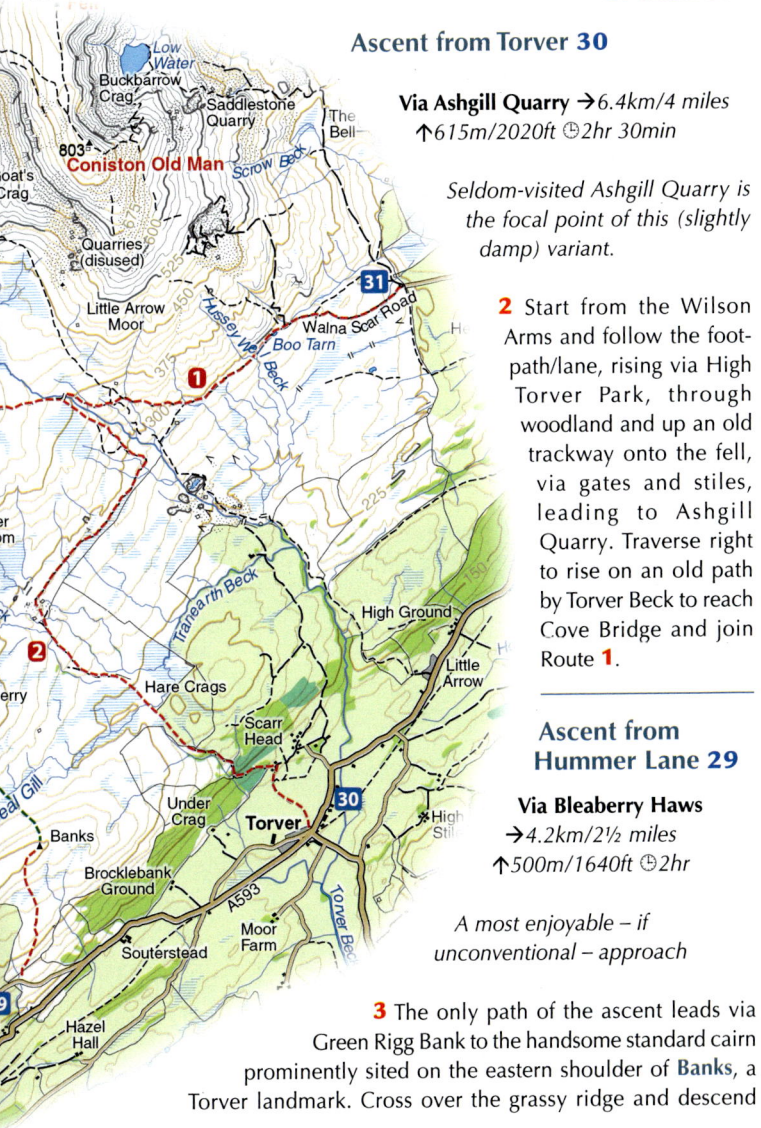

Ascent from Torver 30

Via Ashgill Quarry →*6.4km/4 miles*
↑*615m/2020ft ⏲2hr 30min*

Seldom-visited Ashgill Quarry is the focal point of this (slightly damp) variant.

2 Start from the Wilson Arms and follow the footpath/lane, rising via High Torver Park, through woodland and up an old trackway onto the fell, via gates and stiles, leading to Ashgill Quarry. Traverse right to rise on an old path by Torver Beck to reach Cove Bridge and join Route **1**.

Ascent from Hummer Lane 29

Via Bleaberry Haws
→*4.2km/2½ miles*
↑*500m/1640ft ⏲2hr*

A most enjoyable – if unconventional – approach

3 The only path of the ascent leads via Green Rigg Bank to the handsome standard cairn prominently sited on the eastern shoulder of **Banks**, a Torver landmark. Cross over the grassy ridge and descend northwest into the curiously named damp hollow of Plattocks. Thread your way up through the impeding bracken, taking an old wall as your guide, past a small quarry to the cairn surmounting **Bleaberry Haws**. Slip through the next narrow valley depression, with its small quarry ruin, to embark on the real climb of the day, checking out the oddly eroded, steeply pitched bedrock as you clamber over High Pike Haw. Pass up by a marshy hollow to a sheepfold tucked under Dropping Crag. Step through the outcrops onto the broad ridge to join the rising wall to **White Maiden**. From here the summit of Walna Scar lies around 750 metres to the north, along the ridge.

Link-route via the plantation →*2km/1¼ miles* ⏲*30min*

4 A bridleway, a clearly marked forest track, leads westwards from the forest access gate off Hummer Lane, skipping over **Appletree Worth Beck** via a bridge and skirting the headland of the Knott to meet the road close to Water Yeat Bridge.

Dow Crag and Coniston Old Man from Banks

Ascent from Water Yeat 28

Valley approach →*3.7km/2¼ miles* ↑*460m/1510ft* ⏲*2hr 30min*

This is the perfect approach to Walna Scar as the valley-head mountain. Reversed, this route can also be woven into a circular expedition, using the well-marked bridleway through the Broughton Moor forest (Route 4) as the means of getting back to Hummer Lane, the start of Route 3.

5 Either follow the forest track direct from the recessed forest gate at SD 238 928, advancing to the stile and wooden footbridge through the ravine at **Natty Bridge** or, alternatively, cross Water Yeat Bridge and follow the minor road up to **Stephenson Ground** to find the gated bridleway up the western side of the Lickle gorge, a lovely approach focused on White Pike. Where this then crosses the continuing footpath from Natty Bridge, go east, following the grooved path weaving onto Caw Moss, crossing a small flag bridge, with White Pike dominant. The occasional fellwalker keeps the path discernible as it leads on towards a gateway in a wall with a tarn beyond. Ignore the path and take off up the fellside, keeping this wall close right. This is a simple pathless means of getting onto **White Maiden** and a safe escape route off the ridge in bad weather too. From White Maiden follow the ridge north to the summit.

Via Walna Scar Quarry →*4km/2½ miles* ↑*445m/1460ft* ⏲*2hr 20min*

The dramatic quarries add interest and offer a chance to reflect on the industry and toil of a former era.

6 Alternatively, from **Natty Bridge** (see Route **5**) you can walk on to the natural destination of the Lickle-head path – the Walna Scar Road (Route **7**) – across the base of the spoil banks of Walna Scar Quarry, or cut up from the quarry direct to the subsidiary summit of White Pike. As the bridleway reaches the brow, a little after the turn-off for Route **5**, you come to a fork. Neither path has a mastery of the marshy ground here and bikers have damaged the surface in places. The more commonly followed footpath leads straight on by Dawson's Pike, comes under the slate spoil and follows the intake wall direct to the **Walna Scar Road**. The right-hand bridleway takes you up among the quarry workings and so is the preferred option. The vast quantity of slate tip suggests a major hollowing of the fell and, sure enough, this is what has happened. (If you are lured into the main quarry, the only way out is the way you went in!) Keep up the right-hand side of the workings to get the most stupendous – perhaps fearful – view into the cavity. The rest of the ascent is straightforward, if pathless. On reaching the plateau top slant right to visit the cairn on White Pike, an excellent viewpoint down the Lickle valley to the sea. Follow the ridge northeast to reach the summit.

Ascent from Seathwaite 49

Via the Walna Scar Road →*3.5km/2¼ miles* ↑*520m/1705ft* ⏲*2hr 15min*

The Walna Scar Road offers easy walking and a quick way to the top.

7 The Walna Scar Road branches from the valley road 800 metres north of the Newfield Inn, above Seathwaite Bridge. (There is also a well-marked field-path route via Turner Hall and High Moss (Rucksack Club hut), which takes a great slice out of the road-walking.) The road becomes a rough track after a gate and climbs to a further gate, with a slate tip close at hand. Centuries of wear, compounded by modern traffic (and motorbikes in particular), have taken their toll. Ascend to the saddle and turn right (south) to climb onto the gentle apex of the fell.

Via Gobling Beck →*3.7km/2¼ miles* ↑*615m/2020ft* ⏲*1hr 45min*

The path less trodden

8 An off-road route can be followed almost directly from the Newfield Inn. Embark upon the Park Head Road (bridleway) and then bear left up the old drove-way. From the hurdle-gate at the top cross Yaud Mire and pass Dawson's Pike, by the large quartz outcrop, linking up with Route **6** leading by Walna Scar Quarry.

The Scafells from White Maiden

The summit

An apology for a cairn marks the top of a grassy pillow, but the view is excellent, if constricted by Brown Pike to the north. Tick this one off and speed on to rocky White Maiden and the prow end of the ridge at White Pike for the best fell-top experiences.

Safe descents

The Walna Scar Road is the obvious option, going E (**1**) for Coniston or W (**7**) for the Duddon. Should you be tempted to descend off White Pike, watch out for crags, but do not head NW towards the slate quarries; an ability to fly will be your only salvation from the unprotected edge.

Ridge routes

Caw → *4km/2½ miles ↓185m/605ft ↑75m/245ft ⏱1hr 15min*
Follow the ridge SW, passing the pool in the dip, then accompany the wall off White Maiden. Traverse Caw Moss, heading SW onto the ridge via Pikes, and proceed to the summit.

Dow Crag → *1.6km/1 mile ↓20m/65ft ↑180m/590ft ⏱45min*
Go N over the Walna Scar pass, climbing past cairns on Brown and Buck Pikes. Follow the exciting edge to the cliff-top summit battlement.

22 WETHERLAM 762M/2500FT

Climb it from	Coniston **32**, Tilberthwaite **33** or Little Langdale **40**
Character	A mountain with a great presence and an extraordinary choice of ascents
Fell-friendly route	6
Summit grid ref	NY 288 011
Link it with	Swirl How
Part of	The Swirl Round

Glances to the southern quarter of Lakeland frequently fall upon Wetherlam, a prominent marker for the Coniston Fells. Its four aspects are quite distinct. The northern slopes, tumbling as crags and scree into the Greenburn valley, are steep and austere, and the eastern slopes, initially no less steep, are given extra spice by the imposition of Tilberthwaite Ghyll, its upper ravine draped in larch alpine fashion and flanked by slate quarries. The southern perspective is dominated by two great ridges: the Yewdale Fells, which form the first craggy rebuff above the village of Coniston, and, above, the Lad Stones ridge, which rises imperiously to the summit. Immediately west of this is the wild recess of Red Dell and the

↑ *Looking down Prison Band on Swirl How to Wetherlam*

22 WETHERLAM

strangely neglected ridge of Black Sails. From Swirl How, the pivotal summit on the main ridge, the Prison Band ridge leads east, and a curious saddle, Swirl Hawse, makes the connection with Wetherlam.

Wetherlam is much more than bulky mass. Down the centuries its wealth of copper and dense fine-grained slate has attracted the attention of industrious man. Deep shafts, levels and open quarries penetrate its colourful interior – though none of these are safe for the average inquisitive fellwanderer.

Wetherlam is one of the most complex mountains in the district, not so much in terms of surface features but rather in its hidden depths from its mining past. It also has the greatest array of route choices of any summit among the Southern Fells. Parallel ascents (4, 6) lead up the two southern spurs, mirrored by corresponding valley routes (5, 7). More intrepid walkers might opt for the exhilarating Wetherlam Edge (11) and Steel Edge (12), with a further approach following the lonely Greenburn valley to the north (17) to ascend via Swirl Hawse. Other options explore the fascinating fell country hereabouts, with its rich evidence of copper mining and slate quarrying. Few can reach this boldly individual summit on a decent day with any sense of disappointment.

Ascent from Coniston 32

Aspirations normally focus on gaining the high Lad Stones ridge (Route 4), the natural start/finish to the perennially popular Coniston Skyline walk embracing Swirl How, Brim Fell and Coniston Old Man. There are three lead-in routes to the Hole Rake gap (Routes 1–3), where the ridge effectively begins.

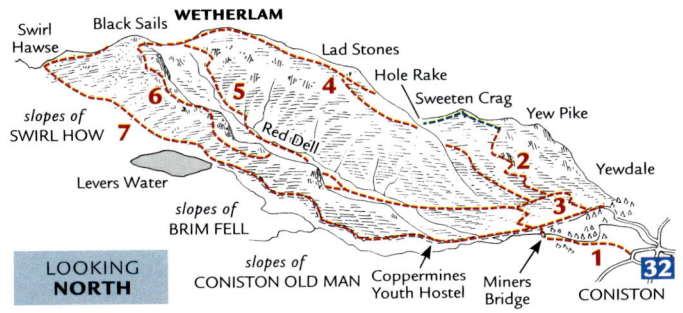

WALKING THE LAKE DISTRICT FELLS – CONISTON

Via Lad Stones →*5.2km/3¼ miles*
↑*730m/2395ft* ⏱*3hr*

1 Turning right above the Sun Hotel, a short walk up the road from the bridge, follow the path from **Dixon Ground**

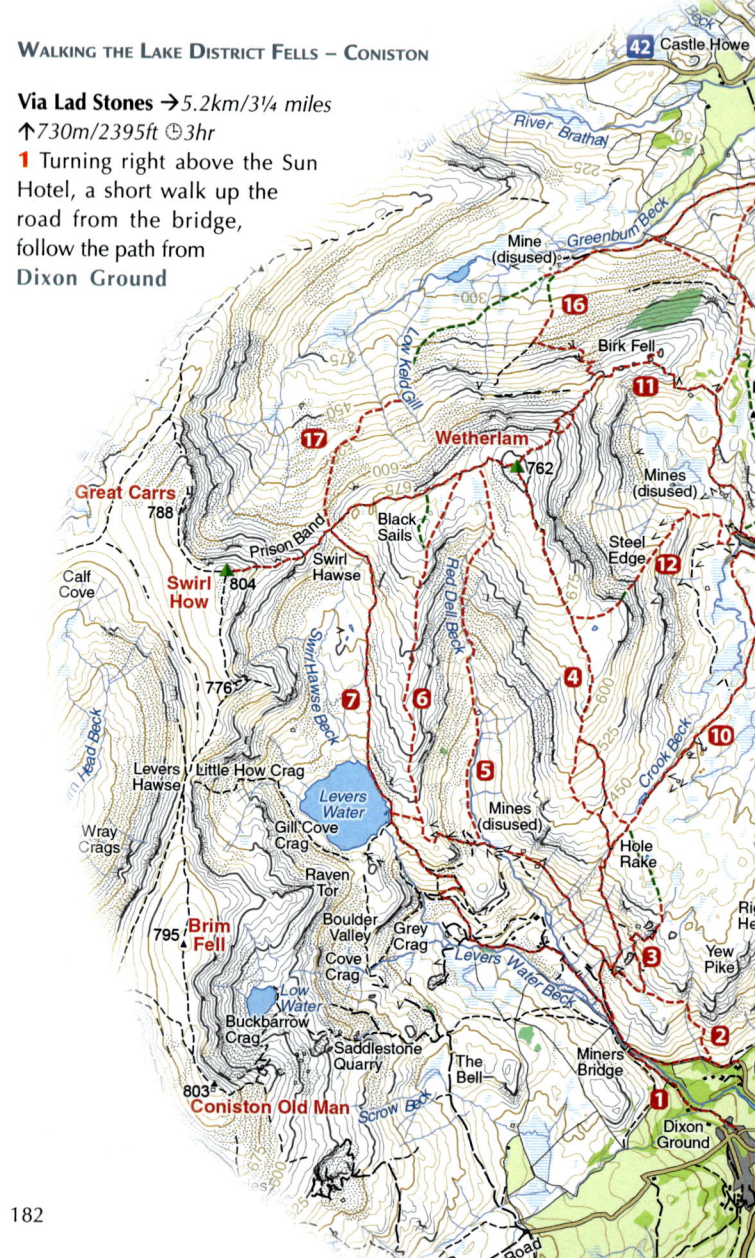

22 WETHERLAM

that leads to **Miners Bridge**. Cross the bridge and go left on the main valley track and, as it levels, fork right on the old quarry track. Be sure to take the third left turn in a zag-zag course, on an incline path to **Hole Rake**.

2 Follow the road access into the Coppermines Valley from beyond the Black Bull and the Ruskin Museum. It soon becomes a rough track. Beyond a cattle grid branch off up the Mouldry Bank slope, contouring round from an old cairn under Rascal How to link with Route **1**.

3 Follow Route **2** up the Mouldry Bank slope then bear up the old quarry path, right, taking care where the quarry has collapsed and removed a chunk of the track. This route winds up through the upper portion of the Blue Quarry onto the fell above. Here either climb over **Sweeten Crag** or find the green path leading northwest by Kitty Crag to **Hole Rake**. (Sweeten Crag is the high point of the undulating rough fell alp that runs from Yew Pike to Yewdale Crag – an absorbing place to wander.)

4 On reaching **Hole Rake** via Route **1**, **2**, or **3**, two paths have developed to the **Lad Stones** ridge: one starts short of the top of the pass, dipping through the gill and weaving onto the ridge-end; the other, a more cautious path, departs over stepping-stones before the rushy tarn, north of the rake. It mounts assuredly onto the ridge northwest through early slabs, turning at a large block of bedrock. On the ridge-top the two paths join and proceed to the summit. It takes far longer than expected, over two pronounced steps in the ridge.

Via Red Dell and Black Sails ➔*6.5km/4 miles* ↑*715m/2345ft*
⏱*3hr 20min*

A rewarding ascent, steeped in the history of the copper industry

5 Take Route **1** to the point where it turns off up to Hole Rake and continue on the quarry track to reach a row of quarrymen's terraces, known as Irish Row. Just past here a path leads right towards **Red Dell**. This is copper-mines country sure enough, with leats (water channels), water-wheel pits and evidence of long-abandoned deep workings: bracken fronds grow around their gaping mouths like lures to a death trap. It's a landscape full of interest – and considerable danger! A path leads on past the site of a 17th-century copper-ore grinding mill into the Red Dell valley. Pass a large

Thriddle incline water-wheel pit

erratic and then a sheepfold before fording **Red Dell Gill**. At its head climb on the east side. A faint trod guides up to cairns leading to the peaty hollow just to the west of the summit.

6 The neglected Black Sails ridge provides a gem of an ascent. Follow Route **5** to the **Red Dell** workings and climb the Thriddle incline, then pass a mine level halfway up with two gate-grilled levels at the top. Go left to the saddle and follow naturally right, up the ridge, with faint evidence of a path. You can also join the ridge from the outflow of **Levers Water** (see Route **7**).

The path tends to avoid the ridge-top, although there is no good reason to do so. At the top the ridge constricts to give a fine view back down Red Dell. You can clamber up to the cairn on **Black Sails** or slant half-right to join the main ridge path from Swirl Hawse (Route **7**) to reach the summit.

Via Swirl Hawse →*7km/4¼ miles* ↑*660m/2165ft* ⏲*3hr 15min*

The steady route up Wetherlam, suitable when poor conditions require a less exposed line or for easy descent

7 The regular track, still used by Burlington's slate lorries and United Utilities' vehicles heading for the Paddy End waterworks, advances up the Church Beck valley from Coniston. The approach is level up to the superbly sited **Coppermines Youth Hostel** then makes a brief steady rise, and then, after the concrete mass of the waterworks, zig-zags up to the outflow of **Levers Water**. Continue up the **Swirl Hawse Beck** valley. Marshy ground is the only hazard en route to the saddle's cairn. At the **Swirl Hawse** saddle a path goes on into the Greenburn Beck valley ahead, a minor trod in comparison with the worn trail at your feet. Go right (east), traversing the north slope of **Black Sails** to reach the summit and consistently enjoying the fabulous views to the north.

To Tilberthwaite via the Yewdale Fells →*2.5km/1½ miles* ↑*255m/835ft* ⏲*2hr*

Two paths from Coniston make good approaches to Tilberthwaite Ghyll, extending the exploration of Wetherlam's eastern foothills.

8 At the northern end of the village, on a loop off the A593, is Holly How Youth Hostel. Pass by the hostel and turn up a path to the left beside **Far End** cottages to join a lateral path from the Coppermines Valley access track as it becomes a rough track. Go through the hand-gate to follow a path climbing directly opposite. The climb, marked with small cairns, is unexpectedly steep and interesting and has a marvellous outlook. Cross the headstream of **White Gill** (a striking water-slide feature from Yewdale), perhaps detouring briefly to visit the **Yewdale Crag** headland, before weaving down through juniper and Penny Rigg slate quarry/mine to the Tilberthwaite road.

9 Alternatively, where Route **8** heads off up the slope, a gentle path threads through the woodland at the foot of the **Yewdale Crag** scarp. Fording

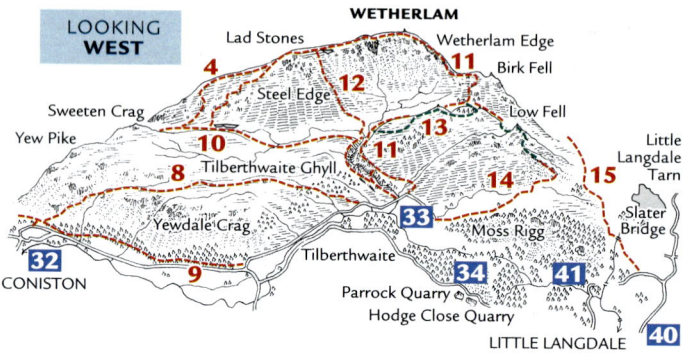

White Gill you may notice on your right, at the edge of the pasture close to the road, a 19th-century lime kiln. In season the continuing path is renowned for its deep-pile carpet of bluebells. On reaching the road junction go left for Tilberthwaite.

Ascent from Low Tilberthwaite 33 or Little Langdale 40

Via Steel Edge or Birk Fell Hawse →*3.5km/2¼ miles* ↑*640m/2100ft*
⏲*2hr 45min*

Rock outcrops allow for short bursts of scrambling of the easiest kind on these exhilarating ascents.

Paths ascend either side of Tilberthwaite Ghyll and connect to one another halfway up via a scenic footbridge.
   10 The path on the south side of the ghyll leads up through minor slate sites worthy of brief inspection and on along Hole Rake to connect with Route **4**.
   11 The path to the north starts from the road bend and curves slowly round towards the ghyll, meeting it above the footbridge at an area of very old copper mines at the head of the ravine. The main route to Birk Fell and Wetherlam Edge goes north, leading round the two shallow combes of Dry Cove, with further evidence of old copper mines. Step onto Birk Fell on a

newly pitched path and find a cairn with a lovely view off to the right. From Birk Fell Hawse the high prow of **Wetherlam Edge** looms. The climb includes several rocky steps but nothing extraordinary. The erosion suggests that the pitching repair work needs to continue, however. Proceed up the ridge to the summit.

12 Alternatively, follow Route **11** to the head of the ravine, cross the footbridge and turn right, then left, onto the base of the **Steel Edge** ridge. Starting as a grassy rigg it narrows impressively to culminate in a spot of hands-on scrambling of the easiest kind, up to the **Lad Stones** ridge-top to join Route **4** near a perfect horseshoe-shaped pool. A word of warning: if you choose to descend by this ridge, do not be lured into the gully on the north side. This looks to be the way but most definitely is not. Its loose angular scree is horrid.

13 As a variation on Route **11**, from the point that the main path on the north side of the ghyll turns north, you can step onto the low ridge on the right, without a path, and hold to the skyline via the little cairned knoll-tops of **Blake Rigg** and **Hawk Rigg**, then easily turn left (south) to rejoin Route **11**.

Looking down Steel Edge

WALKING THE LAKE DISTRICT FELLS – CONISTON

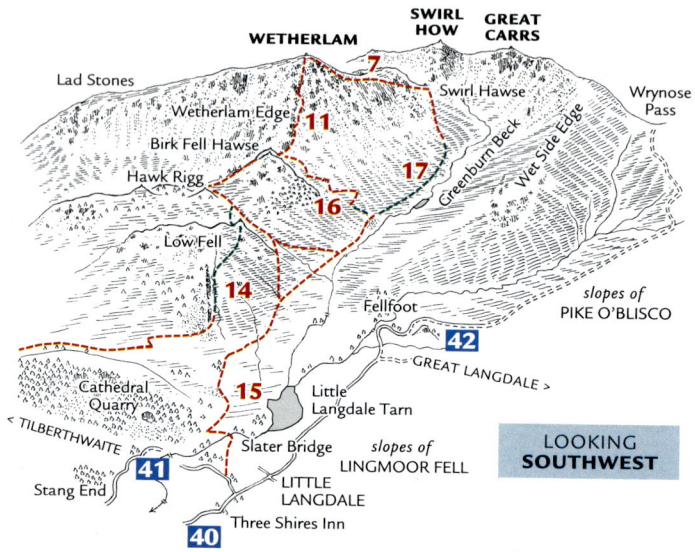

Via Low Fell →*5km/3 miles* ↑*720m/2360ft* ⊕*3hr*

Low Fell gives Wetherlam a firm foot in Little Langdale and offers an intimate connection with the valley.

14 From **High Tilberthwaite** two tracks proceed north. Take the left-hand option. The route begins to descend an old quarry track and forks left. Follow on up to the ridge-end slate tip through a gate. Climb to the mid-point of **Runestone Quarry**. Branch right and climb pathless to the summit of **Low Fell**, which has a wonderful carpet of bilberries and an excellent view of Little Langdale and through the Blea Tarn gap to the Langdale Pikes. A spidery path leads west from the summit, descending Great Intake to reach a ladder-stile. Find a path linking over a small saddle, north of **Hawk Rigg**, back down southwest to the popular path. Go right to climb onto Birk Fell (Route **11**).

22 WETHERLAM

Via the saddle →*4.8km/3 miles* ↑*665m/2180ft* ⏲*3hr 10min*

A further attractive approach from Langdale

15 From the Three Shires Inn make for **Slater Bridge**. Among the trees above you at this point is **Cathedral Quarry**, which is well worth investigating, but be careful and heed the signs if you go in via the tunnel. Pass along the narrow lane by Low and High Hallgarths. Shortly after the old road from Tilberthwaite comes in the track forks. Take the left fork, which rises with a wall to the right. As the wall drifts away a narrow path can be followed left up the bracken slope of Great Intake to a ladder-stile, bound for the saddle next to **Hawk Rigg**, or you can turn left after the gate in the next wall to follow the wall up to the saddle. Pass over the saddle to meet the popular path and turn right, joining Route **11**.

Wetherlam Edge from Hawk Rigg

Via Greenburn Mine →5.2km/3¼ miles ↑660m/2165ft ⏲3hr 15min

Follow in the footsteps of the miners to explore the fell's industrial heritage.

16 From where Route **15** turns off up the slope, the best option is to stay with the valley track alongside **Greenburn Beck**, rising to the old Greenburn mine. It's a protected monument so inspect it respectfully.

Once past the ruins angle half-left, finding a gap in the bracken, to find an engineered miners' path slanting left up the steep fellside. An early cairn indicates a branch path leading half-right up to the Long Crag Level. The main grass path climbs to Pave York Levels. There are three mine adits (entrances) here, one above the other. Weave up the fell, glancing at each dark dank level in turn, the top one probably the most intriguing. A fellwalker's path continues above, rising to **Birk Fell Hawse** and then on to the popular path climbing **Wetherlam Edge** (Route **11**).

Wetherlam from Holme Fell

Via Swirl Hawse →7km/4¼ miles ↑660m/2165ft ⏱3hr 25min

A valley approach following Greenburn Beck leads to a punishing ascent of the valley head.

17 Having followed Route **16** to Greenburn mine, the more usual approach to Wetherlam is to continue up the dale and bear half-left from the reservoir dam. Go up the fellside. Evidence of a path only appears after **Low Keld Gill** and High Keld Gill have been forded. Climb the dry slope beneath the scree to **Swirl Hawse** and turn left to join Route **7**.

The summit

The highest ground is a gentle dome with small rocky protuberances, the unruly summit cairn itself taking advantage of one low plinth. The site deserves a far more elegant pile. Certainly it's a place to consider a wide Lakeland landscape, the deep furrow of Greenburn ensuring an uninhibited prospect. In imperial measurements, the height of the fell has a pleasing neatness – 2500ft.

Safe descents

The ground falls innocently away to the west and south but matters to the north and east need careful attention. The rocky steps of Wetherlam Edge (**11**) face into a biting winter gale but are otherwise none too troublesome. The easier routes are S down the Lad Stones ridge (**4**) or W to Swirl Hawse (**7**).

Ridge route

Swirl How →2km/1¼ miles ↓145m/475ft ↑190m/625ft ⏱1hr 25min

Head W down an early stony slope. Two paths converge to cross peaty ground on the shallow plateau hollow at the head of Red Dell. The clear stony path drifts across the northern flank of Black Sails before descending more steeply to Swirl Hawse, clearly identified by its large cairn. The Prison Band ridge looks tough but is meekly overcome via a series of mock towers – note one particularly strikingly banded specimen a third of the way up. The summit cairn greets you at the top.

WALKING THE LAKE DISTRICT FELLS – CONISTON

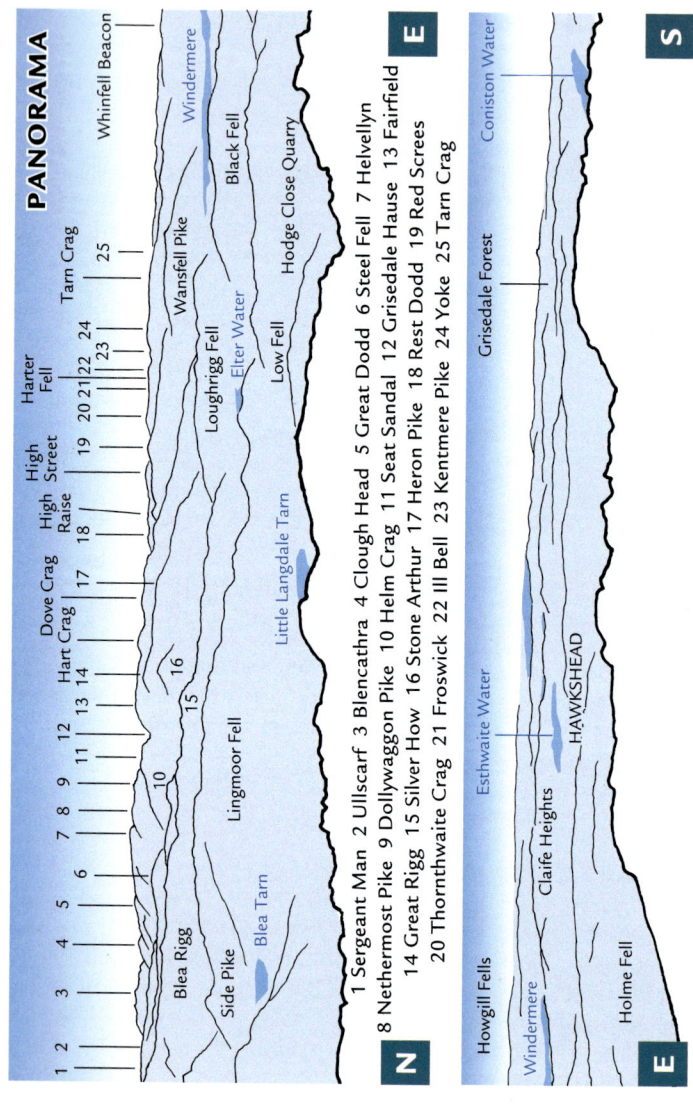

PANORAMA

1 Sergeant Man 2 Ullscarf 3 Blencathra 4 Clough Head 5 Great Dodd 6 Steel Fell 7 Helvellyn 8 Nethermost Pike 9 Dollywaggon Pike 10 Helm Crag 11 Seat Sandal 12 Grisedale Hause 13 Fairfield 14 Great Rigg 15 Silver How 16 Stone Arthur 17 Heron Pike 18 Rest Dodd 19 Red Screes 20 Thornthwaite Crag 21 Froswick 22 Ill Bell 23 Kentmere Pike 24 Yoke 25 Tarn Crag

22 WETHERLAM

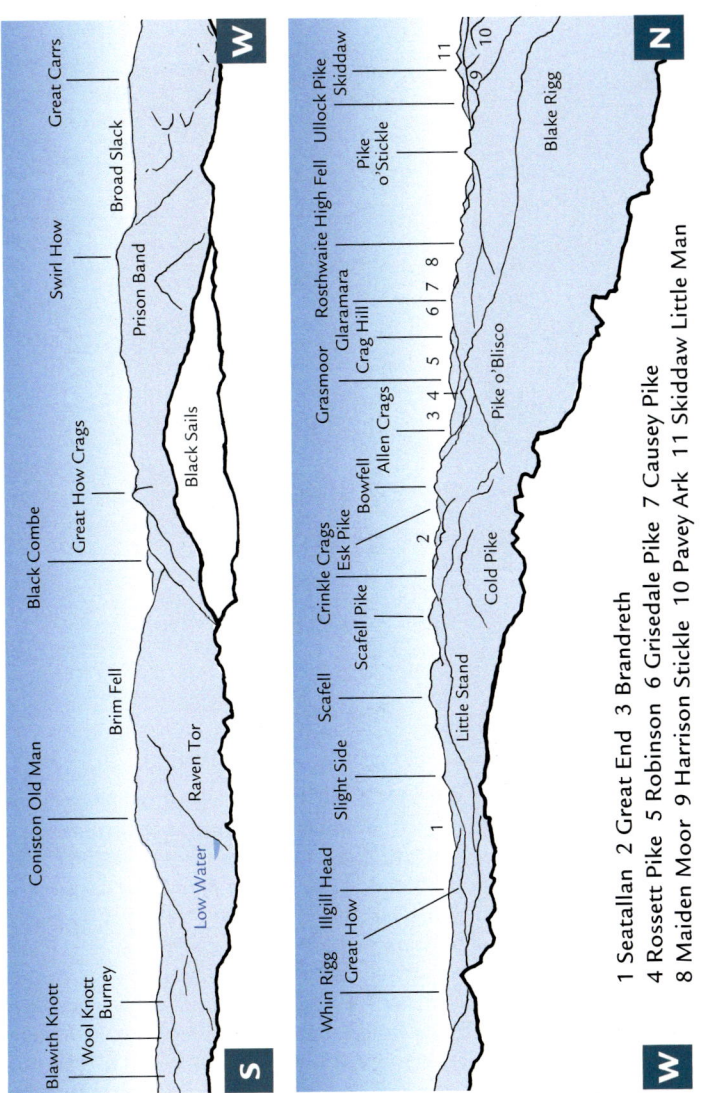

1 Seatallan 2 Great End 3 Brandreth
4 Rossett Pike 5 Robinson 6 Grisedale Pike 7 Causey Pike
8 Maiden Moor 9 Harrison Stickle 10 Pavey Ark 11 Skiddaw Little Man

23 WHITFELL 573M/1880FT

Climb it from	Brackenthwaite **23**, Corneyfell Road (Fell Lane) **14** or Buckbarrow Bridge **15**
Character	A rounded elegant sentinel keeping watch over an old ridge-straddling route
Fell-friendly route	1
Summit grid ref	SD 159 930
Link it with	Buckbarrow or Stainton Pike

The southwesterly rippling ridge that springs from Harter Fell and terminates on Black Combe is focused on Whitfell. The stately guardian of an ancient bridleway, it is the natural target for a fell-climb or a long ridge traverse, with the grace of the main fell contrasting with the chunky mass of Burn Moor tagged on to its west. The summit is engaging, boasting a stout cairn built upon an archaic gathering of stones, whose cultural significance has long been lost.

Routes lead up from east (1) and west (4), from Brackenthwaite and Fell Lane, to the saddle between Whitfell and Stainton Pike, Route 4 including an optional diversion to visit the Rowantree Force ravine. A further route from the west makes a pathless ascent beside Red Gill onto Burn Moor (3). One more route rises up above Buckbarrow Beck (2) from the Corneyfell Road to the south.

↑ *Whitfell from Withe Bottom*

23 WHITFELL

Ascent from Brackenthwaite 23

Direct →3.7km/2¼ miles ↑375m/1230ft ⏱2hr

From pasture to fell

1 A bridleway traverses the ridge from **Bigert Mire**, a very tidy community with six cottages huddling together where once just one farm stood. There is space for one parked car at a pinch. Walk through to the gate and bear up left on the bridle-track, passing a lone-standing barn. The track enters **Bigertmire Pasture** at a gate and begins purposefully enough – well used by a tractor carrying feed to livestock – but the line of the path fades as it rises up the great pasture. Stride up to a kissing-gate in the fence, which seems to be strengthening the broken intake wall, and the path reappears on the other side. Rise to the cairn at the top of the pass and bear left, now with the ridge path, to the summit tumulus.

Loganbeck farm on the approach from the Corneyfell Road to Bigert Mire

Ascent from the Corneyfell Road (Fell Lane or Buckbarrow Bridge) 14 & 15

Via Fell Lane or Burn Moor →4.5km/2¾ miles ↑355m/1165ft ⏱2hr 15min

Routes from the west are devised around the main watercourses draining the fell.

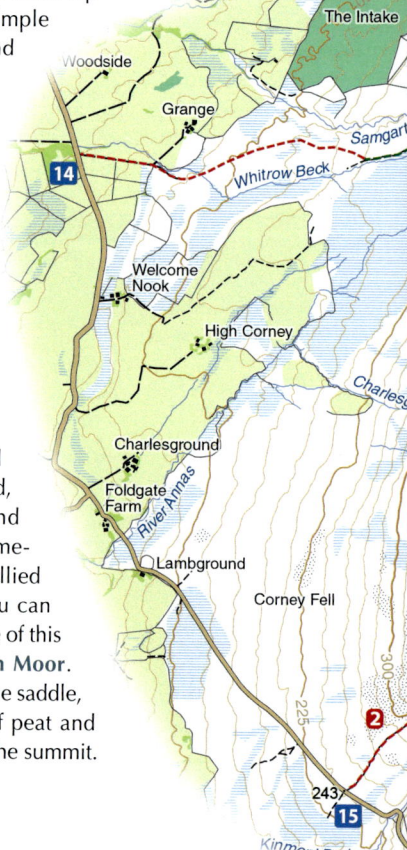

2 From the Corneyfell Road at SD 132 904 a bridle-track, an old peat-cutters' track, climbs to the cairn on Hare Raise then apparently stops. However, the table-top summit has no impediment to a simple traverse other than tough grass, and you can visit the prominent cairn en route to Whitfell's summit tumulus.

3 Park on the verge of the A595 just beyond the entrance to Fell Lane, south of Broad Oak. Follow the lane, ignoring the cattle grid and passing through the facing gate. The bridle-track embarks on a winding course across a rough pasture of rushes and gorse, no more than an intermittent path after the ford, sometimes in doubt, but continuing eastward between **Samgarth** and **Whitrow Becks**. Finding drier ground, draw alongside Whitrow Beck and wander through the intriguing homestead enclosure and as far as the gullied foot of **Red Gill**. From this point you can bear right to follow the left-hand edge of this deeply gullied forked gill onto **Burn Moor**. Sheep trods give some assistance to the saddle, where you pass a small exposure of peat and climb onto easier ground leading to the summit.

23 WHITFELL

4 Alternatively, from **Red Gill**, the bridleway encountered on Route **3**, an engineered green-way, climbs the steeper ground eastward and allows a quick detour left to visit **Rowantree Force**. The path is lost as the ground levels in the broad basin of Withe Bottom but restored as you rise to the small cairn at the highest point of the pass. Join the ridge path and climb right (south) to the summit.

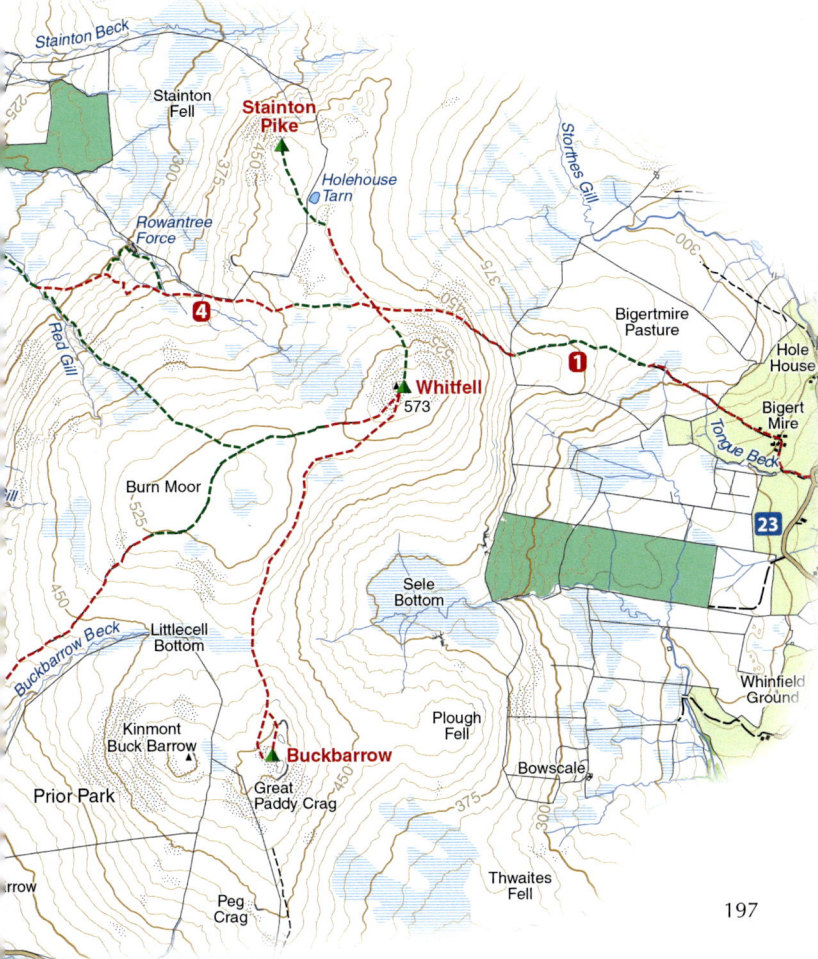

The summit

Rising to a gentle dome, the fell culminates in an ancient cairn. This is a low round pile of rocks some 18 strides wide, upon which has been built a rustic yet quite noble cairn. Inevitably visitors have further adapted the handy stones to fashion a wind shelter, tucked in on the leeward side. Sandwiches consumed, gaze east and south to the Duddon and its spreading estuary. An old Ordnance Survey pillar stands forlornly on a flat patch of ground to the northeast.

Safe descents

Especially in misty conditions, it is best to descend N then track either E (**1**) or W (**4**) with the cross-ridge path.

Ridge routes

Buckbarrow →2.4km/1½ miles ↓95m/310ft ↑70m/230ft ⏲40min
A path descends SW, traversing the east slopes of Burn Moor. Cross the marshy edge of Littlecell Bottom S onto the emerging rocky edge, which leads to the summit.

Whitfell summit, a large cairn resting on a massive tumulus

23 Whitfell

The Pike from Bigert Pasture

Stainton Pike →1.5km/1 mile ↓100m/330ft ↑5m/15ft ⏱25min
Descend N. A path materialises as you cross the old bridleway (now NW) onto the low ridge. Branch half-left to cross the plain fence before Holehouse Tarn. A narrow trod leads to the summit knoll.

WALKING THE LAKE DISTRICT FELLS – CONISTON

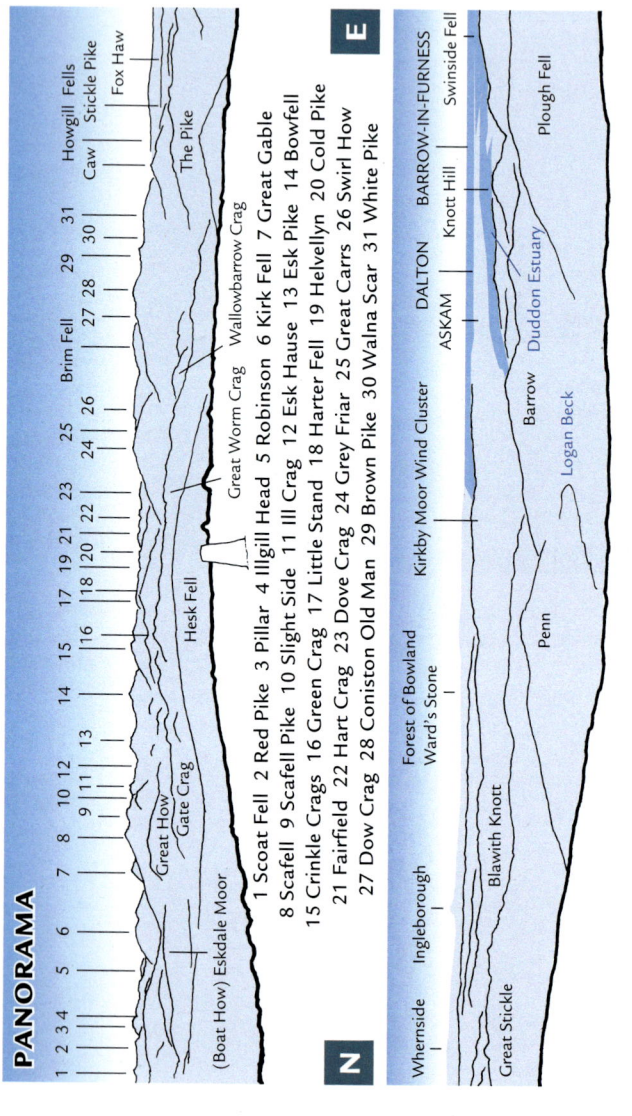

23 WHITFELL

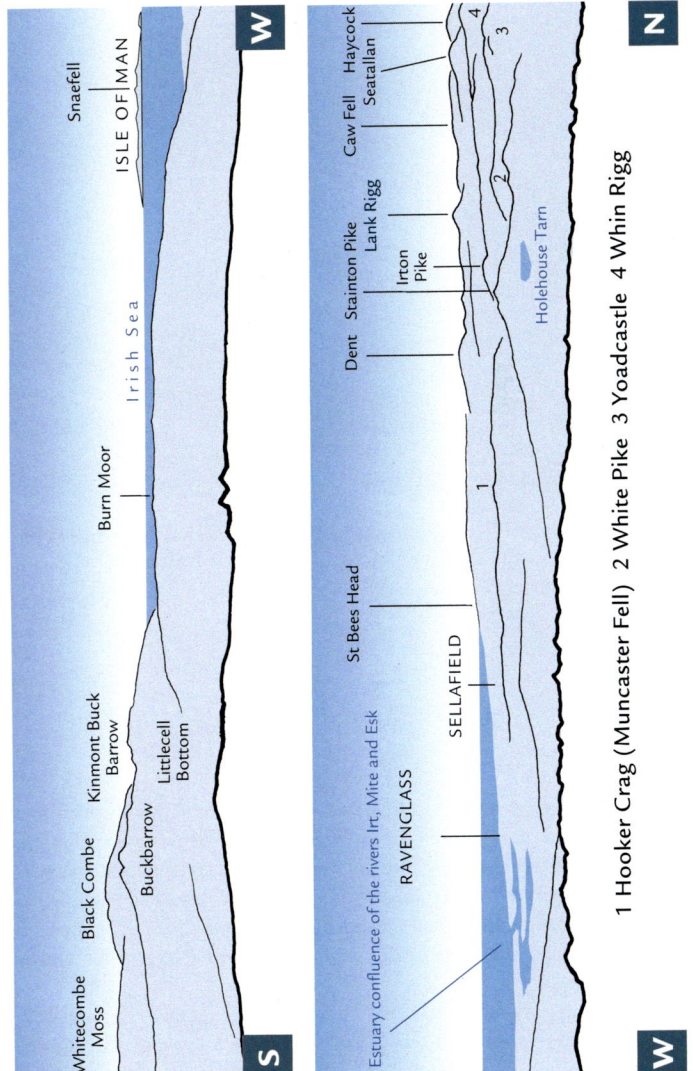

1 Hooker Crag (Muncaster Fell) 2 White Pike 3 Yoadcastle 4 Whin Rigg

24 YOADCASTLE 494M/1621FT

Climb it from	Dyke **13**, Corneyfell Road (Fell Lane) **14**, Brantrake **11** or Birkerfell Road (Devoke Water track-end) **8**
Character	An upthrust knott on the rough moor south of Devoke Water
Fell-friendly route	2
Summit grid ref	SD 157 952
Link it with	Hesk Fell or Stainton Pike

Motorists with an eye for a scenic drive scan their atlases and quickly home in on the Birkerfell Road, delighting in the moorland traverse between Eskdale Green and Ulpha, with the thrilling backdrop of the Scafells in grand perspective. On a good day it can be hard to keep driving, frequent laybys tempting you to pull in and gaze with admiration at the Lakeland alps. Those who park up and wander to the lonely shores of Devoke Water find serenity and solace in the timeless wilderness setting.

The discerning wanderer, with the boots and the will, takes to the fellsides and reaps rich rewards from the discovery of the numerous cairned tops surrounding the lake: Seat How, Rough Crag, Water Crag, Brantrake Crag,

↑ *Yoadcastle from the Stainton Pike ridge path*

Garner Bank, White Pike and the cairnless Rowantree How, scenically the best of the bunch. Nonetheless, although set back and hidden from the immediate arena, Yoadcastle, aloof and inviting, must be considered the ultimate goal of any well-rounded expedition.

Although the Birkerfell Road offers the quickest access (4), Devoke Water can also be approached from the valley floor, from Dyke (1) and Brantrake (3), and from the lake, the summit can be reached by a choice of (pathless) options. One more route leads up from Broad Oak via Stainton Beck (2) then takes a pathless line over the subsidiary outcrops of the Knott and White Pike.

Ascent from Dyke 13 or the Corneyfell Road (Fell Lane) 14
off map S

Via Barnscar →*7.2km/4½ miles* ↑*470m/1540ft* ⏲*3hr 15min*

A squelchy route to Devoke Water, followed by a choice of lines onto the fell-top

1 A small section of old road may be used for parking at the entrance to Dyke Farm. Follow the farm track through the farm buildings. Rising beyond, watch for a gate on the left. The bridleway emerges from the more obvious farm lane. Keep within the walled lane, admiring the pink stonework. A further gate spells a change but not for the better! The next enclosure is traversed by both a bridleway and a footpath. The ground is so rough and wet that horse-riders have been redirected onto the footpath, making the walkers' lot nigh on impossible. Cling on to the wall and hop from tuft to tuft. The fun and games only partially dies down as the path turns right, away from the wall, with the dampest bit paved. But thankfully matters finally improve after the next gate!

A clear green-way rises easily by the obscure remains of the Bronze-Age native settlement of **Barnscar**, traces of field walls and huts lying beneath a dense cover of bracken. The cairned path leads on, with a low ridge on the left, crowned by a cairn – a tempting distraction. A sequence of paired stone markers guide the old path over wet ground towards the western end of **Devoke Water**, overlooked by two Bronze-Age cairns, and the path continues just above the southern shore.

Taking the line that most appeals bear off right onto either **White Pike** or **Stord's Hill**. If you choose Stord's Hill, make sure to climb onto the subsidiary

Devoke Water from the cairn on Woodend Height

top of **Rowantree How** on your way to the great cairn on **Woodend Height**. From here the summit lies a short distance to the south.

Via Stainton Beck →*5.6km/3½ miles* ↑*450m/1475ft* ⏱*2hr 10min*

A straightforward route following Stainton Beck and then the natural rise of the land

2 White Pike can also accessed from Broad Oak. Park by the telephone kiosk opposite Broad Oak Farm, cross the cattle grid and follow the farm access track to Stainton Ground. Although there is a footpath, complete with stiles, it is preferable to follow the farm track, unless you wish

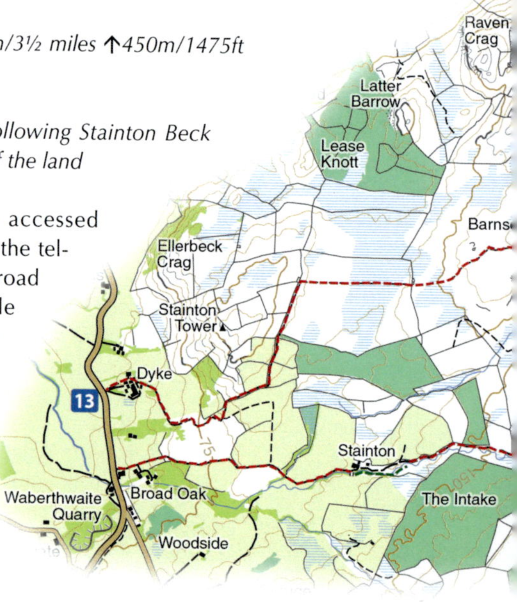

24 YOADCASTLE

to wade through the knee-high water at the Black Beck ford. Cross a ladder-stile, right, and an unusually broad footbridge, immediately before the farmyard gate. Embark on a footpath which hugs **Stainton Beck**, via two fence-stiles, pass **Stainton Ground** and continue through gorse and marshy ground. Reach the open fell via two ladder-stiles and an intermediary low fence-stile. Beat a way through the bracken, without a path. Climb up onto **the Knott** and then, more steeply, to the handsome cairn on White Pike. There is not the slightest hint of a path; it's up to you. Cross the small depression to the southeast to ascend to the summit.

Ascent from Brantrake 11

Via Rough Crag →6km/3¾ miles ↑560m/1835ft ⏱2hr 50min

Rough Crag is a fabulous viewpoint and can be visited en route to Yoadcastle. Be warned: if descending to the west, Linbeck Gill is often tricky to ford.

3 A small parking area beside the River Esk is a handy springboard. From the hand-gate almost opposite keep beside the wall, under the mightily rough fellside of Brantrake Crags. Coming above the old farm, begin a series of hairpins, the original 'brant rake' or steep steps climbing to a saddle where the old peat track dissolves into the combe of Brantrake Moss. Ford the gill, left, and follow on over the cairned top to the east, traipsing round to a large boiler-plate slab composed of a pale rock typical hereabouts. Head south, slipping through a narrow defile at the head of Hare Gill. Pass a pair of spruces, heading up to the cairn on Rough Crag – a fine viewpoint. Visitors often walk round Devoke Water, taking in the neighbouring cairned top of Water Crag to the west, although Linbeck Gill can be deep and troublesome to ford and you will need to cross in order to continue your ascent with Route **1**. Alternatively, from Rough Crag descend southeast to the boathouse approach track to join Route **4**.

Ascent from the Birkerfell Road (Devoke Water track-end) 8

Via Devoke Water →3.7km/2¼ miles ↑255m/835ft ⏱2hr 25min

The shortest approach also benefits from a high start.

4 By parking at the minor junction on the Birkerfell Road you can join the track leading southwest to the tarn, thus avoiding the Brantrake section of the ascent (Route **3**). (As a novel addition, you could include Seat How. Access to the top is only possible from the east.) The track terminates at the ruined Victorian boathouse. A path continues round the southern shore to link with Route **1**, contending with wet ground. The second beck flowing into the

24 YOADCASTLE

tarn, **Hall Beck**, is the clue to the ascent. Climb south over **Rowantree How** onto **Woodend Height**. There are no paths to begin with, symptomatic of all Yoadcastle approaches, but once the high ground is reached there they are, naturally! The main summit lies a short distance to the south of the cairn on Woodend Height.

The summit

On the ground the summit is obvious, although maps tend to be a little vague and the whole mass of adjacent ground carries no distinguishing name. The abrupt summit outcrop is easily mounted to reach a small top with only the tiniest of cairns. All cairn-building effort has apparently been exhausted in creating Woodend Height's sturdy cairn, which is the obvious second port of call, followed by White Pike.

Devoke Water backed by Harter Fell and Seat How

Safe descents

Be wary of the outcrops which form a battlement around White Pike. Otherwise all crags are minor and, while there are no paths off the fell, the gills are universally open-coursed and easy to follow.

Ridge routes

Hesk Fell →*2.4km/1½ miles* ↓*120m/395ft* ↑*100m/330ft* ⏲*50min*
Walk E without the benefit of a tangible path into the broad and exceedingly damp depression at the head of the great bowl of Storthes Gill. Gaining firmer ground, begin the ascent of Hesk Fell, drifting SE onto the featureless top to locate the small heap of stones marking the summit.

Stainton Pike →*2km/1¼ miles* ↓*60m/195ft* ↑*65m/215ft* ⏲*40min*
A path, little better than a sheep track, leads on a gentle curving line S. Crossing a broad saddle, it mounts a shallow bank, from where you need to branch right by a cairn and cross the plain fence to reach the solitary summit cairn, set a little further W than Yoadcastle.

Yoadcastle rising above Eskdale

1 TWO HARD KNOTTS

Start/Finish	Jubilee Bridge **4**
Distance	8km/5 miles
Ascent/Descent	730m/2395ft
Time	5hr
Terrain	Some early rocky terrain above the Roman fort, but largely on clear fell paths
Summits	Border End (Hard Knott) and Harter Fell

A hugely rewarding rocky ramble, whetting your appetite for off-the-beaten-track adventure.

From the cattle grid ascend the steep road. As the left-hand wall climbs away left, follow suit and follow a path which leads to the west gate of **Hardknott Castle** Roman fort. Walk through the middle of the fort, studying the various structural elements with their interpretative panels, to exit via the east gate. Advance up through the open space to the Roman parade ground and angle left to find the heap of stone cleared by the auxiliary garrison in the creation of the parade ground to form an observation dais.

↑ *The Scafells from high on Border End*

Roman granaries

If visibility and conditions are poor, simply follow the footpath along the course of the original Roman road to reach the modern tarmac road at a hairpin, then ascend the road to reach the top of **Hardknott Pass**. However, in fair conditions proceed above the scarp edge on a sheep path, with the great cliff of Yew Crag forming a foreground to the handsome view up Eskdale. Crossing a low wall, leave what remains of the sheep trod to embark on an intuitive route up the outcrop-shielded slope. There are plenty of grassy lines available, avoiding a succession of rock bands, keeping to the left of the upper, more serious, rocky defence to reach the cairn set back from the ultimate prow of **Border End**. The view back down to the Roman fort is superb, but all the way up and from the top the eyes are constantly drawn to the fabulous mountain cirque forming the head of Eskdale, centred on the wildest aspect of the mighty Scafells – an uplifting and constant scenic theme throughout the entire walk.

A path transpires from the cairn along the spine of the little ridge, advancing east to dip into the damp bowl, with the higher mass of the fell northeast. Keep right on the grass path, descending to cross a low broken wall through a gap then coming naturally down to the top of the pass, joining the road to the right of the cairn. Follow the road west down to where a path breaks left opposite Raven Crag. This is, in fact, the old Roman road which leads down to Black Hall and the Duddon.

The way forks; keep right with the bridleway (blue arrow waymark) and slip around the old wall corner, heading to and through a stone-weighted gate.

1 Two Hard Knotts

The continuing path bears left, in partial harmony with the fence. Approaching a hand-gate in the forest fence, fork right, continuing across the marshy ground to now set to work climbing the fell beyond a fence-stile, keeping left of the imposing Demming Crag. A consistent path rises to the great tors on top of **Harter Fell**, the summit of which is accessed from the east side, with the OS column secreted on the west side of the massive rocky crown. This is one of the most rewarding summits in the district, with lovely raw rock underfoot and exciting scenes all around, notably, of course, the Scafells.

Linger long before accepting the inevitable need to leave. Descend west; the path is obvious. Keeping right at a minor cairned fork, cross over two lengths of old wall to ultimately meet the bridleway from the Duddon by a lone rowan. Turn right, descending via two hands-gates and, latterly, two field-gates, to cross the little footbridge. Throughout this final section your attention will be captivated by a majestic prospect of upper Eskdale ahead, with the near pastures of Eskdale forming a lovely contrast below. Follow the bridleway back to the road and your start point. Don't forget, the Woolpack Inn is very close – the perfect post-walk objective!

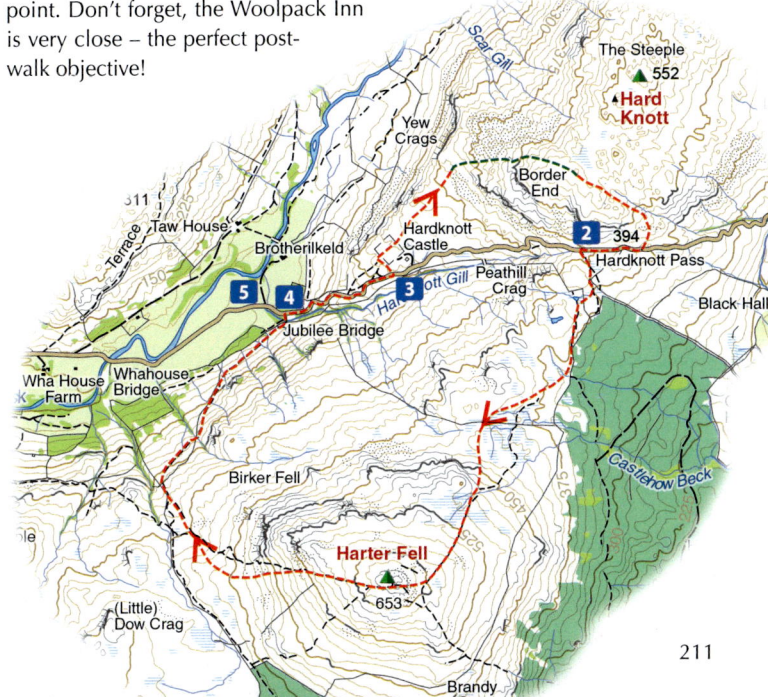

2 THE SWIRL ROUND

Start/Finish	Tilberthwaite Ghyll **33**
Distance	13km/8 miles
Ascent/Descent	1025m/3365ft
Time	6hr
Terrain	Almost entirely on good paths; rock-steps on Steel Edge and Prison Band are easily overcome and the long grassy ridge of Wet Side Edge is a pleasure
Summits	Wetherlam, Swirl How and Great Carrs

Combining the best ascent routes for both Wetherlam and Swirl How in a great horseshoe from the beautiful hidden valley of Tilberthwaite.

From the parking area on the south side of Tilberthwaite Ghyll, climb the inviting flight of slate steps, beside considerable evidence of slate-quarry workings at Horse Crag, notably the deep recessed hollow to the left, which can be inspected, with awe, via a short passage. Higher up, ignore the level path which tries to draw you down to a footbridge and a steep climb onto the cobbled path on the north side of the valley. That cobbled mine access

↑ *Wetherlam from Great Carrs*

2 THE SWIRL ROUND

track can be used as an alternative from Low Tilberthwaite, but far better the southerly way. The southern path comes to a gill and an exciting if modest slate rock-step, after which the path levels as the great combe opens. At the fork bear right to ford Crook Beck by the convenient large boulders.

From this point there are two options: either go straight ahead, with little trace of a path, to the base of the rock slope, or follow the inviting path to but not over the wooden footbridge. Here cut up left above the mine level, through the bracken, to meet the lateral path (the first option). Now climb the slope easily, side-stepping the ice-smoothed outcropping with occasional perched erratic rocks, and arrive at the lovely grassy ridge, the very essence of **Steel Edge**. Ultimately the rock prevails, but what appears daunting from below turns out to be no more than simple rock-steps and loose rusty scree. After the top shallow gully the slope eases onto the fell pasture. Pass to the left of a pool and, as a second larger tarn comes into sight, find the ridge path.

Go right, passing two cairns, to reach the summit of **Wetherlam**, itself a ragged cairn set on irregular outcropping. Turn left (west); a cairn indicates the way (in mist the path you arrived upon looks more obvious, so

Tilberthwaite valley

WALKING THE LAKE DISTRICT FELLS – CONISTON

pay attention!). Descend gradually via stony ground, bypassing the notable subsidiary top of Black Sails. The path comes down into the narrow pass of **Swirl Hawse**, with its great cairn. **Prison Band** looms above; lots of minor rock-steps ensure the climb is far from dull on a popular path which weaves its way irresistibly to the top of **Swirl How**, a metre higher than Coniston Old Man! A sturdy cairn marks the summit and perhaps the top view of the day. The hard work is largely done, though you're still not quite halfway!

The ridge path goes west, then north, through the shallow Top of Broad Slack col with its chasmal view down the Greenburn valley, past the memorial

2 THE SWIRL ROUND

cairn with remnants of Halifax fuselage. Swinging northeast with the ridge, reach the impressively sited cairn on **Great Carrs**, a spot to savour. The descending ridge path is never in doubt. Note the cairn, left, on the adjacent knoll of Hell Gill Pike. Proceed down Wet Side Edge, a simple grassy ridge, ignoring the path that breaks sharp left from a cairn; take guidance from the cairn beyond that directs east along the crest of the broad ridge.

As the ridge becomes steeper find a path that switches right and then down southeast through the bracken to open marshy pasture. A shepherds' track can lure you to a gate with a National Trust 'no path' notice, in which case simply follow the wall right, coming to the short steep bank descending to a footbridge crossing **Greenburn Beck**. Clambering onto the old mine access track, go left via the gate. The stony way merges with the old road from Fellfoot Bridge and almost at once meets a fork in the way. Bear right, signposted Tilberthwaite. This recently resurfaced track rises and passes through gates, before descending to conclude by **High Tilberthwaite** and Low Tilberthwaite, returning you to your starting point.

Great Carrs' summit cairn

3 CONISTON TRIPLE TREAT

Start/Finish	Walna Scar Road fell-gate **31**
Distance	12km/7½ miles
Ascent/Descent	915m/3000ft
Time	5hr
Terrain	A steady ascent culminates on a genuine mountain peak, tripping round by a high pass then delving into a wild cove harbouring a corrie tarn and great rocks.
Summits	Dow Crag, Coniston Old Man and Brim Fell

A scenically rewarding walk taking in the landmark summit of Coniston Old Man.

A tightly winding road leads up from the village of Coniston to a gate onto the common; use the large parking area 100 metres up from the gate. Follow the open track. This is the **Walna Scar Road**, which negotiates two impressive cuttings (the first known as the Rock Gate) – once daunting obstacles for 4x4 vehicles on this now restricted byway, an ancient cross-ridge route to the Duddon valley. Keep faith with the main track, ignoring the right fork that

↑ *Buck Pike on the Dow Crag ridge*

3 Coniston Triple Treat

Torver Beck and Cove Bridge

WALKING THE LAKE DISTRICT FELLS – CONISTON

takes walkers to Goat's Water. The track crosses Cove Bridge, which spans Torver Beck, the outflow of Goat's Water, now becoming steeper as it winds to the top of the pass by a tiny stone shelter.

At the cross-ways go right; the popular ridge path rises to the cairn and low wind-fold on **Brown Pike**, from where you can peer down on Blind Tarn. The ridge invites you onwards, due north, climbing on over Buck Pike. As the ferocious cliffs of Dow Crag become ever more impressive to the right, watch out for the gullies and stubby spur ridges; best steer clear. The final

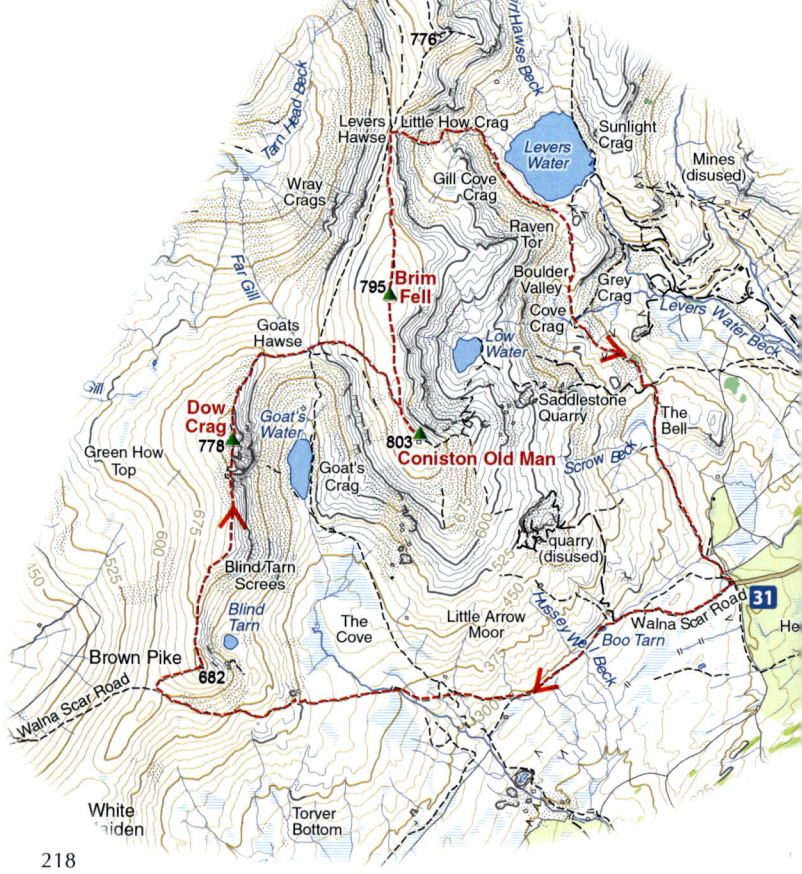

3 Coniston Triple Treat

pull onto the summit of **Dow Crag** can seem difficult. Indeed, some walkers will choose to skirt the rocky upper ground to the left and curve round and approach the summit from the north; it is slightly less problematic, but the abyss no less incredible. There is no scope for a cairn on the tiny summit of fissured bedrock.

The ridge path descends naturally from north to east to slip through the shallow pass of **Goats Hawse**. Clambering on via rocky ground as it ascends, an obvious fork gives the choice of northeast, direct to Levers Hawse, or, better, southwest to reach the popular crown of **Coniston Old Man**, which, with good reason, might be considered the view of the day. About turn and follow the approach but keep north along the ridge over the spacious crest of **Brim Fell**, passing the summit cairn. The path eases down and the ridge narrows to **Levers Hawse**.

In the first dip find a cairn a few metres down to the right guiding the descent path into Gill Cove. Early on this takes advantage of the natural ground, but soon pitching steps are encountered for all they are roughly engineered. The pitching ceases then resumes. As the path slope eases approaching **Levers Water**, veer right. The path contours above the tarn. Coming by the fenced copper-mine shaft, keep up right to enter **Boulder Valley**, with its very angular blocks; these rocks are crag-fallen not glacial erratic in origin. The route heads down to a footbridge, with the stirring crag-tumbling cascades of Low Water Beck holding attention up to the right. Just on the far side of the footbridge stands the biggest of all the boulders in this wild rocky hollow, the Pudding Stone. The path swings left, affording views of the somewhat desolate industrial remnants of the Coppermines Valley down to the left. Soon the regular path coming down from the Old Man is met; go left, then fork right through the gap, now on a secure track leading back to the start.

4 FOX HAW, CAW AND PIKES

Start/Finish	Water Yeat **28**
Distance	9.6km/6 miles
Ascent/Descent	530m/1740ft
Time	4hr 30min
Terrain	Intricate rocky ground – fun in fair weather but ill-suited for cloudy conditions
Summits	The Knott, Fox Haw, Caw and Pikes (Caw)

A wonderful one-fell round, taking in all its rocky ridge connections.

Follow the woodland road down to cross the bridge spanning the River Lickle, no more than a tumbling beck. The road winds up by a long-abandoned potash-kiln to pass through the environs of Stephenson Ground with its handsome stone barns. It then rises, edged by stone flags, comes by Jackson Ground and declines to reach a gate entrance to Carter Ground (blue bridle-way waymark). Follow the open track up to the holiday-let conversions and pass by the old farmhouse, squeezing between the out-barn and house wall then passing up the garden to a gate onto the open fell. When bracken is high keep to the right-hand wall, joining the lateral bridle-track – popular with bikers – at the brow. Go left; the track rises to a ridge-crossing.

↑ *Fox Haw and Caw from the Knott*

4 Fox Haw, Caw and Pikes

Here the route turns right, but before proceeding, a recommended detour goes left along the low ridge to a cairn on **the Knott**, from where you can admire the joyous view down onto the Duddon Estuary. Backtrack, cross the lateral path and ascend the facing ridge onto **Raven's Crag**, characterised by its variety of splintered ice-smoothed outcropping – spot one huge erratic, set on fissured bedrock to the right. The ridge is delightfully and unpredictably meandering, with lots of tantalising craggy knolls to explore, sheep paths your only sure guide. There are a couple of hollows to cross before the primary pull onto **Fox Haw**, with several cairns en route identifying viewpoints, looking either southwest to Stickle Pike or, from Fox Haw, northeast to the crag-defended southern aspect of Caw.

221

The negligible ridge path continues north, reliant on the whims of sheep, down to join the Park Head Road (track). Follow this right, meeting a track coming in from the southeast, and continue down the track until an inviting shelf-path offers relief from the stony trail. This long-abandoned industrial way climbs, then levels before climbing again, coming to the spoil bank and zig-zagging up to the cluster of roofless ruins and the open entrance to a slate mine, the dark dank interior quite uninviting to the casual hill-goer. The route now climbs the final 150m up the right-hand bank, with the tiny gill and cairns indicating the line, latterly swinging left to reach the rock-rib top of **Caw** with its grey-painted Ordnance Survey column. The view is stunning, especially the Duddon aspect towards the Scafells.

Forest track

Descend northeast, ice-smoothed outcropping determining your way. It's all too easy to find yourself heading southeast to the nearer craggy subsidiary top. In mist this section requires a combination of compass and intuition. Reach a grassy saddle before the impressive pull onto the cairn-less rock massif of **Pikes**, another splendid spot to linger. Keep northeast; the succeeding grassy moor, less fraught with rock, leads on to meet the well-used track emanating from the Walna Scar Road. Turn right, descending to cross the new wooden footbridge spanning the infant **Lickle,** and from the gate join a forest track which offers a lovely accompaniment of woodland birdsong to complement the tail end of the trip. After 1.6km watch out for a gentle right curve in the track. Here an unwaymarked footpath heads straight on through the woodland, coming down by a gate to deliver you back to the start point.

MORE TO EXPLORE

Circular
- from Buckbarrow Bridge **15**: Burn Moor – Whitfell – Buckbarrow – Kinmont Buck Barrow
- from Fell Lane **14**: Stainton Pike – Yoadcastle – Woodend Height
- from Broughton Mills **27**: Great Stickle – Stickle Pike – Fox Haw
- from Tom Gill **36**: Tarn Hows – Tom Heights – Black Fell – Holme Fell

Rowantree Force, Stainton Pike

USEFUL CONTACTS

Tourist information

The nearest National Park information centre to the area covered by this guide is in Coniston. There is, however, lots of information available on the National Park website: www.lakedistrict.gov.uk. If you want to talk to someone face to face there is also another information point in Broughton (ring to check opening hours before dropping in).

Coniston
tel 01539 441533

Broughton (community-run)
tel 01229 716115

Accommodation

In addition to the tourist information centres and search engines, the Visit Cumbria website has a good database of local accommodation options: www.visitcumbria.com.

Weather

It is well worth consulting either of these forecasts to gauge the best times to be on the tops.

Lake District Weatherline
tel 0844 846 2444
www.lakedistrictweatherline.co.uk

Mountain Weather Information Service
Full mountain forecasts for 3 days at a time www.mwis.org.uk (choose English and Welsh Forecast/Lake District)
App: Mountain Forecast Viewer

Transport

Traveline
Information on buses, trains and coaches – such as they are
www.traveline.info

Stagecoach
Bus information
www.stagecoachbus.com
App: Stagecoach Bus

Organisations

The National Trust

The National Trust owns 90% of the farms in the national park, as well as historic sites and properties, camp sites and car parks.
www.nationaltrust.org.uk
App: National Trust – Days Out

Fix the Fells

Fix the Fells repairs and maintains 335 upland paths in the national park. Read about their work, volunteer or donate on this website.
www.fixthefells.co.uk

Mountain Rescue

The Lake District Search and Mountain Rescue Association manages 12 teams of volunteers across the national park. The site has useful safety information. Downloading the free OS Locate app will enable you to tell the team your grid ref, whether you have phone signal or not, should you need to call them.
www.ldsamra.org.uk

Other

Visitors curious to know more about the history of mining in the Coniston Coppermines Valley should consult Eric G. Holland's *Coniston Copper Mines: A field guide* or, for greater depth, his *Coniston Copper – A history*, both published by Cicerone Press although now out of print.

A FELLRANGER'S GLOSSARY

Navigational features

Word	Explanation
arête	knife-edge ridge
band	binding strip of land
bank-barn	barn accessible on two levels (often built on a slope or bank)
beck	main stream flowing into and through valleys to lakes and rivers
boiler-plates	non-technical term for exposed broad slabs of rock
cairn/man	small pile of loose stones indicating a path or path junction
clint	block forming part of a natural limestone pavement
combe/cove	hanging valley high in the fells
common	undivided land grazed by several farmers
cop	viewpoint
crag	substantial outcrop of rock
dale	valley
dodd	rounded hilltop
drumlin	large mound that accumulated beneath a melting glacier
dub	dark pool
fell	mountain pasture, frequently attributed to the whole hill
force	waterfall
garth	small enclosure close to farm buildngs
gate	dialect term for a track
ghyll/gill	steeply sloping watercourse
glen	from British term 'glyn' meaning valley
grain	lesser watercourse above a confluence
hag	eroded section of peat moor
hause, saddle, col, dore, scarth	high gap between fells
holm	dry riverside meadow
hope	secluded valley
howe	hill or mound
ill	treacherous
intake	upper limit of valley enclosure
keld	spring
knott	compact or rugged hilltop
laithe	barn in the field or on the fell (rather than next to the farmstead)
ling	heather

A FELLRANGER'S GLOSSARY *continued*

lonnin	quiet lane
man	from Celtic term 'maen' meaning stone marker
mell	bald hill
mere	pool or lake
mire	marshy ground
moraine	residual valley-head pillow-mound debris left after a glacier melts away
nab, naze	hill-spur or nose
ness	promontory
nether	lower
nook	secluded corner
outcrop	crag or obvious collection of rocks
out-gang	shepherd's drove lane to a particular fell pasture
park	enclosed hunting ground
pike	sharp or rocky summit
place	plot of ground
raise	heap of stones
rake	grooved track
ridding	(the action of) clearing
rigg	ridge
roche moutonnée	a 'sheep-back' rock formation created by the passing of a glacier
scale	summer-pasture shieling (hut)
scarp/scar	steep hillside
scree	weathered rock debris beneath a crag
seat	summer pasture/high place
shaw	small wood
sheep-creep	small field-to-field access-hole/gap for sheep
shelter-cairn	circular wind-break wall
shieling	hut built for use while pasturing
sike	small stream
slack	small, shallow or stony valley
sled-gate	track for pony-drawn sledges
slump	sedimentary rock that has slipped, creating dykes (intrusions), fractures or ridges
stang	pole
stead	site of a farm

sty	steep path
swine	pigs
tarn	small mountain pool, from the Norse 'tjorn' meaning tear
thwaite	clearing
tongue	'a low jutting ridge'
traverse	walking route across the fells
trig point	Ordnance Survey triangulation column
trod	path created by animals
wash-fold	sheepfold where sheep were once gathered for washing in the beck
water	feeder lake to a river
wath	ford
whin	gorse
wick	inlet or bay or subsidiary farm
wray	secluded corner
yeat	gate

Place names

Name	Explanation
Bigert Mire	'barley-field marsh'
Coppycow	coppy = coppiced woodland (now sadly replaced by conifers)
Devoke (Water)	'the little black one', from the effect the peaty waters have on its native stock of brown trout which remain small and very dark
Duddon (River)	'deep dark valley'
Esk	'source'
Hooker (Crag)	'hollow marsh' (from 'hol' and 'kerr')
Lickle (River)	'looping pooled watercourse'
Littlecell Bottom	'willow hollow'
Natty (Bridge)	'chattering stream'
Stoupdale	from 'stoup', a form of Cumbrian stone gatepost; the valley may have been a source of such stone
Sunkenkirk	'crouched standing stones'
Tranearth	'ground frequented by great cranes' (now only found in continental Europe)
Troutal	'trout hall'
Wainscarth	'waggon pass'; the former name for Hardknott Pass
Whincop	'gorse viewpoint'

A FELLRANGER'S GLOSSARY *continued*

Fell names
Just the more intriguing ones...

Name	Explanation
Caw	'crow hill'
Buckbarrow	'the gathering place of young bucks' (red deer)
Coniston Old Man	'high boundary stone' (marking the edge of a small Viking kingdom centred on Coniston Water)
Dow Crag	'cliffs frequented by doves'
Harter Fell	'stag hill'
Hesk Fell	'hill of the ash trees'
Holme Fell	from a local surname
Kinmont Buck Barrow	Kinmont = 'ceann monaidh' (Gaelic) = 'head of the moor'
Muncaster Fell	'stronghold on a headland', on the site of a Roman viewing station
Stainton Pike	from a local surname
Stickle Pike	'steep pointed peak'
Swirl How	'windswept hill'
Wallowbarrow Crag	'deer-wallow hill'
Yoadcastle	'old horse fort'

THE LAKE DISTRICT FELLS

Fell name	Height	Volume
Allen Crags	784m/2572ft	Borrowdale
Angletarn Pikes	567m/1860ft	Mardale and the Far East
Ard Crags	581m/1906ft	Buttermere
Armboth Fell	479m/1572ft	Borrowdale
Arnison Crag	434m/1424ft	Patterdale
Arthur's Pike	533m/1749ft	Mardale and the Far East
Bakestall	673m/2208ft	Keswick
Bannerdale Crags	683m/2241ft	Keswick
Barf	468m/1535ft	Keswick
Barrow	456m/1496ft	Buttermere
Base Brown	646m/2119ft	Borrowdale
Beda Fell	509m/1670ft	Mardale and the Far East
Bell Crags	558m/1831ft	Borrowdale
Binsey	447m/1467ft	Keswick
Birkhouse Moor	718m/2356ft	Patterdale
Birks	622m/2241ft	Patterdale
Black Combe	600m/1969ft	Coniston
Black Fell	322m/1056ft	Coniston
Blake Fell	573m/1880ft	Buttermere
Bleaberry Fell	589m/1932ft	Borrowdale
Blea Rigg	556m/1824ft	Langdale
Blencathra	868m/2848ft	Keswick
Bonscale Pike	529m/1736ft	Mardale and the Far East
Bowfell	903m/2963ft	Langdale
Bowscale Fell	702m/2303ft	Keswick
Brae Fell	586m/1923ft	Keswick
Brandreth	715m/2346ft	Borrowdale
Branstree	713m/2339ft	Mardale and the Far East
Brim Fell	795m/2608ft	Coniston

THE LAKE DISTRICT FELLS *continued*

Fell name	Height	Volume
Brock Crags	561m/1841ft	Mardale and the Far East
Broom Fell	511m/1676ft	Keswick
Buckbarrow (Corney Fell)	549m/1801ft	Coniston
Buckbarrow (Wast Water)	430m/1411ft	Wasdale
Calf Crag	537m/1762ft	Langdale
Carl Side	746m/2448ft	Keswick
Carrock Fell	662m/2172ft	Keswick
Castle Crag	290m/951ft	Borrowdale
Catbells	451m/1480ft	Borrowdale
Catstycam	890m/2920ft	Patterdale
Caudale Moor	764m/2507ft	Mardale and the Far East
Causey Pike	637m/2090ft	Buttermere
Caw	529m/1736ft	Coniston
Caw Fell	697m/2287ft	Wasdale
Clough Head	726m/2386ft	Patterdale
Cold Pike	701m/2300ft	Langdale
Coniston Old Man	803m/2635ft	Coniston
Crag Fell	523m/1716ft	Wasdale
Crag Hill	839m/2753ft	Buttermere
Crinkle Crags	860m/2822ft	Langdale
Dale Head	753m/2470ft	Buttermere
Dodd	502m/1647ft	Keswick
Dollywaggon Pike	858m/2815ft	Patterdale
Dove Crag	792m/2599ft	Patterdale
Dow Crag	778m/2552ft	Coniston
Eagle Crag	520m/1706ft	Borrowdale
Eskdale Moor	337m/1105ft	Wasdale
Esk Pike	885m/2904ft	Langdale
Fairfield	873m/2864ft	Patterdale

Fell name	Height	Volume
Fellbarrow	416m/1365ft	Buttermere
Fleetwith Pike	648m/2126ft	Buttermere
Froswick	720m/2362ft	Mardale and the Far East
Gavel Fell	526m/1726ft	Buttermere
Gibson Knott	421m/1381ft	Langdale
Glaramara	783m/2569ft	Borrowdale
Glenridding Dodd	442m/1450ft	Patterdale
Gowbarrow Fell	481m/1578ft	Patterdale
Grange Fell	416m/1365ft	Borrowdale
Grasmoor	852m/2795ft	Buttermere
Gray Crag	697m/2287ft	Mardale and the Far East
Grayrigg Forest	494m/1621ft	Mardale and the Far East
Graystones	456m/1496ft	Keswick
Great Borne	616m/2021ft	Buttermere
Great Calva	690m/2264ft	Keswick
Great Carrs	788m/2585ft	Coniston
Great Cockup	526m/1726ft	Keswick
Great Crag	452m/1483ft	Borrowdale
Great Dodd	857m/2812ft	Patterdale
Great End	907m/2976ft	Borrowdale, Langdale, Wasdale
Great Gable	899m/2949ft	Borrowdale, Wasdale
Great How	523m/1716ft	Wasdale
Great Mell Fell	537m/1762ft	Patterdale
Great Rigg	767m/2516ft	Patterdale
Great Sca Fell	651m/2136ft	Keswick
Great Worm Crag	427m/1401ft	Coniston
Green Crag	489m/1604ft	Coniston
Green Gable	801m/2628ft	Borrowdale
Grey Crag	638m/2093ft	Mardale and the Far East

THE LAKE DISTRICT FELLS *continued*

Fell name	Height	Volume
Grey Friar	772m/2533ft	Coniston
Grey Knotts	697m/2287ft	Borrowdale
Grike	488m/1601ft	Wasdale
Grisedale Pike	791m/2595ft	Buttermere
Hallin Fell	388m/1273ft	Mardale and the Far East
Hard Knott	552m/1811ft	Coniston
Harrison Stickle	736m/2415ft	Langdale
Hart Crag	822m/2697ft	Patterdale
Harter Fell (Eskdale)	653m/2142ft	Coniston
Harter Fell (Mardale)	778m/2553ft	Mardale and the Far East
Hart Side	758m/2487ft	Patterdale
Hartsop above How	586m/1923ft	Patterdale
Hartsop Dodd	618m/2028ft	Mardale and the Far East
Haycock	798m/2618ft	Wasdale
Haystacks	598m/1962ft	Buttermere
Helm Crag	405m/1329ft	Langdale
Helvellyn	950m/3116ft	Patterdale
Hen Comb	509m/1670ft	Buttermere
Heron Pike	621m/2037ft	Patterdale
Hesk Fell	476m/1562ft	Coniston
High Crag	744m/2441ft	Buttermere
High Hartsop Dodd	519m/1703ft	Patterdale
High Pike (Caldbeck)	658m/2159ft	Keswick
High Pike (Scandale Fell)	656m/2152ft	Patterdale
High Raise (Central Fells)	762m/2500ft	Langdale
High Raise (Haweswater)	802m/2631ft	Mardale and the Far East
High Rigg	355m/1165ft	Borrowdale
High Seat	608m/1995ft	Borrowdale
High Spy	653m/2142ft	Borrowdale

Fell name	Height	Volume
High Stile	807m/2648ft	Buttermere
High Street	828m/2717ft	Mardale and the Far East
High Tove	515m/1690ft	Borrowdale
Hindscarth	727m/2385ft	Buttermere
Holme Fell	317m/1040ft	Coniston
Hopegill Head	770m/2526ft	Buttermere
Ill Bell	757m/2484ft	Mardale and the Far East
Illgill Head	609m/1998ft	Wasdale
Iron Crag	640m/2100ft	Wasdale
Kentmere Pike	730m/2395ft	Mardale and the Far East
Kidsty Pike	780m/2559ft	Mardale and the Far East
Kirk Fell	802m/2631ft	Wasdale
Knock Murton	447m/1467ft	Buttermere
Knott	710m/2329ft	Keswick
Knott Rigg	556m/1824ft	Buttermere
Lank Rigg	541m/1775ft	Wasdale
Latrigg	368m/1207ft	Keswick
Ling Fell	373m/1224ft	Keswick
Lingmell	807m/2649ft	Wasdale
Lingmoor Fell	470m/1542ft	Langdale
Little Hart Crag	637m/2090ft	Patterdale
Little Mell Fell	505m/1657ft	Patterdale
Little Stand	739m/2426ft	Langdale
Loadpot Hill	671m/2201ft	Mardale and the Far East
Loft Crag	682m/2237ft	Langdale
Longlands Fell	483m/1585ft	Keswick
Long Side	734m/2408ft	Keswick
Lonscale Fell	715m/2346ft	Keswick
Lord's Seat	552m/1811ft	Keswick

THE LAKE DISTRICT FELLS *continued*

Fell name	Height	Volume
Loughrigg Fell	335m/1099ft	Langdale
Low Fell	423m/1388ft	Buttermere
Low Pike	507m/1663ft	Patterdale
Maiden Moor	576m/1890ft	Borrowdale
Mardale Ill Bell	761m/2497ft	Mardale and the Far East
Meal Fell	550m/1804ft	Keswick
Mellbreak	512m/1680ft	Buttermere
Middle Dodd	653m/2143ft	Patterdale
Middle Fell	585m/1919ft	Wasdale
Muncaster Fell	231m/758ft	Coniston
Nab Scar	450m/1476ft	Patterdale
Nethermost Pike	891m/2923ft	Patterdale
Outerside	568m/1863ft	Buttermere
Pavey Ark	697m/2287ft	Langdale
Pike o'Blisco	705m/2313ft	Langdale
Pike o'Stickle	708m/2323ft	Langdale
Pillar	892m/2926ft	Wasdale
Place Fell	657m/2155ft	Mardale and the Far East
Raise	884m/2900ft	Patterdale
Rampsgill Head	792m/2598ft	Mardale and the Far East
Rannerdale Knotts	355m/1165ft	Buttermere
Raven Crag	463m/1519ft	Borrowdale
Red Pike (Buttermere)	755m/2477ft	Buttermere
Red Pike (Wasdale)	828m/2717ft	Wasdale
Red Screes	777m/2549ft	Patterdale
Rest Dodd	697m/2287ft	Mardale and the Far East
Robinson	737m/2418ft	Buttermere
Rossett Pike	651m/2136ft	Langdale
Rosthwaite Fell	551m/1808ft	Borrowdale

Fell name	Height	Volume
Sail	771m/2529ft	Buttermere
Sale Fell	359m/1178ft	Keswick
Sallows	516m/1693ft	Mardale and the Far East
Scafell	964m/3163ft	Wasdale
Scafell Pike	977m/3206ft	Borrowdale, Langdale, Wasdale
Scar Crags	672m/2205ft	Buttermere
Scoat Fell	843m/2766ft	Wasdale
Seatallan	693m/2274ft	Wasdale
Seathwaite Fell	631m/2070ft	Borrowdale
Seat Sandal	736m/2415ft	Patterdale
Selside Pike	655m/2149ft	Mardale and the Far East
Sergeant Man	736m/2414ft	Langdale
Sergeant's Crag	574m/1883ft	Borrowdale
Sheffield Pike	675m/2215ft	Patterdale
Shipman Knotts	587m/1926ft	Mardale and the Far East
Silver How	395m/1296ft	Langdale
Skiddaw	931m/3054ft	Keswick
Skiddaw Little Man	865m/2838ft	Keswick
Slight Side	762m/2500ft	Wasdale
Souther Fell	522m/1713ft	Keswick
Stainton Pike	498m/1634ft	Coniston
Starling Dodd	635m/2083ft	Buttermere
Steel Fell	553m/1814ft	Langdale
Steel Knotts	433m/1421ft	Mardale and the Far East
Steeple	819m/2687ft	Wasdale
Stickle Pike	376m/1234ft	Coniston
Stone Arthur	503m/1650ft	Patterdale
St Sunday Crag	841m/2759ft	Patterdale
Stybarrow Dodd	846m/2776ft	Patterdale

THE LAKE DISTRICT FELLS *continued*

Fell name	Height	Volume
Swirl How	804m/2638ft	Coniston
Tarn Crag (Easedale)	485m/1591ft	Langdale
Tarn Crag (Longsleddale)	664m/2179ft	Mardale and the Far East
Thornthwaite Crag	784m/2572ft	Mardale and the Far East
Thunacar Knott	723m/2372ft	Langdale
Troutbeck Tongue	363m/1191ft	Mardale and the Far East
Ullock Pike	690m/2264ft	Keswick
Ullscarf	726m/2382ft	Borrowdale
Walla Crag	379m/1243ft	Borrowdale
Wallowbarrow Crag	292m/958ft	Coniston
Walna Scar	621m/2037ft	Coniston
Wandope	772m/2533ft	Buttermere
Wansfell	489m/1604ft	Mardale and the Far East
Watson's Dodd	789m/2589ft	Patterdale
Wether Hill	673m/2208ft	Mardale and the Far East
Wetherlam	762m/2500ft	Coniston
Whinfell Beacon	472m/1549ft	Mardale and the Far East
Whinlatter	517m/1696ft	Keswick
Whin Rigg	536m/1759ft	Wasdale
Whiteless Pike	660m/2165ft	Buttermere
Whiteside	707m/2320ft	Buttermere
White Side	863m/2831ft	Patterdale
Whitfell	573m/1880ft	Coniston
Winterscleugh	464m/1522ft	Mardale and the Far East
Yewbarrow	628m/2060ft	Wasdale
Yoadcastle	494m/1621ft	Coniston
Yoke	706m/2316ft	Mardale and the Far East

LISTING OF CICERONE GUIDES

BRITISH ISLES CHALLENGES, COLLECTIONS AND ACTIVITIES

Cycling Land's End to John o'Groats
The Big Rounds
The Book of the Bivvy
The Book of the Bothy
The C2C Cycle Route
The End to End Cycle Route
The Mountains of England and Wales: Vol 1 Wales
The Mountains of England and Wales: Vol 2 England
The National Trails
Three Peaks, Ten Tors
Walking The End to End Trail

SCOTLAND

Backpacker's Britain: Northern Scotland
Ben Nevis and Glen Coe
Cycle Touring in Northern Scotland
Cycling in the Hebrides
Great Mountain Days in Southern and Central Scotland
Mountain Biking in Southern and Central Scotland
Mountain Biking in West and North West Scotland
Not the West Highland Way
Scotland
Scotland's Best Small Mountains
Scotland's Mountain Ridges
Skye's Cuillin Ridge Traverse
The Ayrshire and Arran Coastal Paths
The Borders Abbeys Way
The Great Glen Way
The Great Glen Way Map Booklet
The Hebridean Way
The Hebrides
The Isle of Mull
The Isle of Skye
The Skye Trail
The Southern Upland Way
The Speyside Way
The Speyside Way Map Booklet
The West Highland Way
The West Highland Way Map Booklet
Walking Highland Perthshire
Walking in Scotland's Far North
Walking in the Angus Glens
Walking in the Cairngorms
Walking in the Ochils, Campsie Fells and Lomond Hills
Walking in the Pentland Hills
Walking in the Scottish Borders
Walking in the Southern Uplands
Walking in Torridon
Walking Loch Lomond and the Trossachs
Walking on Arran
Walking on Harris and Lewis
Walking on Jura, Islay and Colonsay
Walking on Rum and the Small Isles
Walking on the Orkney and Shetland Isles
Walking on Uist and Barra
Walking the Cape Wrath Trail
Walking the Corbetts Vol 1 South of the Great Glen
Walking the Corbetts Vol 2 North of the Great Glen
Walking the Galloway Hills
Walking the Munros Vol 1 – Southern, Central and Western Highlands
Walking the Munros Vol 2 – Northern Highlands and the Cairngorms
Winter Climbs Ben Nevis and Glen Coe
Winter Climbs in the Cairngorms

NORTHERN ENGLAND TRAILS

Hadrian's Wall Path
Hadrian's Wall Path Map Booklet
Pennine Way Map Booklet
The Coast to Coast Map Booklet
The Coast to Coast Walk
The Dales Way
The Dales Way Map Booklet
The Pennine Way

NORTH EAST ENGLAND, YORKSHIRE DALES AND PENNINES

Cycling in the Yorkshire Dales
Great Mountain Days in the Pennines
Mountain Biking in the Yorkshire Dales
St Oswald's Way and St Cuthbert's Way
The Cleveland Way and the Yorkshire Wolds Way
The Cleveland Way Map Booklet
The North York Moors
The Reivers Way
The Teesdale Way
Trail and Fell Running in the Yorkshire Dales
Walking in County Durham
Walking in Northumberland
Walking in the North Pennines
Walking in the Yorkshire Dales: North and East
Walking in the Yorkshire Dales: South and West

NORTH WEST ENGLAND AND THE ISLE OF MAN

Cycling the Pennine Bridleway
Cycling the Way of the Roses
Hadrian's Cycleway
Isle of Man Coastal Path
The Lancashire Cycleway
The Lune Valley and Howgills
Walking in Cumbria's Eden Valley
Walking in Lancashire
Walking in the Forest of Bowland and Pendle
Walking on the Isle of Man
Walking on the West Pennine Moors
Walks in Silverdale and Arnside

LAKE DISTRICT

Cycling in the Lake District
Great Mountain Days in the Lake District
Lake District Winter Climbs
Lake District: High Level and Fell Walks
Lake District: Low Level and Lake Walks
Mountain Biking in the Lake District
Outdoor Adventures with Children – Lake District
Scrambles in the Lake District – North
Scrambles in the Lake District – South
The Cumbria Way
Trail and Fell Running in the Lake District
Walking the Lake District Fells – Borrowdale
Walking the Lake District Fells – Buttermere
Walking the Lake District Fells – Coniston
Walking the Lake District Fells – Keswick
Walking the Lake District Fells – Langdale
Walking the Lake District Fells – Mardale and the Far East
Walking the Lake District Fells – Patterdale
Walking the Lake District Fells – Wasdale

DERBYSHIRE, PEAK DISTRICT AND MIDLANDS

Cycling in the Peak District
Dark Peak Walks
Scrambles in the Dark Peak
Walking in Derbyshire
Walking in the Peak District – White Peak East
White Peak Walks: The Southern Dales

SOUTHERN ENGLAND

20 Classic Sportive Rides in South East England
20 Classic Sportive Rides in South West England

LISTING OF CICERONE GUIDES *continued*

Cycling in the Cotswolds
Mountain Biking on the North Downs
Mountain Biking on the South Downs
Suffolk Coast and Heath Walks
The Cotswold Way
The Cotswold Way Map Booklet
The Great Stones Way
The Kennet and Avon Canal
The Lea Valley Walk
The North Downs Way
The North Downs Way Map Booklet
The Peddars Way and Norfolk Coast path
The Pilgrims' Way
The Ridgeway Map Booklet
The Ridgeway National Trail
The South Downs Way
The South Downs Way Map Booklet
The South West Coast Path
The South West Coast Path Map Booklets
  Vol 1: Minehead to St Ives
  Vol 2: St Ives to Plymouth
  Vol 3: Plymouth to Poole
The Thames Path
The Thames Path Map Booklet
The Two Moors Way
Two Moors Way Map Booklet
Walking Hampshire's Test Way
Walking in Cornwall
Walking in Essex
Walking in Kent
Walking in London
Walking in Norfolk
Walking in the Chilterns
Walking in the Cotswolds
Walking in the New Forest
Walking in the North Wessex Downs
Walking in the Thames Valley
Walking on Dartmoor
Walking on Guernsey
Walking on Jersey
Walking on the Isle of Wight
Walking the Jurassic Coast
Walks in the South Downs National Park

WALES AND WELSH BORDERS

Cycle Touring in Wales
Cycling Lon Las Cymru
Glyndwr's Way
Great Mountain Days in Snowdonia
Hillwalking in Shropshire
Hillwalking in Wales – Vols 1&2
Mountain Walking in Snowdonia
Offa's Dyke Path
Offa's Dyke Path Map Booklet

Ridges of Snowdonia
Scrambles in Snowdonia
Snowdonia: 30 Low-level and easy walks – North
Snowdonia: 30 Low-level and easy walks – South
The Cambrian Way
The Ceredigion and Snowdonia Coast Paths
The Pembrokeshire Coast Path
The Severn Way
The Snowdonia Way
The Wales Coast Path
The Wye Valley Walk
Walking in Carmarthenshire
Walking in Pembrokeshire
Walking in the Forest of Dean
Walking in the Wye Valley
Walking on the Brecon Beacons
Walking on the Gower
Walking the Shropshire Way

INTERNATIONAL CHALLENGES, COLLECTIONS AND ACTIVITIES

Canyoning in the Alps
Europe's High Points
The Via Francigena Canterbury to Rome – Part 2

AFRICA

Kilimanjaro
The High Atlas
Walking in the Drakensberg
Walks and Scrambles in the Moroccan Anti-Atlas

ALPS CROSS-BORDER ROUTES

100 Hut Walks in the Alps
Alpine Ski Mountaineering Vol 1 – Western Alps
Alpine Ski Mountaineering Vol 2 – Central and Eastern Alps
Chamonix to Zermatt
The Karnischer Hohenweg
The Tour of the Bernina
Tour of Monte Rosa
Tour of the Matterhorn
Trail Running – Chamonix and the Mont Blanc region
Trekking in the Alps
Trekking in the Silvretta and Ratikon Alps
Trekking Munich to Venice
Trekking the Tour of Mont Blanc
Walking in the Alps

PYRENEES AND FRANCE/SPAIN CROSS-BORDER ROUTES

Shorter Treks in the Pyrenees
The GR10 Trail
The GR11 Trail
The Pyrenean Haute Route

The Pyrenees
Walks and Climbs in the Pyrenees

AUSTRIA

Innsbruck Mountain Adventures
The Adlerweg
Trekking in Austria's Hohe Tauern
Trekking in the Stubai Alps
Trekking in the Zillertal Alps
Walking in Austria
Walking in the Salzkammergut: the Austrian Lake District

EASTERN EUROPE

The Danube Cycleway Vol 2
The High Tatras
The Mountains of Romania
Walking in Bulgaria's National Parks
Walking in Hungary

FRANCE, BELGIUM AND LUXEMBOURG

Chamonix Mountain Adventures
Cycle Touring in France
Cycling London to Paris
Cycling the Canal de la Garonne
Cycling the Canal du Midi
Mont Blanc Walks
Mountain Adventures in the Maurienne
Short Treks on Corsica
The GR20 Corsica
The GR5 Trail
The GR5 Trail – Benelux and Lorraine
The GR5 Trail – Vosges and Jura
The Grand Traverse of the Massif Central
The Loire Cycle Route
The Moselle Cycle Route
The River Rhone Cycle Route
The Robert Louis Stevenson Trail
The Way of St James – Le Puy to the Pyrenees
Tour of the Queyras
Trekking the Robert Louis Stevenson Trail
Vanoise Ski Touring
Via Ferratas of the French Alps
Walking in Corsica
Walking in Provence – East
Walking in Provence – West
Walking in the Ardennes
Walking in the Auvergne
Walking in the Briançonnais
Walking in the Dordogne
Walking in the Haute Savoie: North
Walking in the Haute Savoie: South

GERMANY

Hiking and Cycling in the Black Forest
The Danube Cycleway Vol 1

The Rhine Cycle Route
The Westweg
Walking in the Bavarian Alps

HIMALAYA

Annapurna
Everest: A Trekker's Guide
The Mount Kailash Trek
Trekking in Bhutan
Trekking in Ladakh
Trekking in the Himalaya

IRELAND

The Wild Atlantic Way and Western Ireland

ITALY

Italy's Sibillini National Park
Shorter Walks in the Dolomites
Ski Touring and Snowshoeing in the Dolomites
The Way of St Francis
Trekking in the Apennines
Trekking in the Dolomites
Trekking the Giants' Trail: Alta Via 1 through the Italian Pennine Alps
Via Ferratas of the Italian Dolomites Vols 1&2
Walking and Trekking in the Gran Paradiso
Walking in Abruzzo
Walking in Italy's Cinque Terre
Walking in Italy's Stelvio National Park
Walking in Sardinia
Walking in Sicily
Walking in the Dolomites
Walking in Tuscany
Walking in Umbria
Walking Lake Como and Maggiore
Walking Lake Garda and Iseo
Walking on the Amalfi Coast
Walking the Via Francigena Pilgrim Route – Part 3
Walks and Treks in the Maritime Alps

JAPAN, ASIA AND AUSTRALIA

Hiking and Trekking in the Japan Alps and Mount Fuji
Hiking the Overland Track
Japan's Kumano Kodo Pilgrimage
Trekking in Tajikistan

MEDITERRANEAN

The High Mountains of Crete
Trekking in Greece
Treks and Climbs in Wadi Rum, Jordan
Walking and Trekking in Zagori
Walking and Trekking on Corfu
Walking in Cyprus

Walking on Malta
Walking on the Greek Islands – the Cyclades

NORTH AMERICA

The John Muir Trail
The Pacific Crest Trail

SOUTH AMERICA

Aconcagua and the Southern Andes
Hiking and Biking Peru's Inca Trails
Torres del Paine

SCANDINAVIA, ICELAND AND GREENLAND

Trekking in Greenland – The Arctic Circle Trail
Trekking in Southern Norway
Trekking the Kungsleden
Walking and Trekking in Iceland
Walking in Norway

SLOVENIA, CROATIA, MONTENEGRO AND ALBANIA

Mountain Biking in Slovenia
The Islands of Croatia
The Julian Alps of Slovenia
The Mountains of Montenegro
The Peaks of the Balkans Trail
The Slovene Mountain Trail
Walking in Slovenia: The Karavanke
Walks and Treks in Croatia

SPAIN AND PORTUGAL

Camino de Santiago: Camino Frances
Coastal Walks in Andalucia
Cycle Touring in Spain
Cycling the Camino de Santiago
Mountain Walking in Mallorca
Mountain Walking in Southern Catalunya
Portugal's Rota Vicentina
Spain's Sendero Historico: The GR1
The Andalucian Coast to Coast Walk
The Camino del Norte and Camino Primitivo
The Camino Ingles and Ruta do Mar
The Camino Portugues
The Mountains of Nerja
The Mountains of Ronda and Grazalema
The Sierras of Extremadura
Trekking in Mallorca
Trekking in the Canary Islands
Walking and Trekking in the Sierra Nevada
Walking in Andalucia
Walking in Menorca
Walking in Portugal
Walking in the Algarve

Walking in the Cordillera Cantabrica
Walking on Gran Canaria
Walking on La Gomera and El Hierro
Walking on La Palma
Walking on Lanzarote and Fuerteventura
Walking on Madeira
Walking on Tenerife
Walking on the Azores
Walking on the Costa Blanca
Walking the Camino dos Faros

SWITZERLAND

Switzerland's Jura Crest Trail
The Swiss Alpine Pass Route – Via Alpina Route 1
The Swiss Alps
Tour of the Jungfrau Region
Walking in the Bernese Oberland
Walking in the Engadine – Switzerland
Walking in the Valais

TECHNIQUES

Fastpacking
Geocaching in the UK
Map and Compass
Outdoor Photography
Polar Exploration
The Mountain Hut Book

MINI GUIDES

Alpine Flowers
Navigation
Pocket First Aid and Wilderness Medicine
Snow

MOUNTAIN LITERATURE

8000 metres
A Walk in the Clouds
Abode of the Gods
Fifty Years of Adventure
The Pennine Way – the Path, the People, the Journey
Unjustifiable Risk?

For full information on all our guides, books and eBooks, visit our website:
www.cicerone.co.uk

Explore the world with Cicerone

walking • trekking • mountaineering • climbing • mountain biking • cycling • via ferratas • scrambling • trail running • skills and techniques

For over 50 years, Cicerone have built up an outstanding collection of nearly 400 guides, inspiring all sorts of amazing experiences.

www.cicerone.co.uk – where adventures begin

- Our **website** is a treasure-trove for every outdoor adventurer. You can buy books or read inspiring articles and trip reports, get technical advice, check for updates, and view videos, photographs and mapping for routes and treks.

- **Register this book** or any other Cicerone guide in your member's library on our website and you can choose to automatically access updates and GPX files for your books, if available.

- Our **fortnightly newsletters** will update you on new publications and articles and keep you informed of other news and events. You can also follow us on Facebook, Twitter and Instagram.

We hope you have enjoyed using this guidebook. If you have any comments you would like to share, please contact us using the form on our website or via email, so that we can provide the best experience for future customers.

CICERONE

Juniper House, Murley Moss Business Village, Oxenholme Road, Kendal LA9 7RL

✉ info@cicerone.co.uk   cicerone.co.uk